BRITAIN'S LAST TOMMIES

Also by Richard van Emden:

Boy Soldiers of the Great War
All Quiet on the Home Front
Last Man Standing
The Trench
Prisoners of the Kaiser
Veterans: The Last Survivors of the Great War
Tickled to Death to Go

BRITAIN'S LAST TOMMIES

Final Memories from Soldiers of the
1914-18 War
In Their Own Words

RICHARD VAN EMDEN

Pen & Sword
MILITARY

First published in Great Britain in 2005 by
Pen & Sword Military
An imprint of
Pen & Sword Books Ltd
47 Church Street
Barnsley
South Yorkshire
S70 2AS

Copyright © Richard van Emden, 2005

ISBN 1 84415 315 0

Printed and bound in England
By CPI UK

Pen & Sword Books Ltd incorporates the Imprints of Pen & Sword Aviation,
Pen & Sword Maritime, Pen & Sword Military, Wharncliffe Local History,
Pen & Sword Select, Pen & Sword Military Classics and Leo Cooper.

For a complete list of Pen & Sword titles please contact
PEN & SWORD BOOKS LIMITED
47 Church Street, Barnsley, South Yorkshire, S70 2AS, England
E-mail: enquiries@pen-and-sword.co.uk
Website: www.pen-and-sword.co.uk

Dedicated to Matthew, whoever he was

CONTENTS

ACKNOWLEDGEMENTS

I owe a particular thank you to all the staff at Pen & Sword Books who have worked tirelessly to help produce this book under relentless time pressures, and particularly to Roni Wilkinson for his encouragement and willingness to go beyond the call of duty to typeset this book at speed; thanks also to Jon Wilkinson for the excellent jacket design which ensured that this book will stand out amongst so many others on the military book shelf. I am also grateful to everyone at Pen & Sword, and especially to Charles Hewitt and Paula Brennan for their enthusiasm for and belief in the book. I would also like to thank the photographer Roderick Field for his excellent pictures.

As always, I would like to highlight the help of my very good friend Taff Gillingham who was always on hand to answer my technical questions, as well as many other queries of a more general nature, from his undoubted expertise. I would also like to thank Jeremy Banning for his invaluable help chasing down facts and figures for me, proving what an excellent researcher he is. I am also grateful to the staff of the Sound Archive at the Imperial War Museum, particularly Richard McDonough, Richard Hughes and Lucy Farrow for their kind help and for providing, usually at short notice, the recordings of Frank Sumpter, Joe Armstrong, G B Jameson, Joe Yarwood, Norman Dillon and Clarrie Jarman, from which extra details were garnered which augmented my own tape recordings. In the same vein, I would like to thank Vic and Diane Piuk, my friends on the Somme, for very useful extra material from their recordings of the remarkable Richard Hawkins.

A huge thank you also goes to Ryan Gearing and his partner Sarah, for all their help and kindness, and to Richard McCoombe as well as to all those who regularly offer me support and ideas, including Peter Barton, Denis Goodwin, Steve Humphries and Nick Fear. Once again, I would like to thank my wife, Anna, for putting up with interminable hassle, my agent Jane Turnbull for all her care and devotion and my mother, Joan van Emden, who has once more proved herself indispensable with her wealth of knowledge of the English language, and willingness to check my text.

This is the last purely oral history I will write on the Great War, and I would like to send my absolute heartfelt thanks to all those veterans, living or dead, who have given their time and effort to let me write about them and their memories. I have been given twenty years of enjoyment and fascination talking to these men, and it is a debt I can never replay.

INTRODUCTION

O N MY WALL AT HOME, I have a list of the last surviving veterans who served on the Western Front. Seven years ago, their names filled a 71-page spreadsheet, with approximately six or seven names to a page. Three years ago, they filled several pages of A4. Now, in August 2005, their six names cover barely one.

They are:

Henry Allingham, born 1896: Mechanic, Western Front 1917-1918

Alfred Anderson, born 1896: Infantryman, Western Front 1914-1916

Harold Lawton, born 1899: Infantryman, Western Front 1918

Harry Patch, born 1898: Infantryman, Western Front 1917

George Rice, born 1897: Infantryman, Western Front 1918

William Young, born 1900: Wireless Operator, Western Front 1918

In addition, there are three veterans of the navy: **Kenneth Cummings**, **Claude Choules**, and **William Stone**; one of the Merchant Navy: **Nicholas Swarbrick**; and five men who were in uniform but did not serve abroad. (**Sydney Lucas, Bob Rudd, Bert Clark, Harry Newcombe, and William Roberts**.)

This year, we have lost William Elder, Charles Watson, Gerald Stickells, Alfred Finnigan, Albert 'Smiler' Marshall, Cecil Withers, and Fred Lloyd; last year, Edward Rayns, Arthur Halestrap, Arthur Barraclough, Jim Lovell, Arthur Naylor, Percy Wilson, John Oborne, Jonas Hart, William Burnett, John Ross, Jasper Hankinson, Albert Dye, Albert Williams, Henry Fancourt, Tom Kirk, Ernest Issacs, and Harry Ward – twenty-four in all, far more than survive. It is for this reason that I have written these stories now; there will be no opportunity to write another such book.

It is an oral history. Over the last twenty years, I have met and recorded nearly 270 servicemen; I owe them all a huge debt of gratitude. It has been my aim to offer to the reader many of the best stories that I have heard since 1990. The 90s were the last decade in which we were fortunate enough to have a large number of Great War survivors, and as such 1990 is not simply an arbitrary cut-off point for stories. Nevertheless, in writing a book that calls itself Britain's Last Tommies, I would be disingenuous if I included those who had died perhaps ten years before that date. Every man who appears in this book lived well into his nineties, indeed, of the sixty-three quoted, fifty-two lived to reach their hundredth birthday, and nineteen lived to 105 or more. The average age of the men in this book is over 103, and rising!

In an old file, I came across a statistic that in 1990 there were 39,000 surviving servicemen of the Great War. Where this figure came from, I now have no idea, but it does not seem an unreasonable number. If approximately 6 million men served in the forces between 1914 and 1919, then 39,000 represents the last 0.65 per cent, a number small enough for these men to be called the last Tommies. This said, I have weighted the book decisively in favour of those who are either still alive or have died in the last ten years, that is, at least 80 years since the start of the Great War.

We have had more than our fair share of time with these men. Their generation has lived far longer than was expected of any previous one. In 1986, during the BBC broadcast from France to commemorate the 70th anniversary of the Battle of the Somme, a reporter noted that "soon these men will be gone." If he was talking about the Somme, his prediction was nineteen years in the fulfilling. When Albert "Smiler" Marshall died on 16 May this year, he took with him the last living memories of the battle of 1916: while serving with the yeomanry, he had waited behind the lines on 1 July, ready to exploit the expected break-through which never came. Later that month, he dug trenches and buried the dead between the village of Contalmaison and Mametz Wood. If, on the other hand, the reporter meant all those who served in the Great War, then we are still waiting for the inevitable. These six represent approximately one in every million men who served abroad. In the past, when one died, another was found to keep alive the memory of those days. No new veterans have come to light in the last year, and it now seems unlikely that any more will. These six are the last.

There are not enough interviewees to fill a book entitled *Britain's Last Tommies*, if, by Last Tommies, the reader infers that these men are alive, and, of course, there is no guarantee that on publication any of them will still be with us. There is an inherent risk in putting the face of a veteran on the cover: the power of Harry Patch's image is empirically strong, but it is even stronger when we know that the 107-year-old soldier is still alive. Life and death have come full circle. Once, back in the trenches, these men counted their lives in minutes or hours, as Harry, a survivor of the fighting near Ypres, has always asserted. His fervent wish when he saw the sun rising was to watch it set, and that was his yardstick for life. Harry was lucky to have survived the war, a war that took his friends. Ninety years on, his life, as well as that of the other veterans, has returned once again to the precipice.

When I began speaking to former servicemen back in the 1980s, it was almost possible to identify an old soldier by his demeanour. Back then, the youngest were in their mid to late eighties, and I met several who were out shopping or for an afternoon stroll, including a ninety-four year old Gallipoli veteran enjoying the sun near the castle keep in Newcastle upon Tyne. For the next few years, old people's homes were an excellent place to find interviewees and often, while visiting one, I discovered that a second and even a third lived in the same home. In November 1997, I was fortunate enough to meet Walter Green, a 100-year-old former private of the 20th Durham Light Infantry, who happened to mention, in the course of our conversation, that another centenarian lived just down the hall. His name was Alfred Cramp, a private in the same regiment but of the 12th Battalion.

Word of mouth introduced me to others. A friend, knowing my interest, told me he had just shared a bus trip from Edinburgh to Newcastle with a then ninety-one year old man called Robbie Burns, "the only Robbie Burns in Whitley Bay", the old soldier said, which made him easy to find. More recently, others have came to light through connections within the Great War forum, and latterly the award of the Légion d'Honneur by the French to the last surviving veterans, and the press campaign that followed, uncovered many more.

As they have grown older, so their names have appeared in the press when a significant milestone was reached, perhaps a 70th wedding anniversary or, more commonly, a hundredth birthday. One magazine for the caring industry ran features on improvements to homes and the latest technology or guidelines for the business of looking after the elderly. The interest of the magazine to me was a small monthly editorial piece that encouraged owners of homes to nominate their residents for a special bunch of flowers as they reached their 100th birthday. The name and address was given in each case and, while most nominees were women, every now and again a man's name was published. In June 1998, Harry Patch's name appeared in one such list.

Occasionally, a veteran was found by pure chance. In 2002 I met Alfred Lloyd, then aged 104, after a conversation I had with a dealer at a postcard fair was overheard by a man flicking through cards. Noting my interest in the Great War, he asked if I would like to meet an old soldier in Uckfield. At that time there were fewer than 100 alive, and yet Alfred Lloyd was not generally recognized.

Finally, the internet opened other doors to the last survivors, through websites dedicated to the Great War or, more obliquely, through the power of search engines that have enormously enhanced the opportunities for 'instant' research. The last I discovered, in late 2004, was found simply by typing into Google, 'Happy Birthday, age 105, born 1899." In a split second I was looking at a newspaper report in Oldham, wishing their local man, Arthur Naylor, a happy 105th birthday. With the cooperation of the paper and his family, I was delighted to meet Arthur shortly before he died.

It was wishful thinking to believe that these men would go on forever, that there would always be new veterans to take the place of those who died. Most who are still alive are phlegmatic about their continued existence. When once they clung on to life, now they are amused and not a little surprised that, although their generation has gone, they live on. Some are ready to go and do not fear the end. Utterly worn out, they see no purpose to their continued survival. Smiler Marshall was ready, his spirit fading even though his body, tired by 108 years of struggle, would not quite give up. Cecil Withers, who died this year aged 106, voiced his fear that death, when so close, was not an edifying prospect. Yet when he died in April, he did so, like Smiler, with dignity and strength, calling out loud on Jesus to take him.

Harry Patch has no intention of going anywhere just yet. He has found profound companionship with Doris, many years his junior. Doris, born and raised in the east end of London, is feisty and a good match for Harry. Fun to be with, and utterly devoted to Harry, as he is to her, she has given him a new lease of life. When he recently went into hospital for a slight infection, a friend asked him, "Now, you're not going to do anything silly, are you, Harry?" Twigging what she meant, he replied, in his strong Somerset accent, "No chance!" Former mechanic Henry Allingham is happy to stick around, too. At his 109th birthday party in June this year, there was a popular consensus that a similar event must be held in a year's time. "Is that all right, Henry?" Henry concurred with a smile, and crossed fingers thrust in the air.

The veterans have slipped away, but now their individual passing has become the stuff of newspaper columns and television news-bites, while at the same time there are web pages devoted to the slightly morbid speculation as to how many are left worldwide.

Survivors have reached borderline celebrity status, and most have enjoyed the limelight. Harry has a cider named after him, Patch's Pride, and his portrait has been painted by the former international wicketkeeper and artist, Jack Russell. Alfred Anderson has been painted, too, while a sculptor is currently capturing his features in bronze. Henry Allingham has visited Buckingham Palace, with other Great War soldiers, and has appeared on television innumerable times.

The physical stamina of many can be amazing. When I met 101-year-old Royce Mckenzie in Doncaster, I called at his home to find no one in. Wondering what to do next, I stood at the front door, turned and saw a man, hands in pockets, saunter across the road and introduce himself as Royce. He apologized for being late; he'd just been down to the bookies. Centenarian James Hudson offered to drive me to his golf club for lunch; sadly, my jeans precluded the trip. At 103, Jack Rogers became 'Britain's oldest columnist' writing for his local newspaper in Lincoln, while GB Jameson was going down to the local baths for a swim, aged 106. Edgar Cranmer, aged 99, played football with his great grandson in the back garden; Stan Clayton was catching a bus into town to do his weekly shopping in the market when he was well past 100 years, and continued to drink at his local pub until shortly before his death.

If the spirit is willing and the body can be made to follow, veterans have opportunities galore to enjoy themselves, and who can blame them? The media turned out in force for Henry's birthday in June, for great age has always fascinated the public. Great age with charm – and Henry has both in abundance - is manna from heaven for the press.

Just a couple of weeks behind Henry in the age game is Alfred Anderson. When I visited him recently, he was watching snooker on television. From his armchair ten feet away, Alfred was perfectly able to follow progress as the balls rolled across the green baize and to listen to the hushed commentary. One concession to age is a walking stick that he has sensibly decided to use round the house, after a recent fall; apart from that, he appears pretty fit and well. Harry Patch's movements are more halting. He can walk with difficulty, but his hearing is good and his eyesight excellent, as befits a former machine gunner. His recent cataract operation was needed to help his reading; his long sight was hardly impaired in the first place.

A couple of years ago, when coming back from the battlefields of Belgium and France, the coach party we were travelling with stopped at Calais. Everyone was given an hour and a half for lunch, so a few of us, along with Harry, decamped to a cheap and cheerful restaurant with rock music videos pumped from a television in the corner of the dining area. The music and the fast cut images were obtrusive enough to catch the eye, and I watched as Harry considered the Red Hot Chilly Peppers. As the band members launched themselves in the air, guitars blazing, the drummer thrashing away, I saw Harry's face. It revealed only a mild curiosity; and slight incomprehension. I leant over to Harry. "It's only pop music." Harry smiled. He may simply have been wondering where these young men got their energy from. It is precisely the same question that these old soldiers are themselves asked, time and again. What long-life battery do they run that keeps them going for so long? Most oblige with "a tot of rum in the morning"; "a glass of sherry at night"; "my family were all long-lived. Have you met my sister? She is 105." But the reality is invariably more mundane; there is no magic. One centenarian concluded, "I just keep breathing."

What does a man like Harry, then aged 105, make of the world around him, when he was born before controlled flight, when telephones and electricity were still in their infancy, and television and radios, never mind pop music, were a generation away? Normally the loss of keen senses inhibits an individual's ability to make an accurate assessment; not so Harry, not so Alfred, but they are the exceptions. Only a very few maintain all their faculties and senses intact for so long.

The cycle of life returns most people to the manifestations of infancy, without their ever reaching a remarkable age. As hearing goes and sight fails, veterans too have been forced into wheelchairs and old folks' homes, too often ignored or patronized, at which point many are happy to go. Some have ended up in semi-isolation, talked about, talked over and around. Henry has chosen to live independently; he tried a residential home but did not like it, and has adamantly maintained his independence. It means that, even now, there are days between visits when no one talks to him and life is hard.

In recent years, as their uncourted celebrity has grown, they have received well-deserved attention. At Henry's birthday, local schoolchildren played classical instruments, Eastbourne's town mayor presented cards, and members of the forces paid tribute to his service. As Britain's oldest man, he was a major attraction, and Henry loved every minute of it.

Only in the last decade have veterans become the honoured guests, invited as a matter of course to take centre stage. I recently heard a friend's story. A teacher, with a long-term interest in the war, he is also a man not known for being backward in coming forward. A few years ago when veterans were scarce but not rare, he was in the town of Ypres where he spotted and spoke to a soldier of the Great War. The annual commemorations around Armistice time were in full swing, and, knowing that there was a church service the following morning, my friend asked, without any authority, if the old soldier would like to attend. The gentleman said that he would and they agreed to meet the following morning. They did, and, as promised, my friend walked up to the door as the great and the good made their way into the chapel. As they approached, they were greeted by a steward.

"I have a veteran here who would like to attend the service."

"Does he have a ticket?" asked the steward.

"Yes, he has a ticket. He has a bayonet scar down the side of his face."

"I'm afraid he can't come in without a ticket," the steward replied.

"Well, if he's not going in, then no one is going in."

Using his body and outstretched arms to barricade the doorway, my friend stood implacable, moral indignation to the fore. To everyone's surprise, he barred entry to anyone still outside the chapel. The steward, as amazed as anyone at the turn of events, retreated to consult with someone inside, and returned. Apparently it would be all right for the old gentleman to attend after all.

I saw no point in writing just quotes with no commentary. What would we learn about these men by doing so, however stirring the individual stories might be? If this is the last oral history of these soldiers, then there is a duty of care to create something more three-dimensional. I saw no great worth in relating lives which, though they ran to great length, were frequently placid and relatively uneventful in comparison with 1914-1918. The war years were, in the vast majority of cases, the most extraordinary times of their lives. Most may have abhorred what they went through, but equally they "wouldn't have missed it for the world", as many have told me, too many for the apparently contrary sentiments to have been an aberration. The war took an enormous amount from these men, but equally it gave much in self-confidence, camaraderie, love, and the work ethic.

Listening to tape after tape of interviews, I found that it became clear which men had an aptitude for story telling and which had not. In my desire to meet as many old soldiers as I could, I sometimes failed to visit again those whose stories deserved much wider exploration. Often they lived too far away, and realistically a single visit was only ever likely to be possible. Listening to the tapes, however, I am frustrated that on many occasions I did not follow a story up, or ask an interviewee to go over the details again for greater clarity. When ninety-six-year-old Alfred Genower, ex-King's Royal Rifle Corps, told me that his brother John was murdered in a POW camp, I hardly commented; I was interested in what Alfred had done. During the interview, Alfred again mentioned the incident, but once more I failed to appreciate its importance. The murder of Able Seaman John Genower in Brandenburg POW camp was one of the sensations of the war, and a Government White Paper was published on the events surrounding his death. An outraged press also followed the story, and while the incident did not have the seismic repercussions felt after the killing of Nurse Edith Cavell, it was still hugely significant politically, and I missed it. The recording of history is as much in the comprehension as it is in the telling.

For this reason, there are those who appear fleetingly in this book, men who, no doubt, had other stories to tell had there been more opportunity. Nevertheless, there is no sense in including stories of no great cogency simply because the veteran is alive or has recently died.

In a very small number of cases, I have recounted stories previously published in another book I wrote: *Veterans, the last Survivors of the Great War*. When I wrote it, I did so in the belief that that was the last opportunity to record the memories of that generation. The majority of those interviewed were aged 100 or more, but even then the numbers of survivors ran into four figures. This book is due to be published in paperback and although it was tempting to take key stories from it, I have largely refrained, except when new and important historical information has come to my attention, shedding new light on a story.

I have chosen stories that give a balanced overview of the war years. I have not set out to cover every campaign but to give a flavour of the war, giving as much store to quirky or humorous incidents – as much a part of life at the front – as I have to famous battles. I have concentrated on the Western Front, as the principal crucible of conflict, although the Gallipoli campaign features to a lesser extent.

For the most part, the text follows a fairly strict chronology. However, when writing a book such as this there is always a tension between keeping stories strictly as they occurred or placing them in such a way as to make some accommodation with the narrative flow. In many instances, this does not matter. A man's reaction to a wounded colleague is not on the whole governed by time. However, the unfolding of a campaign and the participation of an individual's unit in that battle, is clearly part of an ordered history. There are many books that follow the precise history of a battle; this book is designed to be more impressionistic.

The title *Britain's Last Tommies*, is not restricted to the infantry but is meant to include all survivors of the war. For this reason, interviews with members of the Royal Navy have been included, specifically two men who served on the Western Front and at Gallipoli with the Royal Naval Division, and two with the Royal Naval Air Service before its amalgamation with the Royal Flying Corps to form the Royal Air Force.

The soldiers, airmen and sailors featured in this book have been given their rank and regiment as was appropriate at the time. Many servicemen were promoted and/or transferred during their service, and this is reflected in the text as and when it applied to them. G B Jameson, for example, begins the book as a Lance Corporal in the Northumberland Hussars, and finishes the war as an acting Captain, Royal Field Artillery; Cecil Withers begins the book serving with the East Surrey Regiment but finishes the war with the Royal Fusiliers.

The vast majority of memories that appear in this book have been taken from the taped interviews I conducted with Great War veterans. Sometimes, when the Imperial War Museum has interviewed the same men, I have listened to tapes held in their sound archive. Where there are new pertinent details, I have, where possible, amalgamated them into my text to give the fullest recollection of an incident. Very occasionally, where someone has given a story that seems particularly relevant to the structure of this book, and which I have not heard before, I have included it too. However, as this is my own tribute to the last survivors of the Great War, there are no recollections from servicemen whom I did not myself meet or interview. In the cases where the gentleman has died this year, during the preparation of this book, or who is still alive at the time of publishing, their names have been emboldened.

Each man is identified with his rank, number, unit and date of birth and death. Where known, information as to the platoon, company or battery is also given.

It has been an honour, and a joy, to have met these men, and their influence on me has been profound. I have spent many thousands of hours with veterans, and have travelled across the globe to meet them, as well as accompanying some back to the battlefields of France and Flanders. In all this time, it would be impossible not to notice moments that were funny, sad, heart-rending or plain ridiculous, initiated by, or involving, veterans. Often these observations were made during the swirl of publicity that accompanies any old soldier who has crossed the Channel in recent years, or as they gathered together for a reunion in Britain. At times, the most poignant moments came in the quiet of a living room, or the busy environment of an old folks' home.This book is dedicated to a man I never met, although on several occasions I sat within yards of him. I know only his first name, Matthew, and that he died around 1987, but I have never forgotten the poignancy of his last difficult months and the events surrounding his death.

I was visiting James Cripps, who lived in the seaside town of Whitley Bay, in a residential home formed of two terraced houses knocked together, where James was happy enough. The staff seemed pleasant, but there appeared little for the residents to do other than sit and read or watch a large television that was endlessly switched on, volume up, positioned diagonally across one corner of the room so all could see. As is typical with homes, the residents had their favourite seats, and James sat in a high-backed chair nearest the far door that led out in to the narrow hallway of the conjoined terraced house. Here was the head of a staircase that led up to the bedrooms.

I saw James, a former rifleman in the 8th Rifle Brigade, many times before he mentioned that he was not the only veteran of the Great War living there; the other was a man named Matthew. Matthew was bedridden and blind. He lived in a room tucked behind the stairs at the far end of the hallway. A door, I think painted ochre, remained almost permanently closed. Matthew was not in a position to talk, James told me, and he deemed it preferable that I should not ask to meet him.

And then one day, James told me that Matthew had died. James seemed quite matter of fact about it; he must have known it was for the best. When, later that afternoon, I left, I spoke to a member of staff and said that I was sorry to hear that Matthew had died. Yes, said the girl, it was very sad, but what had moved her more was what James had done. James, she told me, had stood up and pushed his zimmer frame out into the hallway. Mild curiosity made her follow him, and she watched as James made his slow, faltering way towards the closed door of Matthew's room. Indifferent to, or more likely unaware of, the fact that anyone was watching, James had stood erect, faced the closed door and saluted, pausing for a moment in silence before making his way back to the sitting room and the television. One old soldier's unspoken tribute to the passing of another.

The last official reunion of Great War servicemen took place at the National Archives at Kew in April 2003. Nine veterans attended the final meeting: Conrad Leonard, 23rd Middlesex Regiment; Jack Davis, 6th Duke of Cornwall's Light Infantry; Henry Allingham, No 9 Squadron, Royal Naval Air Service; Bill Stone, Royal Navy; Smiler Marshall, 1/1st Essex Yeomanry; Walter Humphrey, 15th London Regiment; Tommy Thomson, 1st Battalion, Honourable Artillery Company; Harry Patch, 7th Duke of Cornwall's Light Infantry; Fred Lloyd, Army Veterinary Corps.

Over the page is a final roll call of Great War veterans. The only criterion for inclusion in the list is that the veteran had to have been alive on 1 January 2000. Their average age is over 106 years.

1. Last Old Contemptible and holder of the 1914 Mons Star and Bar
PRIVATE ALFRED ANDERSON, No1643, 1/5th Black Watch, 25 June 1896 -
Still alive aged 109

2. Last Kitchener Volunteer, September 1914
PRIVATE JOHN EDWARD DAVIS, No12482, 6th Duke of Cornwall's Light
Infantry, 1 March 1895 – 20 July 2003
Died aged 108

3. Last British Gallipoli survivor
SAPPER PERCY GEORGE GORING, No1426, 484th (East Anglian) Field
Company Royal Engineers, 19 December 1894 – 27 July 2001
Died aged 106

4. Last Jutland survivor*
MIDSHIPMAN HENRY ST JOHN FANCOURT, HMS *Princess Royal*,
1 April 1900 – 8 January 2004
Died aged 103

5. Last 1 July 1916 survivor**
PRIVATE CHARLES VICTOR HOLMAN MM, No41946, 1st Essex Regiment, 26
February 1898 – 13 January 2002
Died aged 103

6. Last survivor of the campaign in the Middle East
DRIVER ALBERT EDWARD DYE, No091566, 52nd Division Army Service
Corps, 1 October 1896 – 7 September 2004
Died aged 107

7. Last holder of the Distinguished Conduct Medal
SAPPER PERCY JOSEPH CLARKE, No3060, 1/3rd London Field Company
Royal Engineers, 22 August 1895 – 8 May 2000
Died aged 104

8. Last holder of the Military Cross
2ND LIEUTENANT ARTHUR BROADBENT MORTIMER, 1/8th West Yorkshire
Regiment, 21 March 1898 – 25 December 2000
Died aged 102

---

* Henry Allingham was present at Jutland but did not play an active part in the battle.
** Albert 'Smiler' Marshall was present on 1 July 1916 but did not play an active part in the battle that day.

9. Last holder of the Military Medal

LANCE CORPORAL JAMES LOVELL, No220739, 8th Royal Berkshire
Regiment, 10 February1899 – 27 January 2004
Died aged 104

10. Last Cavalryman, last veteran of the Somme, 1916 and holder of the 12914/15 Star

TROOPER ALBERT ELLIOTT 'SMILER' MARSHALL, No1771, 1/1st Essex
Yeomanry, 15 March 1897 – 16 May 2005
Died aged 108

11. Last Artilleryman

DRIVER WILLIAM ELDER, No78452, 120th Heavy Battery, Royal Garrison
Artillery, 5 May 1897 – 22 June 2005
Dicd aged 108

12. Last Royal Engineer

SAPPER ARTHUR HALESTRAP, No316620, 138 Brigade, 46th Division Royal
Engineers Signals, 8 September 1898 – 2 April 2004
Died aged 105

13. Last veteran, Royal Flying Corps

A/CORPORAL WILLIAM ALEXANDER SMILLIE YOUNG, No119941, Royal
Flying Corps attd, 14th Brigade Royal Horse Artillery, 4 January 1900 -
Still alive aged 105

14. Last veteran, Royal Naval Air Service

MECHANIC HENRY WILLIAM ALLINGHAM, No8289, 9 Squadron, Royal
Naval Air Service, 6 June 1896 -
Still alive aged 109

15. Last Army Officer

LIEUTENANT NORMAN PORTEOUS, 13th Royal Scots,
9 September 1898 – 3 September 2003
Died aged 104

16. Last Naval Officer
MIDSHIPMAN KENNETH CUMMINGS, HMS *Morea*, 6 March 1900 -
Still alive aged 105

17. Last Prisoner of War
PRIVATE HAROLD WALTER LAWTON, No41648, 1/4th East Yorkshire
Regiment, 27 July 1899-
Still alive aged 106

18. Last 1914-1918 Chelsea Pensioner
PRIVATE ALBERT ALEXANDRE, No2043, 1st Royal Guernsey Light Infantry, 6
October 1901 – 14 January 2002
Died aged 100

19. Last veteran of Passchendaele (3rd Ypres), and last veteran to visit the Western Front (21 September 2004)
PRIVATE HENRY JOHN PATCH, No29295, 7th Duke of Cornwall's Light
Infantry, 17 June 1898 -
Still alive aged 107

20 Last veteran of the 1914-1918 war to lose a son in the 1939-1945 war
A/LANCE CORPORAL CECIL CLARENCE WITHERS, No16230, 7th East Surrey
Regiment, 9 June 1898 – 17 April 2005
Died aged 106

CHAPTER ONE

1914

RECORDING THE PAST

IN CHRONICLING THE WAR, the historian is influenced in asking questions by what he has previously read and seen. There is a tendency to put them in such a way as to make it appear that we expected veterans, instead of saving their own skins - or those of their friends – to walk around the trenches sponging up experiences and images so that they could fill in the details for future writers. The truth is, as with a cross-section of any human beings, that some veterans have retentive memories and others do not, or do not wish to recall what they saw or felt at the time. Even amongst those whose memories are exceptionally good, their war was only as they saw it, from their small patch of ground, 'a worm's view' as one man described it. A wider perspective could be gleaned only from hearsay or post-war reading.

"You see what you see then," Smiler Marshall once told me. "You don't go off to investigate, or go along the ruddy trench counting." On another occasion, frustrated but always good natured, he answered, "You asked me what I felt? I didn't feel anything, see my meaning?" Smiler recalled what he saw, and what he described felt authentic. He had little recollection of places or dates that in any case can sometimes suggest reading in retrospect. But while a village was often little more than a muddy hole in the ground, his memory for people's names was excellent because these were the men he served with, his comrades and friends.

Memories can be surprising. Asking an old soldier detailed questions about injuries and medical treatment belies the fact that at that time he was likely to have been in extreme pain and somewhat more preoccupied with his physical condition than with consigning dates and place names to memory. It seems facile to ask a veteran who had his arm amputated at a Base Hospital from which port he left to come home, but it is possible that for some reason or other he remembers, and therefore the question is legitimate. There are men who found the experience of war so exhilarating (as well as terrifying) that they retained information they themselves wondered at. "Now why should I remember that?" they muse. As a historian, you feel duty bound to ask questions just in case the veteran saw more than expected, for any reason.

Equally, it is too easy for the historian to fall into the trap of seeing the war as overly personalized, an interviewee revisiting events only as they affected him, unlikely to see the war's effects in a broader context. Too often their answers proved particularly disarming. Reginald Spraggins MM, who served with the 11th Suffolk Regiment, was badly wounded three times during the war, badly enough to be sent back to Britain for treatment on each occasion. The first time he was hit by three machine gun bullets; three months later he was back in France. The second time he was hit in the shoulder and the back by shrapnel, for which he spent just three weeks in hospital. Then, in 1918, he was shot again. As he was being treated, he was wounded in the shoulder by shrapnel, and his arm was so badly smashed that it later had to be amputated. Venturing that he must have felt personally targeted by the Germans, and particularly the artillery, he replied, "Why? There were plenty of us getting killed, people being killed all round. The shell that got me, killed several others. I felt lucky to be alive."

In the best and most exhilarating interviews, there can be a sudden connection between interviewee and interviewer, a closeness that allows the veteran to speak openly in a way he may never have done before, even to his close family. Harry Patch had not only not spoken about his war for 81 years, he had refused ever to broach the subject. Then something changed his mind – to this day he doesn't really know what. Yet when I met him in 1998, his first description of his service lasted for just five minutes, after which he felt that there was nothing more to say. Crucially, he allowed me to ask questions, and gradually a whole world of recollections and anger was reopened. It was a great privilege to be the first one to hear him, and a special bond has grown between us.

In recent years, as the pool of survivors has become smaller, so the same soldiers have been interviewed again and again, increasingly by the media, which have their own idea of what the stories should be: muddy trenches half filled with water, in a moonscape battlefield; behind the lines, incompetent Generals ordering up hopeless attacks, the death of a generation with just a handful left to tell the tale. In such a media world, veterans, as the eminent historian Richard Holmes wrote, can easily become "General Issue, neatly packed with what we wanted to hear."

When the Imperial War Museum opened its Trench Experience back in 1990, a dozen veterans were invited down to give their seal of approval. "It's very well done, but we were always soaking wet and always lousy," one veteran explained. In truth, the soldiers were almost always lousy but they were not 'always' soaking wet. "Much safer than any trench I've ever been in," ventured another. True, but there were quiet parts of the line, too. The problem is not that rats as big as cats did not exist, or that men were not lousy and frequently soaking wet, it is just that these memories and the images they have created in the public consciousness have grown to the exclusion of all others.

A few veterans began to have had enough of talking about the war. One such was Robert Renwick. I had visited him on three or four occasions, and early on he had been more than willing to talk about his memories. However, on my last couple of visits I detected a weariness unattributable just to his age; he was 100 years old. I was by no means his only visitor, and he had talked his war out. I asked him if he would appear on a documentary we were making and he agreed, though not without hesitation. This would be the last interview he would do. Sadly, he died peacefully just days before we had arranged to call.

It was easy to forget that these old soldiers had had lives other than those intense years fighting in the trenches. Sometimes they were annoyed that all people wanted to talk about was the war. "I'm sick of talking about it" is a comment I have heard more than once. Nevertheless, the months or years they spent on the Western Front or elsewhere were frequently the most prominent in their minds. George Louth was 'bored' with talking about the war, and if approached, he would often decline. But ask him about the rest of his life, about his farming, and George himself would turn the conversation towards his time in France; he could never escape that cataclysmic period of his life and, as much as he hated what he had suffered, he needed people to know and appreciate what he had gone through.

Any thorough study of the Great War, whatever aspect it chooses to investigate, must draw on every source of archive material, from the diaries of the time, the books written soon afterwards, and the memories recorded decades later. All sources have their value. The soldiers wrote what they felt at the time, but that does not mean it is absolute truth. It is the truth as conceived then, but time, and the new perspective time brings, can often alter impressions of events. Many years after the war, a veteran of the Somme wrote, "So many things are seen more clearly now that the passing years have allowed the mud of action to settle at the bottom of the pool of life."

Equally, as the passage of time often dulls memory, events can become jumbled and recollections distorted, so that actions become contracted into one. Amid this confusion, the war itself can be re-interpreted, under the influence of modern fads and fashions. The 1960s dour re-appraisal of the senior command undoubtedly fed the receptive minds of surviving veterans to believe that the war was futile, and that they were simply cannon fodder, but such bitterness did not start in the 1960s, or even in the late 1920s; it was born at least amongst some during the war years. Harry Fellows, a veteran of the battle of Loos, made it known that he and his friends referred to Field Marshall Haig as "the butcher", right or wrong. Regardless of how history is interpreted, it is almost impossible, when two million men were serving in the field, that this or that version is the only true one.

With oft-retold anecdotes, it is possible to subsume another man's story and believe one was actually there. One veteran told me of an incident in late 1914 which he described with remarkable detail, a cavalry-on-cavalry engagement which simply was not borne out by the regimental war diary or by the veteran's own service papers, which survive at the National Archives in Kew. Was he lying, or had he subsumed someone else's story? I like to think it was the latter, but I have never repeated it because there is more than a question mark over the truth.

In a similar way, a collective memory may not be entirely accurate. Kitchener's famous recruiting poster is recalled by veterans from all parts of the country as highly influential in their enlistment. Yet the poster was published only in the London region, and was not systematically distributed nationwide. Sometimes, such collective memory reinforces the individual's reminiscence: so, every soldier who boarded a cattle truck in France remembered the words painted on the side: 40 HOMMES, 8 CHEVAUX. If they served on the Somme, they remembered the leaning Madonna on top of Albert Basilica, and if they passed through the Bull Ring training camp at Etaples, they all recalled the harsh discipline. These were images and memories that men carried with them for the rest of their lives.

Even those soldiers blest with the finest memories can get details wrong. Cecil Withers, who died earlier this year aged 106, was convinced that he had served in the 12th East Surrey Regiment. Right up to a few weeks before his death, he remained lucid and articulate, with one of the best memories I have come across in the last decade. He had, nevertheless, forgotten the seemingly unforgettable, for while researching his story, I discovered that he had, in fact, served in the 7th Battalion. On my next visit I quizzed him. Was he sure he had served in the 12th? He was positive. I read him a list of officers from each battalion, and he recognized none from the 12th and many from the 7th Battalion. When I told him the results, he was taken aback. How many years he had lived with this false memory, he naturally could not recall, but for a long time. Somewhere along the line the facts had altered, probably, as far as I can guess, because the 7th Battalion was part of the 12th Division.

The easy accessibility of war-time records makes the checking of many stories relatively easy and I have frequently been pleasantly surprised how accurate some of those memories have been, given the passage of time. Indeed, on occasion I have discovered that a private's own personal recollections, that may have appeared to contradict the accepted view of events, have in fact proved correct. The release of surviving personal records at the National Archives in the late 1990s, on the assumption that there were no veterans still alive, has allowed historians a valuable new tool in scrutinizing stories. Inevitably, in a few instances, veterans have been made the victims of their own longevity when personal papers give access to stories that might otherwise have remained lost.

Mostly the revelations are inconsequential, but they might not have been. Arthur Barraclough, for instance, was recorded as having flat feet at the time of his enlistment. "Yes, I did, but how do you know that?" asked Arthur in surprise when I commented on the fact. When Andrew Bowie was training at Invergordon, he was brought before the Colonel who asked why he had a bad mark, a fine in a civil court, against his record. Unable to recollect ever appearing in court on any charge, he asked the Colonel what the offence was, but the Colonel was unable or unwilling to explain. From the records it was clear that, after being called up under the provisions of the Derby Scheme, he had been fined for appearing two days late at the barracks. Andrew was greatly relieved at the inconsequential nature of the penalty, clearing up an incident "that's been worrying me for over eighty years." The surviving records also show that Vic Cole was reduced to the ranks on three occasions for various altercations and once for being drunk on active service. On the third occasion, after a Field General Court Martial, Vic was paraded in front of the battalion to have his Lance Corporal's stripe stripped from his arm. Far from being ashamed of this incident, Vic suggested it as a way in which a fellow veteran might recollect him.

"If he remembers," he said cheerfully, "that would be me."

THE OUTBREAK OF WAR

According to popular sentiment, it was all going to be so easy. The war, widely expected by the general public for a decade or more, had finally arrived, and when news filtered through, any private fears, any attempts at public demonstrations against it, were lost amid the Union Jacks and the carefree singing and dancing. In one or two places the mood turned ugly, and Germans and German businesses were attacked but, for the most part, news of the arrival of war was taken in good part. The reality of the situation, the massive German conscript army that was marching towards France through poor defenceless Belgium, was forgotten; the professional British Army would go to the continent to deliver a bloody nose to the Germans, and return home triumphant. The war, it was widely assumed, would be over by Christmas. It was a popular notion, not least amongst the tens of thousands of young boys who clamoured to leave boring, poorly paid jobs in order to enlist. If their parents disapproved, they would say that they would be home before the turkey or goose hit the oven, and the chances were that they would never see active service. A few months in the countryside, breathing fresh air and being paid for it, was reason enough to allow a son to go to war; parents would be spoilsports to stop it, and downright unpatriotic into the bargain

When the Archduke Ferdinand, heir to the Austro-Hungarian throne, and his wife were assassinated in Sarajevo by a young Serbian nationalist, Gavrilo Princip, few people even gave the murders a thought, let alone believed it to be of any great consequence. Why should they? In the summer months of July and August, as workers sweltered in their factories and a lucky few took their annual week's holiday, a handful of gunshots hundreds of miles away could not be important.

Unknown to most British people, however, there was a pre-war system of alliances, which would spell the end of peace as they knew it. After the assassination, Austria, backed by its more powerful ally Germany, used the opportunity to give Serbia an ultimatum that would effectively subjugate the small Balkan power to her neighbour. Serbia, in turn, appealed to her old ally Russia for support, and it was given. Russia had an agreement with France dating back to 1892 that, if Russia should enter a European war, France would come to her aid. Since 1904, this system of alliances had been extended to Britain. Her 'splendid isolation' had been broken first when she agreed a treaty with Japan in 1902, and two years later, France and Britain had signed an entente cordiale, including an understanding that in a general conflict with Germany, Britain would side with her neighbour. It was an understanding, but not a guaranteed commitment.

In the desire to avoid war on two fronts, the Germans struck out at France by sending three armies through Belgium, a country whose neutrality was guaranteed by Britain, as well as other nations, including Germany. The pressure to become involved was too great. Britain issued an ultimatum to Germany to withdraw and when, at on 11o'clock on the evening of 4 August, the ultimatum expired, Britain became involved in her first conflict on mainland Europe for almost a century.

As the regular army mobilized and set sail for France, the new Secretary of State for War, Lord Kitchener, made his now famous appeal for volunteers. The public might be under the misapprehension that the war would be short, but the iconic Field Marshal was not. He knew, as did other senior commanders, that the war would last beyond Christmas, and probably beyond one or two Christmases after that. Kitchener appealed for an initial 100,000 recruits who would be trained to take the field later in the war. In the meantime the regular army and the territorials would hold the line. This new civilian army was not expected to be fully ready for action until 1917, but losses at the front ensured its deployment long before that date.

Kitchener's public standing was immense, at a time when military men figured large in the popular consciousness. Britain's standing in the world was largely due to, and depended on, courageous and patriotic soldiers who upheld the nation's honour and prestige around the globe. Kitchener had won his public spurs in crucial victories at the tail end of the nineteenth century at the Battle of Omdurman, and Khartoum and his name had become synonymous with steadfastness and courage. His appeal met with a resounding response from the men of Britain, who flocked in large numbers to recruiting stations across the country. However, it was only with the news of the first setback of the war, the Battle of Mons and the subsequent retreat almost to the gates of Paris, that there was the largest flood of recruits. Men who had held back from enlisting on a wait-and-see basis now found that their country really did need them, and urgently.

The summer months of 1914 had seen the army on manoeuvres, both the regular army and the territorials training at camps across Britain. The ranks of the territorials were filled with young lads keen to have a two-week break from work, and the summer camp was a chance to see friends and have a good time. In Scotland, Alfred Anderson, today aged 109, had just finished his annual stay at Monzie Camp near Crieff. He had been looking forward to his two weeks of freedom from work at his father's joinery in Newtyle. Alfred, one of six children, had joined the territorials in 1912 with other local lads and was eighteen when war broke out. Another such lad was George

Rice, now aged 108, from Birmingham. He was enjoying his break in Wales with the Durham Light Infantry when news came of war.

The regular army had set sail for France, sending an Expeditionary Force of six divisions, numbering 80,000 men. The first units began to arrive on the continent within ten days of mobilization, a remarkable feat in itself, and these were moved cautiously northeast until they reached the small Belgian town of Mons. Cavalry were then sent forward, scouring the countryside in an attempt to make contact with the enemy. The first skirmishes took place on the morning of 22 August but it was not until the following day that the fighting began in earnest, as the Germans attacked British infantry deployed along the bank of the Mons-Condé Canal. In fierce exchanges, the Germans suffered grievous losses, but their numbers were overwhelming and the British were forced to withdraw for fear of being enveloped by enemy troops crossing further down the Canal. A retreat from Mons began that would not be halted for two weeks, by which time the BEF had been forced to march over 200 miles to the southeast of Paris. The Germans followed closely behind, but in doing so committed a gross tactical error. The pre-war blueprint for an invasion of France, known as the Schlieffen Plan, had included the encirclement and capture of Paris, in order to knock France out of the conflict. By failing to seize the capital and following the BEF instead, the Germans swung their forces east in an attempt to rout the British, overstretching their own supply lines, and forcing their equally exhausted troops to carry on the chase all the way to the River Marne. This opened up the German army to an assault from the flank. The French Sixth Army, which had been withdrawn to defend Paris, was now ordered east to attack the Germans, taking the enemy by complete surprise. The Germans were forced to retire to the first defensible position, a ridge known as the Chemin des Dames. As the Germans fell back, the Allies advanced again, but were incapable of shifting the Germans from the ridge. Both sides dug in on the Aisne. It was the beginning of trench warfare.

Unwilling to accede to a static war, both sides began to try to outflank each other, moving northwest in a struggle to envelop each other's forces. As both sides moved diagonally across northern France, they passed over the rolling countryside of the Somme, which was to play such a major role in the war two years later. The inevitable result of any outflanking manoeuvre was effectively a race to the sea, and at Nieuport on the Belgium coast, both sides settled with nowhere else to go. Behind them were hundreds of miles of front that would now be dug and fortified in a line of trenches, which would eventually run from the Belgian coast through to the Swiss Alps.

The Germans might have been dealt a formidable blow on the Marne but their numerical advantage was still an impressive weapon even if many of their best troops had been killed or wounded. Their firepower was also pre-eminent and in chaotic fighting near the Belgium town of Ypres, the BEF fought to hold the line as the Germans pressed for a breakthrough in the late autumn and early winter of 1914. The British regular army, supported by rapidly deployed units of the territorial army, hung on, although at times it was touch and go. By December, the Germans called a halt to their offensives and dug in for winter.

At home, recruits for Kitchener's new army shivered with cold and slept in makeshift camps hastily constructed in the aftermath of the huge civilian response to the call to arms. Nearly one million men had enlisted by the end of the year, four times the number of the old regular army, which had relied on having half of its men abroad and in foreign billets at any time. Recruitment had been over-successful: men had been drawn from right across the social spectrum, many leaving jobs vital to the British war economy in order to enlist. They now sat in tents and huts waiting for equipment. For months, these eager recruits were marched around, sporting not much more than the civilian clothes they had joined up in and using broomsticks for rifles. Morale was good at first, but in the autumn of 1914 it began to slip, as men saw little immediate prospect of service other than to flounder in the mud that inevitably surrounded camps when thousands of pairs of feet ground green fields into soup. To be serving with your friends was a good enough jape for younger recruits, but for older soldiers with families to support at home, the excitement of going to war was beginning to wear off. Separation allowances to loved ones back home were being indifferently paid as the authorities worked to set up payment schemes; dissatisfaction and resentment would grow unless conditions improved rapidly.

As the war became bogged down in the winter mud, it was evident that it would not be over quickly; instead, it was hoped that 1915 would bring victory. A Christmas gift from Princess Mary to the soldiers at the front, came with various gifts in an embossed brass tin accompanied by a photograph of the princess, and a message wishing the men a merry Christmas and a victorious New Year.

At home, the pressure on men who had not enlisted was growing, sometimes unfairly. Stan Clayton, a twenty year old from Sheffield, had family commitments which kept him at home, not least a critically ill brother. He had resisted the pressure to enlist so far, but name-calling was on the increase from people who knew little of Stan's predicament. Then, just before New Year, Stan's brother died. He was now free to enlist. Albert ['Smiler'] Marshall, aged seventeen, from the Essex village of Elmstead Market, had begun work as a shipwright's apprentice straight from school, before becoming a stable boy on a country estate. As he was under age, he had faced no pressure to enlist, particularly after his elder brother had joined up. Albert was keen to do his bit, however, and just before Christmas he made his way to the recruiting office.

THE EXPECTATION OF WAR

Private Percy Victor Johnson, No39931, 21st London Regiment,
1 March 1899-May 2002
When I was a youngster, I was helping a greengrocer to get food out
on a stall when who should come down the Oxford Road on horseback
but King George. And who should be with him but the Kaiser, stuck
up there wearing a great big cape and a helmet and wonderful medals
on his chest. Well, our own King George, he looked absolutely way out
of his depth. When I got home I told my father and he said, "Oh,
there's going to be a war, and not so very long either. That bloke's not
over here for nothing." This was in about 1913. A year later, my father
went off to fight in the Great War with his three brothers and in time
I followed him.

Lance Corporal Victor Thomas Cole, No1308, 7th Queen's Own
(Royal West Kent Regiment), 2 January 1897-20 November 1995
About this time [1913] in the grounds of the Crystal Palace there was
a terrific open air floodlight display. "The Invasion", as it was called,
featured a life-size English village complete with church and pub.
Village folk walked slowly from the former and others drank beer
outside the latter. Into this peaceful rural scene suddenly a German
plane swooped (it ran down a wire) and dropped some bombs which
exploded with appropriate noise and a great deal of smoke. When the
air cleared it was seen that German soldiers occupied the village. All
ended happily when the Territorials arrived and routed the enemy.

Private Arthur James Burge, No202813, 1st East Surrey Regiment,
19 June 1895-17 August 1999
My housemaster at Malvern, the geography teacher, always started the
beginning of term very patriotically. He'd got a map that showed in red
all the possessions of the Empire, and where we kept order in the
world. He would give us a talk that always finished with: "Now, boys,

if your country is ever in danger you should be willing to give up your life for her." He said that every term and I never forgot it.

Sapper Arthur Halestrap, No316620, 138 Brigade, 46th Division Royal Engineers, 8 September 1898-2 April 2004

History was well taught, and we knew all about the Crimea and Florence Nightingale and all the notable figures of those days. Living in Southampton, seafaring was particularly in our blood and the might of the British Navy was always in our mind. Every year there was a big review of the Navy at Spit Head, and we were taken round the fleet in a paddle steamer to see what it was like. There seemed to be hundreds of ships of all sizes from little pinnaces rushing about right up to giant battleships.

A distant relative of my mother's was related to Nelson's Captain on the *Victory*, and we had to go and visit her and kneel and she would bless us. As the Royal family used to dress their children in sailor suits, so we would all follow the tradition. I had a blouse with a big collar with three white stripes on it and short trousers. That was the sort of thing that happened when I was a boy.

My father was in the volunteers and his brothers were in the South African war. I remember, at the age of three, the excitement when letters came from the front. Whilst we were at school, we were told all the current events, and they were full of war. We knew that a conflict was being prepared and was inevitable. The only thing that we were troubled about was who would be our allies.

[Ed. Many men in Southampton worked in maritime industries. Arthur's father worked for the White Star shipping line, as did his neighbour. As a young lad, Arthur had the run of the White Star ships that docked in the port, including HMS Titanic, *which Arthur was allowed to visit and walk round. Shortly afterwards, the ship sank, taking with it Arthur's neighbour who served as an engineer.]*

WAR

Private Cecil Clarence Withers, No16230, 7th East Surrey Regiment, 9 June 1898-17 April 2005

I was in the scout camp at St Mary Cray near Orpington, the night war was declared, 4 August 1914, and our scoutmaster told us the news. The boys, oh, they did put their hands together, "Hooray", you know. "England is at war with Germany," he said, and we clapped hands because we knew we would be fighting for the right things. After that, they dissolved the scouts, and our scoutmaster, who was in the territorials, went away to France and was killed. He was a very nice chap.

Private Arthur Burge, 1st East Surrey Regiment, 1895-1999

I was staying with a German family over the summer when, on 1 August 1914, my father sent a telegram, "Return home immediately." Herr Professor Dr Berne banged on my room door, and said I had half an hour to get packed to catch the train from Metz. I grabbed everything, I never had time to wash, or have a cup of tea. He walked me to the station and off I went to London. I had my suspicions that war was breaking out; there had been so much talk. On the way to the station, the professor asked me if I could lend him two sovereigns, which I did. I didn't know why he asked. After the war, when we made claims against the Germans for reparation, I claimed the two sovereigns and got them back through the offices of Rothschilds.

Private George Francis Rice, No238217, 1/5th Duke of Wellington's Regiment, 18 June 1897-

I was away on our annual summer camp when the war broke out. I was a member of what was known as the Special Reserve and we were on a fifteen-day exercise. The weather was gorgeous, and the scenery beautiful. There were stories in the newspapers of trouble abroad but we didn't take much notice. It was good at camp, and we were quite happy there. I found it exciting; it was like a holiday. I went up a hill for a walk to have a good view of where we were and, as I went, a bugle sounded and I saw a lot of people running about down below. I thought, "I wonder what that is?" and went down to see. Well, blow me down, the war had started – and I was in it whether I wanted it or not."

Private Alfred Anderson, No1643, A Company, 1/5th Black Watch, 25 June 1896-

As members of the territorials, we had our annual camp when we were able to get away from work and enjoy some time with good friends. July 1914 was my third summer training, this time at Monzie Camp near Crieff. The weather was hot and on route marches, we wore short sleeves. One evening, just before our summer camp finished, a group of us were talking one night when we heard loud cheering from the officers' marquee, and we wondered what it was. We were told war had been declared and were advised that we would get call-up papers. I told my parents, and my father took the news very, very badly. The first thing he said was, "You're only a laddie apprentice, you can't go to war." I said, "I'm not going to war. I'm just going to Dundee drill hall." Mum didn't say much; she was too upset.

Corporal George Brumwell Jameson, No242 A Squadron, 1/1st Northumberland Yeomanry, 19 December 1892-2 March 1999
We wanted to go to war. It was something one felt one had to do, it was a duty we owed to the country. Just as my forebears had fought in the Boer War, so I was going to go to this one. You didn't question what you were doing. There was no animosity against the Germans, not as far as we were concerned. We used to say at the time that the German soldier had to do his duty just as we had to do ours. But the Germans had no justification for attacking France by coming through Belgium. We thought that Belgium was sacrosanct, so to speak, but they were egged on by the Kaiser's self-aggrandisement and that led them to do what they did. We thought we had a better army altogether

and once we got down to business, we would wipe them out.

Able Seaman Alfred George Bastin, L8/2717, D Company, Hawke Battalion, Royal Naval Volunteer Reserve (RNVR), 30 July 1896-February 1997

I enlisted in the Royal Naval Volunteer Reserve as a drummer boy in July 1912, shortly before my sixteenth birthday. I was one of four children and we lived near Waterloo Station where my father worked printing tickets for the railway. My elder brother joined the East Surreys and was sent to India and my younger brother went to France. At one point all three of my father's sons were in uniform and serving during a time of war, a fact of which my father was very proud.

On 3 August 1914, I'd been out in Hyde Park to listen to the band, which I used to do every Sunday. I got home about half past nine and as I opened the door, on the floor were two envelopes. I thought, "What on earth is this, on a Sunday night?" One was from the naval volunteers mobilizing me, telling me to report to headquarters, and the other was from the Custom House appointing me to a job somewhere on the east coast. I got into my uniform and went down to headquarters, and people kept drifting in asking me who I was, and my rank. "I'm a drummer boy in the bugle band." "All right, stand on the gate and announce the new arrivals as they come in." I stood at the gate until midnight before they let me go home, telling me to report back in the morning.

A few days later, Lord Kitchener made his appeal for men and quite a number of them were miners from Yorkshire who came down to London. Well, the following month, when they were forming the 1st Naval Division, as we became known, they found that we weren't completely up to strength, and these poor blokes who only been in the army for three or four weeks and had only just been taught how to handle a bloody rifle, were given to us, with no training at all. We were gradually being fitted out, but half these men had khaki trousers and blue jackets and they had to go out to Belgium like that.

Corporal Ernest Albert Doran, No2152, 2nd London Regiment (Royal Fusiliers), 25 February 1893-May 1996

I never had the slightest intention of going to fight for King and Country. It is true I joined up in August 1914, but that was only because we thought the war would be over by Christmas. We thought that by going to Malta we would have a nice holiday in the Mediterranean for a few months, then we'd come back, the war would be over, and we could get back to work.

This is how it happened. I went to work on the Monday morning as usual, and a group of us were having a cup of coffee in Lyons. Anyway, this chap came over to us and said, "How would you fellows like to go to Malta?" So we all said, "Oh, yes we'd all like to go," so the whole office enlisted, eight or nine of us. This man worked with us but he was also a member of a territorial battalion in the London Regiment, and so he took us off to Vincent Square near Victoria to enlist. I went back into the office until 4pm that afternoon to clear up any loose ends - that was on the Monday - and four days after I joined, we sailed. The authorities needed to transfer regular battalions from Malta and we were shipped out there to take their place.

Private Francis 'Frank' Edward Sumpter, No5345, A Company 1st Rifle Brigade, 13 October 1897-31 July 1999

I was ordered with a few men to go to Parkstone Quay, Harwich, as guard of honour to Prince Lichnowsky, the German ambassador to London, because although the BEF had set off for France, he hadn't left the country then. We went to Harwich, and the sergeant major came along, and lined up the troops to present arms. Then he looked at me and said, "Not you, you're too young, get back," so I dropped out. Instead, I had a bird's eye view of proceedings and saw the embassy staff with all their baggage and prams, quite a retinue of them, leaving the country.

Lance Corporal Joseph Armstrong, No2123, B Coy, 1st Loyal North Lancashire Regiment, Special Reserve, 12 April 1895-July 1997

I was called up on 6 August and arrived at Fulwood Barracks in Preston on the 8 August, before I was sent south to Felixstowe. As soon as I got there, they put me in the Military Police. I was walking along the promenade one morning when I was told the Company Officer wanted to see me. I'd heard that the first draft was going out to France and I thought, "Oh good, I'm going to be on the first draft," and I was quite pleased about that. When I got there, a Colour Sergeant and an officer greeted me and said, "Armstrong, you're a first class shot, they want a musketry instructor at Fulwood Barracks. You'll be given another stripe and when you get there you'll be made a Staff Sergeant." Then the officer looked at me. "Armstrong, you don't look too pleased. What's the matter?"

"I thought you were going to tell me I was on the first draft, Sir."

"What draft? Which draft?"

"Sir, I understand the first draft is to go out."

"Armstrong, you mean to tell me that you'd rather go across there amongst all that blood and shit?"

He must have thought I was crackers, but he could see that I was determined to go, so he said, "Put him on the draft, Colour Sergeant." The next day we were marched down to Felixstowe Station as the band played "Let auld acquaintance be forgot," and were put on a train to Southampton to set sail for St Nazaire.

Private Alfred Anderson, 1/5th Black Watch, 1896-

The quartermaster sergeant called out the roll. He was sitting at a table in the middle of the hall and he just took us as we were in the roll book, so I was about the first to volunteer because my name is A. Anderson. I didn't sign anything. You had to declare your willingness to go abroad in front of the others. That was enough. Only one or two said they couldn't volunteer for home reasons, parents to support and things like that, but very few refused to go. We did have talks amongst ourselves about it and the main thing I remember was that we would stick together. We had drilled together, been at camps with the same fellows, what else could you do? You couldn't say "I'm not staying with the battalion."

One of the lads who volunteered was Fred Geekie, who was aged only sixteen. I knew him well as we grew up in the same town of Newtyle, before his family moved to the high street in Forfar. Everybody was aware of his age, but nobody said anything. Several of us told him privately that he was too young to go, but he said, "I want to keep with the boys." It was natural, of course, I mean we had been brought up with each other. The Sergeants didn't want to know and so Geekie went out with the battalion. He was killed towards the end of the war.

EMBARKATION

Sapper Arthur Halestrap, 46th Division Royal Engineers, 1898-2004
The troops used to come through Southampton to embark at the docks, and it was tremendously exciting to watch the men march through the town, and to see the remounts going through, one man leading three horses. Of course we were always excited if one broke away and ran off. The Scottish regiments were the most impressive. To hear the pipes and to see all these huge lines of troops in their kilts all going the same direction, it was wonderful. Everyone would turn out and cheer them on their way, giving them chocolate, fruit and tins of milk.

Trooper Benjamin George Clouting, No8292, 4th Troop, C Squadron, 4th (Royal Irish) Dragoon Guards, 15 September 1897-13 August 1990
It was dark below deck, for with the threat of submarine attack, all

lights had been dimmed, and portholes closed and firmly screwed shut. Up on deck, there was a strict order banning all smoking, but the crossing was calm, and the night warm enough so that many troopers seemed content to just sleep where they liked up on deck.

It was light when we pulled into Boulogne, and we excitedly crowded along the ship's railing to get some early impressions. Walking along the quay were French soldiers wearing their blue jackets, red trousers, and peak caps. "Blimey," said one man, "even the postmen have got bayonets."

Private Alfred Anderson, 1/5th Black Watch, 1896-

We were told mid-afternoon that we were getting a few hours off to go home and say goodbye to our parents. We went to where the transport was, a lorry and two horses and a driver, Dundee to Newtyle. It took about two hours to get there; it's a nice flat road, you see, and we trotted all the way. I saw some of my relatives and I said my goodbyes and mother gave me a bible; then it was back on the transport

The battalion left at 7am. On the train south, the officers sat in the first class compartments with corridors whereas we had empty guards' vans. We didn't worry about the toilets when we were travelling through the country, we just slid the doors back and urinated straight out the side of the wagon.

There were only two stops and one was at York. When we got there, the platform was practically lined with people, and we thought they were a reception and that we were going to be given some refreshments. They were in fact the station staff and were there to keep us on the train. We were for getting out, but they held up their hands, and said, "Don't come out, you can't come out," and we found out why. The engine needed water and we had to reverse to the pumps. Next time we came to the station, we went right through.

Able Seaman Alfred Bastin, Hawke Battalion, Royal Naval Volunteer Reserve, 1896-1997

We left Kingsdown Camp on the afternoon of 4 October, and went along to Dover to embark for Dunkirk. At Dover, all the kit bags were placed on the foredeck of the troop ship. The men were in a holiday mood. We were mostly reservists, Saturday night sailors, they called us, part of the London Division, but I for one wasn't worried at all. I was eighteen years old and thought the whole thing a great adventure.

We landed in Belgium and boarded trains that moved us up towards Antwerp from where refugees were pouring away, an incredible sight, with their belongings on their backs. We marched up towards the trenches, which had been prepared for us to defend the town, when suddenly we were given orders to step aside. A motor car came along at a fair pace and who should be in it but General Seeley and Winston Churchill no less, the First Lord of the Admiralty!

RECRUITING A NEW ARMY

[Ed. Some men wanted to volunteer straightaway; others were more circumspect, and waited to see what would happen. After the retreat from Mons, recruitment soared, in a mixture of enthusiasm and patriotism. Amongst those recruited in early September were Vic Cole and Jack Davis.

Vic Cole was a seventeen-year-old lad undertaking an apprenticeship at the Clapham School of Telegraphy. On the evening of 4 August, he had walked up the Mall and stood outside the gates of Buckingham Palace as war was declared. A month later, he enlisted in the 7th Queen's Own (Royal West Kent Regiment).

Jack Davis, a nineteen-year-old boy from London, was working at the National Liberal Club in Whitehall. He, like Vic, responded to Kitchener's call, enlisting with his friends en masse at New Scotland

Yard. Vic lived to 98 years old, Jack 108, briefly holding the title of Britain's oldest man.]

2nd Lieutenant Richard Maurice Hawkins, 16 Platoon, D Company, 11th Royal Fusiliers, 8 March 1895-26 November 1994
The war broke out and as a young man it was my duty to enlist. I was apprentice to Hoffmanns, a ball-bearing company, and I went into the office one day and said that like all young men I must join up. The boss called me a number of rather unpleasant things, saying that I was an ungrateful so and so. I didn't have much of a vocabulary but I told him what I thought of him and left.

Kitchener had no trouble in finding the first hundred thousand volunteers. Damn it, you couldn't get into the ruddy army, there was such a rush to get in and defeat the enemy, and prevent him from taking over this country. I went to London many times to get into the army and couldn't. The crowds were too big.

In school we'd been in the cadet corps, and we knew how to behave; we knew what we'd got to do. It was our duty, nothing out of the ordinary, it was obvious. The morale was tremendous; we were anxious to get on with the job. After all, if you see somebody breaking into your home you've got to give him a clout, haven't you, get rid of him, and that's what the Germans were trying to do. It was only natural that we wanted to go to France and stop this nonsense.

Private Edward 'Ted' Francis No1114, 1 Platoon, A Company, 16th Royal Warwickshire Regiment, 30 June 1896-24 March 1996
Birmingham people were excited, laughing, joking. Young people, like myself, were saying, "We'll show those Germans, we'll push them back home, how dare they walk over little Belgium." We were anxious to get to France and have a go at them. I worked at a small factory making envelopes and stationery, but it was a boring kind of job and so I didn't want much pushing. The girls, they said, "Oh Ted, you can't stop here now," and they practically ushered me out of the factory. The

talk then was that it would all be over by Christmas, so we were quite impatient to get into the army. It may have been obvious to the senior officers that it was going to be a long war, but not to us.

Lance Corporal Vic Cole, 7th Queen's Own (Royal West Kent Regiment), 1897-1995

I got home and met George Pulley, who was a bit of a lad, and he said, "Yes, I'm going to join the army." They were having a recruitment meeting at the top of Anerley Hill by the south tower of the Crystal Palace, and the speaker was going on about this Kaiser and keeping the Germans off the green fields of old England, and telling us how beautiful it was to be in the army. So George said, "Come on, then, let's join up." There was an old touring car there and a chap saying, "Come on, young fellows, join the army", so we climbed into the car and it took us along the Crystal Place Parade and down the hill to Bromley Drill Hall. We were driven to a nearby pub, and shown to an upstairs room with several long tables, where we signed on for the duration of the war.

Private John 'Jack' Davis, No12482, D Company, 6th Duke of Cornwall's Light Infantry, 1 March 1895-20 July 2003

I was in the Boys' Brigade and was a member of an athletics club too, so I both accepted discipline and had an organised life. The call of the army quite naturally attracted me. I enlisted in New Scotland Yard with thirty of my colleagues, en masse, because our manager at the Liberal Club was a patriotic Frenchman and so we had no difficulty in joining up and letting the women take over our jobs. Then we had a night out, the group of us, for once you accepted the traditional king's shilling, you're in. So, it being our last night of freedom, we made the best of it with the boys.

Private Ted Francis, 16th Royal Warwickshire Regiment, 1896-1996

When I went to enlist, I was amazed to see a long queue of young men about the same age as myself, all laughing and joking, and I thought it was more like a queue for a music-hall than to be a soldier.

I passed easily into the army. You see, my brother and I used to practise weightlifting. Every Sunday morning we used to lift astonishing weights from the floor to above our heads, in the region of a hundredweight with single right hand lifts, first to the shoulder and then up and down. When I enlisted at the Town Hall in Birmingham, the doctor told me to strip. He just had one look at me and said, "Huh, wish they was all like that, my job would be easy, put your clothes on."

When I came home, my mother and father were waiting for me. I'd been spotted queuing by a customer who drank in Dad's pub. Oh, they tore me off a strip - my father wasn't as angry because he understood my feelings, but my mother, she said, "You little fool, don't you understand there's only thieves and vagabonds join the army – you go back and tell them that you've changed your mind and you're not going to join their army." I said, "Mother, I can't do that. I've made an oath to defend the King and Country and accepted the King's shilling and that's that. I can't go back on it, and I don't want to." "Well," mother said, "I suppose you'll be off to France in a day or two and I shan't see you again." I said, "Oh no, mother, we've got to be trained, we'll be at least five or six months in England yet."

She was very inquisitive to know more. Where would we train? But the upshot was that she was much more amenable to me being a soldier. "That's all right, the outing will do you good. I know you'll be home for Christmas because they all say it will be over by then, and to have you here at Christmas, that's all I want." I little realized that that was the last time I should see my mother, because in less than no time I had to go back for her funeral. She died of heart failure.

Private Joseph Henry Yarwood, No68405, 94th Field Ambulance, Royal Army Medical Corps (RAMC), 9 May1896-4 August 1995
It was common to invite a well-known sportsman to come to a particular town, and they'd organize this meeting – of course it was a

recruiting meeting – and they would talk about how they were going to have their own local regiment. The man would say, "Now, boys, we're all going to become part of one regiment, the Swansea volunteers, or whatever, and you're invited to join," and that was very successful. Of course it was nice to go and join up with your pals, because you'd got somebody you knew with you, somebody you could rely on, a much happier feeling than if you were going into a strange crowd.

[Ed. The raw recruits had to be trained before they went to France, a process that was expected to take the best part of a year. For many, it was rather like the Scout camps of their youth, an enjoyable opportunity to be with others of a similar age and background. Those who were to undertake initial training of this eager rabble were in many cases old regular soldiers, some well into their seventieth year. Their first impressions must have proved sobering.]

Private Robert Burns, No14141, 16th Platoon, D Company, 7th Cameron Highlanders, 12 November 1895-29 October 2000
We thought the war would be over before we went out to France. We thought, six months at most, and we had to be trained first and how long that would take we had no idea. We were young, and we thought little more than that we would get in some fun before we had to go back to work. At 18 or 19 one is not very clever, nor very learned, I didn't know anything about world affairs or politics. We listened to what other people were doing and thought, "Why can't we do that?" We had absolutely no idea as to what was going to happen. Later, when we were in France, we'd joke, "So when's this six months up then?"

We were all in it together, pals. "Where do you come from?" "What do you do?" "Where did you work?" "Any cigarettes? Got a light?" "Are you married? No? Any girls?" "Oh yes, half a dozen!"

The training was good fun, shoulder arms, stand easy, nothing to it, it was most enjoyable, as long as one was physically fit. I'll let you into a little secret, too. My pal told me, "If you fail your rifle practice, know what they say? You go back the next day. If you pass your rifle practice you're on a five mile run." So I made it my duty to fail my rifle practice, miss the target. So I went back to the ranges, while those who passed had to go for a long run.

There were three of us who stuck together. One of them was a farmer's son, he didn't have much of an education but he was a real friend, he knew all about life, animal life and human life. He called me Palindrome Burns because my regimental number was 14141.

2nd Lieutenant Norman Margrave Dillon, 14th Northumberland Fusiliers, 27 July 1896-17 October 1997

I was studying to be a mining engineer, but I was glad to get out of the mines when the Secretary of State for War made his appeal for volunteers. I was 18 and one month when I received my commission from the War Office and, after acquiring a uniform, received instructions to report to the 14th Battalion at Berkhamstead. Everyone was in billets, but nobody knew where anything was, so I was told simply to turn up on a local football field at 8 the next morning. There I found 200 men drawn up in squares. They were nearly all miners from the Morpeth area, and had been told to go in their old clothes because uniforms would be issued to them. As I wondered what to do, an old soldier with Boer War ribbons on his chest approached and gravely saluted me, asking, "Are you our new officer?" I told him I didn't know. "I think you are, Sir, as we haven't got any." He asked for instructions but I was completely ignorant of military procedure and, not knowing what to do, I suggested the men should sit down, and then, seeing other companies dispersing, I told him to "Carry on, Sergeant Major," - he was in fact a corporal - and told him to end the parade, not knowing how to do it myself.

After breakfast, I slipped away from my billet and the first thing I did was to go to the railway station, to Smith's bookstall, and there I found various books of a military nature and picked up a War Office manual called "Infantry Training". Set out quite clearly was the whole procedure of falling-in a company and how to manoeuvre it around the parade ground. I spent a lot of time with this manual, drilling imaginary troops represented by matchsticks, until I was fairly proficient. I learnt a new movement each day and then tried it out on the men. We got along famously. They hadn't a clue I was pulling the wool over their eyes, and that I was always just one step ahead of them.

Lance Corporal Vic Cole, 7th Queen's Own (Royal West Kent Regiment), 1897-1995
We had some old timers with the 7th Battalion. The first Major we had, I believe, had Crimean War medals on, and if they weren't Crimean, then they were from the Afghan wars of the 1870s. Major Whittaker was his name and he was at least seventy-five years old. From just a mob wandering round, we were sorted out into sections and platoons. He came out and said, "Attention! Shoulder arms!" and another officer, one of the younger ones, said quietly, "Sir, Sir, it's slope arms." 'Shoulder arms' was the order he used to give way back in the last century. We had wooden guns, cut out into shape, just to learn rifle drill; it was a long time before we got our real rifles.

2nd Lieutenant Richard Hawkins, 11th Royal Fusiliers, 1895-1994
I was on parade with my company one morning, and Major Walters came in, nothing to do but he'd come back to serve his country. I said, "Um, excuse me, Sir, what medals are represented by those little ribbons that you're wearing?" "Well," he said, "one is the King's South African Medal and the other's the Queen's. I'm not quite sure which is which. All I can tell you is that my life was never in danger for one moment. I'm not sure I ever heard a shot fired."

2nd Lieutenant Norman Dillon, 14th Northumberland Fusiliers, 1896-1997

Our training consisted mainly of route marches. There were no uniforms at this time and authority had only been given for the local purchase of boots. As a result, the men's clothing was a scandal, shirt tails sticking out of old trousers. One day I was drilling my platoon when Brigadier General Armstrong rode up on his horse and abused me because my men were clad in rags and tatters. There were plenty of uniforms available in the stores and I had only to ask for them. This was untrue: we did not receive any uniforms for some time after this, and then they were dismal affairs of blue, mass-produced in haste.

Private James William Wilson, No11727, A Company,
7th Leicestershire Regiment, 10 September, 1896 – fl.1998

We were sent to Aldershot, where we were quickly sorted out and began training the first day we arrived. Physical exercise was undertaken on Salisbury Plain, and parades outside the barracks in civilian clothes. I was only a kid but a number of men in the battalion were real tough Yorkshire miners. We had no uniforms and our civilian shoes soon wore out before we ever received boots, in fact the miners said they would refuse to parade again if they didn't get proper boots. After a time, we were given uniforms but not khaki, there was no khaki to be had, so they gave us a red uniform with navy blue cuffs and white braiding, ceremonial uniform you might say. At Christmas we were allowed to go home, and I can remember it to this day, I was walking up Granby Street, fancying myself a soldier, and an elderly gentleman stopped me and said, "Excuse me, Sir, are you going to France in that uniform?" I said, "I've got no other." Do you know, we didn't get khaki until March 1915.

Lance Corporal Vic Cole, 7th Queen's Own (Royal West Kent Regiment), 1897-1995

The signals officer approached a sergeant and told him he wanted some men to be signallers, so the sergeant said to us one by one, "Well, what are you? Boy Scout? Good. OK, you. What are you?" And he came to me and I said, "Wireless operator." "Oh, we don't want you," he said, dismissing me out of hand. He didn't know anything about it, didn't know there was such a thing as wireless. I thought, "That's funny," until the officer said, "Right, is there anyone else?" And I said, "Yes, Sir, I know morse and semaphore," so he said, "Why didn't you say? OK, well, come on then!"

We practised morse code using flags. We'd go out with the section and form a square and signal to each other. I had messages all written out, "Enemy attacking such and such, send reinforcements" and this would be signalled round the square and we would see if the same message came back. The blokes were pretty good because they used to like it and it was better than company drilling, marching up and down all day. As the training progressed, the telephones came in, and morse became morse by sound instead of sight. The telephones came with thin copper wire, number 18 size, just japanned over black. On manoeuvres it used to get entangled in everything and the infantry used to curse us as they frequently got emmeshed in the stuff. Later, we got D3 cable and a dry cell battery to which you added water to make it active, and they lasted about two or three weeks.

Because of my knowledge, I was made a lance corporal, and on my suggestion we went out for a bit of a march with the signals section around Purfleet. It was an agricultural area, fields bounded by dirt road tracks and telegraph poles, plenty of room to muck about. We had two sets of climbing irons so we could scale the telegraph poles. There were two terminals on the D3 telephone, and we put wire round one terminal on the phone. One terminal went to the line and the other went to earth or was clipped onto some railings. Then one man would scale the telegraph pole and clip onto one of the telephone wires and the rest of the section would go up the road a couple of hundred yards and clip onto the wire to see if we could get through.

There was a permanent current on the wire and when we tuned in, we could listen to civilians talking on the telephone. It was great fun.

We had call signs: "Is that AK1?" and we would hear:

"I say, Gladys, whatever's that terrible noise on the wire?"

"I don't know, it must be the soldiers, dear."

"Er, sorry, madam, um, troops on manoeuvres."

2nd Lieutenant Norman Dillon, 14th Northumberland Fusiliers, 1896-1997

My company commander and his second in command chose two furrows next to each other, and, like the rest of us, got some fitful sleep. There was no more rain, and as it was only late September, it was not too cold. However, next morning when we gathered shivering round a small fire and had some tea and bully beef, my No.1 complained of heavy rain. "It must have been wet last night. I was lying in a furrow next to Jones and when I woke up my trousers were completely soaked." Nobody said anything, but our suspicions were confirmed when his second in command arrived and said, "My word, it was cold last night, it affected my bladder. I couldn't be bothered to get up so I just turned over and let fly."

INTO ACTION

[Ed. Even before the nucleus of a New Army began to form in Britain, the regular army was venturing towards the Belgian town of Mons. Ahead of the infantry rode the cavalry, which cautiously moved forward, probing for evidence of the enemy who, they were reliably informed, were marching south in huge numbers. On the night of 21 August, C Squadron of the 4th Dragoon Guards were sent north to see if contact could be made. Among their number was a sixteen-year-old trooper. He was about to witness the first action of the British Expeditionary Force on the continent.]

Trooper Ben Clouting, 4th (Royal Irish) Dragoon Guards, 1897-1990
All four troops of C Squadron were on outpost that night with two troops on standby, saddled up, ready to move at a moment's notice. Our troop was in a cornfield, along the back of which ran a wood. Everything was still and quiet; everyone was tense. We tied the horses' reins round our wrists, while those too nervous to rest talked to each other in whispers. A few of us slackened our horses' girths to let them breathe freely. But silence was the order, and, as horses were prone to play with their loose bit bars, we held or tied handkerchiefs around the bars to muffle any sound.

At about 6.30am, we arrived at a farm on the corner of a staggered crossroads and began watering our horses in a trough. There were already a few people about and, as we waited, a farm worker came in saying he'd seen four German cavalrymen coming down the road.

There was a flurry of action, and a plan was hatched to capture the patrol as it passed. Four men from 4th Troop were dismounted and ordered to fire a volley of shots into the patrol at close quarters. This would be followed by 2nd Troop charging forward and bagging the remainder. I believe a man was sent out behind a hedge to signal when the Germans were about to arrive, but in his excitement he ran to grab his horse and gave his position away.

The Germans turned their horses to go back and the 1st Troop of C Squadron, led by Captain Hornby, went after them, while the rest of the Squadron followed on in support at a fast canter. As the Germans retired into the village, they met up with a larger group of cavalrymen, and, owing to the congestion, were soon caught by the 1st Troop. We arrived after the Germans had scattered, with the main body splitting off and carrying on up the main road. We continued to give chase, our horses slipping all over the place as we clattered along the square-set stones of the road.

Our chase continued for perhaps a mile or more, until we found ourselves flying up a wide tree-lined road. The Germans, reaching the crest of the road, turned and, though they were still mounted, began firing back down the hill. The order came, "Action front, dismount. Get the horses under cover!" In one movement the Troop returned their swords, reached for their rifles and dismounted, dashing for cover. Glancing up the hill, I saw several Germans filling the road. They made a perfect target, and Thomas, the first into action, shot one from his horse.

As far as I am aware, we came out of the action with three prisoners, all suffering from sword wounds. We suffered no casualties except among the horses, one of which had a bullet wound to her stomach. She managed to bring her man out, but she was finished, and was poleaxed in a nearby village.

[Ed. The first shot fired by the British Army on mainland Europe since the Battle of Waterloo ninety-nine years earlier, took place outside the walls of a once-grandiose house one mile north of the village of Casteau, in Belgium. In May 1990, as part of the Old Contemptibles' final pilgrimage to France and Belgium, Ben revisited the spot where the fighting had taken place and stood next to the field where he had taken the horses under cover. It was the first time he had returned there in over 75 years. Ben was seriously ill but he was determined to make the trip and never once let on how poorly he was. On his return, he went into hospital where he died ten weeks later.]

Private Michael Lally, 2nd Manchester Regiment, 2 September 1894–13 April 1999

We were meant to be deployed along the Mons-Condé Canal, but in the end we were held in reserve, so we didn't see much action that day and our casualties were light. The battalion received orders to fall back from the Canal to a little village nearby called Dour, from where we could see fires burning in the direction of Mons, and people were streaming away from the fighting, trying to get away with whatever they could carry with them on farm carts and prams. They were terrified and we felt that we had let them down.

Trooper Ben Clouting, 4th (Royal Irish) Dragoon Guards, 1897-1990
There was complete confusion during the retreat from Mons, for no sooner had the BEF been forced to pull back than the roads became clogged with entire families on the move. Horses, trucks, handcarts, and carriages poured onto every highway, accompanied by the old and the young, all carrying anything they could manage, and all moving at walking pace. We felt sorry for them, but there was nothing we could do.

It was hot, dry and dusty, and very quickly the horses began to look exhausted and dishevelled. Where we could, we rode along the road's soft, unmetalled edges, for the paving stones were very hard on their legs, but our horses soon began to drop their heads, and wouldn't shake themselves as they normally did. Many were so tired, they fell asleep standing up, their legs buckling and taking the skin off their knees. To ease the horses' burden, excess kit was dumped. Shirts, spare socks and other laundry were all thrown away along with our greatcoats.

Private Michael Lally, 2nd Manchester Regiment, 1894-1999
As we retreated down the road, the Military Police were asking, "What division? What regiment?" It was a bloody shambles. That retreat from Mons was the worst part of the war. As we marched south our feet became horribly blistered and sore, I had to wrap puttees round my feet. Later I saw other lads throw their boots away. We ended up in a field just south of Le Cateau. After taking a message on the field telephone, the captain came over and said, "We're all on our own now, lads. Keep going."

Trooper Ben Clouting, 4th (Royal Irish) Dragoon Guards, 1897-1990

The infantry reservists found the going unbearable. Many had been called up after five years on the reserve and had not marched in all that time. Their feet simply weren't up to the stone-set roads, in stiff, unbroken boots. Blood oozed through shoe soles, or from bits of rag tied round blistered feet. In grim determination, they hobbled along in ones and twos, often hanging on to our stirrup leathers to keep going. At any halt, men fell asleep instantaneously, and required a good shake or the prod of a sergeant's boot to wake them again. History judged the Retreat heroic, but from where I was sitting, it was a shambles.

[Ed. The regular army fought a rolling retreat to the River Marne, south east of Paris, before the tables were turned and the German army, exhausted and over-stretched, was forced to retire to the Chemin des Dames. Within weeks of the outbreak of war, Britain would require its territorial forces to take the field, the first units leaving for France in September. Others followed soon after.]

Corporal G B Jameson, 1/1st Northumberland Yeomanry, 1892-1999
We rode into Zeebrugge. It was dead quiet, blackout everywhere, but the clatter of the horses' hooves soon brought the people out. "Oh, they're British", and they flung open every blessed place and showered us with oranges and apples and plied us with wine and loaves of bread. We made a triumphant arrival into Zeebrugge, girls kissing us, we had a marvellous time.

Towards the end of the day, the squadron was quartered in a field, with the horses tied up on picket lines in a square. It was a beautiful evening, a lovely azure blue sky, dead quiet. We lay there, with our heads resting on our saddles, our waterproof sheets on the ground with a blanket and greatcoat on top. There is nothing more thrilling than to sleep out and then wake in the fresh air of an early dawn. There was no thought of a war. Suddenly, away to one side somebody started to play an air from Cavaleria Rusticana on a fiddle and then presently a light baritone took up the refrain and started to sing. These two men were both members of Gosforth Troop: one was Billy Elliot, he had been an associate of the Gosforth Amateur Dramatics Society in Newcastle, the other was Alf Carrick, a member of the operatic society. To lie there with that lovely sky above you and hear that beautiful music wafting all around, and the chomp, chomp of the horses eating, I've never forgotten that, nothing like it, amazing.

[Ed. Eleven Old Contemptibles made the final pilgrimage to the battlefields in 1990. Even fifteen years ago, the average age of those who went was over 95. As well as Ben Clouting, G B Jameson, Frank Sumpter, Joe Armstrong and Fred Dixon also made the trip. G B had dislocated his hip but despite being in great pain, he was determined to go back and although he was forced into a wheel chair for the first and only time in his life he, like Ben, never once complained of his discomfort.]

Lance Corporal Joe Armstrong, 1st Loyal North Lancashire Regiment, 1895-1997

We were jogging along on the train, some of us on the footboards and some on the roof, when a couple of hundred yards ahead I saw some beautiful peach trees, I got up and quickly made my way along the top of the train towards the engine, where I climbed down to the footboards and jumped off. The trees belonged to a house and in the garden was a mother and a daughter. I pointed to the peaches and the mother pointed to my cap badge. Without arguing, because I'd got the train to think of, I let her have my cap badge and I grabbed a few peaches, just managing to leap onto the footboard at the back of the train.

Corporal G B Jameson, 1/1st Northumberland Yeomanry, 1892-1999

Naturally, wherever we went we were looking for food. It was very chancy, as we were so often detached from our supplies and to a large degree they were very slow coming forward. Anyway, as a Corporal I was told to take my patrol up the Menin Road and to push on as far as I could and look for Germans. Under no circumstances had I to get embroiled, but to find and ascertain the enemy's strength. Anyway, we arrived at Gheleveldt Château and I said to my fellows, "Go downstairs and see if you can find some food," while I went upstairs. I remember seeing two small bronze medallions which had fallen off a wall. One showed the Cloth Hall in Ypres, the other showed a man called Edward Pecker. I took those medallions as souvenirs and carried them right through the war. The Château was spick and span, but there was no food at all, not a scrap in the place anywhere, but what we did find was champagne in the cellars. So, we helped ourselves to a couple of bottles each and stuffed them into the strapping round the saddle. But champagne doesn't ride well on horseback and as we rode off, the corks began popping, champagne spewing all over the horses' flanks and in the end we lost the lot.

Lance Corporal Joe Armstrong, 1st Loyal North Lancashire Regiment, 1895-1997
The company officer decided to have a kit inspection while the battalion was out on reserve. We had to show our tin of bully beef, packet of biscuits and tea and sugar, well, by this time, half of us had eaten them. We had to be punished, so what did the officer do? He turned to Regimental Sergeant Major Thompson and ordered him to bring two earthenware jars, each containing two gallons of rum – the nights had been getting cold and he'd started putting rum in the early morning tea – and he ordered the RSM to take the cork out and pour the four gallons onto the ground. He should have been shot.

Out on reserve, Thompson had his own little dugout. Next morning when he got up, he found a tent peg and attached to it was a field postcard, on which was written:
This place marks the spot
Where many a young soldier lost his tot
It was poured out in damn dirty fashion
Because he had eaten his emergency rations.

Thompson went crackers.

Trooper Ben Clouting, 4th (Royal Irish)Dragoon Guards, 1897-1990

Clean water was of great importance to a regiment on the move, and whenever possible, water bottles were kept topped up. On one occasion, the Squadron turned into a stream, and the horses, tired and thirsty, went to drink, but we were told to "Ride on", so on we went. The water was less than a foot deep, clear and inviting, and it seemed such a waste. Several troopers did try to get water into their enamelled bottles, removing the cork and slinging them over into the stream as they rode, tipping and dipping them in the water, but with little success.

Able Seaman Alf Bastin, Hawke Battalion Royal Naval Volunteer Reserve, 1896-1997

The first job when we got settled in the trenches was to post guards, and, my name being Bastin, I was at the top of the bloody list. At 11 o'clock at night I was called out and stood on a corner on guard, rifle ready. I could see a bit of firing going on round about, but nothing near us, and from where I was standing I could actually see the boats in Antwerp harbour all alight. It was beautiful to see. An officer came round occasionally for reports. "Anything doing?" "No, Sir, plenty of firing going on, you can see for yourself, Sir."

It was shortly after this, that things began to liven up. Without warning we were ordered to mount the trenches and fire twenty rounds straight ahead, point blank, on open range, which meant we didn't have to use the sights. We didn't know what we were firing at, no idea at all, but as soon we'd finished, we were given orders to fall in on the road and were marched off to a yard and told to board cattle trucks. When we were all loaded up, off we went, where to, no one had any idea.

Corporal G B Jameson, 1/1st Northumberland Yeomanry, 1892-1999

Before the Battle of Ypres, the squadron was taking shelter in Sanctuary Wood. The Germans were shelling the wood at the time, with splinters of hot metal flying about. The infantry were filtering up through the trees to dig trenches. I was holding my horse, and one of these fellows said to me, "Give me a light, chum." I struck my tinder lighter and leant under the horse's head while he lit his cigarette, just as a shell burst overhead. The man immediately fell dead while my horse had a chunk of shrapnel down its nearside. I discovered too that a chunk of metal was also embedded in the rolled greatcoat strapped to the back of my saddle, and the canvas water bucket that was slung over the sword hilt was punctured and no good. I was untouched but my horse had a nasty gash from about the girth to the stifle down its ribs, as though somebody had taken a red-hot poker down its side. I was lucky. My war might have ended in its first week.

Lance Corporal Joe Armstrong, 1st Loyal North Lancashire Regiment, 1895-1997

We were told to fix bayonets because we were going to charge. I was behind a hedge with a chap next to me ready to move off, when there was an explosion and he was hit in the knee by a piece of shell. I looked and could see his leg was hanging on with a few bits of skin. I got hold of him and dragged him to safety. He emptied his water bottle as I used his bandage to stem the flow of blood; he then emptied my water bottle and I used my bandage. I'm only sorry now I didn't know about tourniquets. I got him on my shoulder and made off towards our lines, when I heard somebody shout, "Go back you bloody fool, go back." In my confusion I had been walking towards the German trenches. They could have shot me easily, but they must have taken pity on me. I walked back and put him behind a tree, but what could I do? I'll always remember that the man was a cockney because he turned to me and said, "Gor blimey, mate, you aint half a toff." And with that he just got hold of his leg and tore it off and threw it round the tree. I had to leave him; no doubt he died. There weren't stretcher bearers around, but perhaps the blood would have congealed enough to save his life, I don't know. By the time I got back the bayonet charge had been made. When I got to the German line, the men were already busy reversing the trench, building up the parapet with dead bodies.

Private Frank Sumpter, 1st Rifle Brigade, 1897-1999
The Germans were eighty yards on the far side of Ploegsteert Wood. We were inside the wood, dug in, when General Hunter-Weston turned up. He appeared to object to us being inside the wood and having listening patrols out in front. He wanted us at the front of the wood instead, so he ordered an attack. "We won't get to Berlin like this," I actually heard him say that to one of our platoon officers.

The next morning over the top we went. I hadn't gone twenty yards when the man next to me got a bullet through his head and his brains splashed right across my shoulders. That was my first experience of war. We rushed forward but when we got outside the edge of the wood we found we couldn't get into the fields beyond because there was a ditch full of water, so we lay down and kept up a field of fire until we were told what to do. It was noticed that further along, there was a gateway with a culvert going over the ditch into the field. Orders were given to do mutual advance, one man at a time.

Our officer gave the command, "Get ready, go!" and each time up the man would get and run like hell and go through the culvert and drop the other side. All the time, our officer lay with his revolver over his arm to frighten the boys into going. As soon as a man got up, the bullets came zup, zup, zup, like a shower of needles from a pine forest when the wind blows, and inevitably two or three were hit as they ran forward into the ploughed field beyond. Half the platoon had gone over when it came to my turn. I ran because nobody refused and because I knew the officer was there with his revolver if I didn't. Once across, we opened fire so that the other half could come on until the entire platoon was across and lying in the mud. Then the order was given, "At the sound of the whistle, you'll go forward at the double." But you couldn't double because as you picked your feet up there was half a hundredweight of clay stuck to your boots. We got as far as we could, and no further. We'd done nothing but got ourselves into a mess.

Able Seaman Alf Bastin, Hawke Battalion, Royal Naval Volunteer Reserve, 1896-1997

We'd gone about thirty miles when all of a sudden the train stopped in a railway siding. "What the hell is going on here?" we wondered. We soon found out. We were surrounded by Germans. Orders were issued to get out of the train and line up on the road, giving up our arms and our bayonets as we did so. We'd been captured and we were dumbstruck. There was one officer with us, Lieutenant Crossman, a naval volunteer, something to do with the Breweries, and he started going mad. This officer did not hand in his revolver and when we got orders to march off, he suddenly stood up in the middle of the road and shouted, "Come on, boys, let's make a dash for it!" and started firing his weapon. What a bloody fool he was, because he was immediately shot and we all quickly lay down in the road. He was carted off, dead I presume, and we were marched away. I suppose there must have been at least a thousand of us on that train.

Private Frank Sumpter, 1st Rifle Brigade, 1897-1999

Early in the morning, I did a foolish thing. I was only sixteen, it was dark and I put my hand round and felt a skin of frost coming onto the clay. "If my rifle bolt freezes and they counter attack, I won't be able to fire", I thought, not knowing in my ignorance that the bolt wouldn't freeze. So I opened the butt trap of my rifle and took the oil bottle out and on top of the bottle there was a spoon. I oiled the bolt; I tried it and it was lovely. I got the bottle and looked round for the lid but couldn't find it. I must have squashed it into the mud, so I put the bottle back into the butt trap of the rifle closed, it down and thought, "Right, I'll tell the Sergeant Major tomorrow and get another one." At 3am we got the order to retire.

On the way back, we were told to pick up the wounded. A pile of stretchers had been brought up to the edge of the wood, and every four men were to take a stretcher. We found one man wounded in the leg, but there was another fellow whom we wouldn't touch. His stomach had been torn and his intestines were exposed, so they used his webbing to try and bolt him in, to keep his stomach from falling on the ground when they took him away. We carried the other man, but it was an awful thing to do, to carry a stretcher through a forest with all the earth churned up and with roots sticking out of the ground. One of the team would slip and the wounded man would fall off the stretcher. We'd put him on again and then someone else would fall. What a job!

Lance Corporal Joe Armstrong, 1st Loyal North Lancashire Regiment, 1895-1997

After the bayonet charge, two companies were told to dig in, and not to retire and not to advance, no matter what happened. The other two companies consolidated the position behind. My company was forward of the other two, and I said to an officer, "Are we right at the front, Sir?" And he said, "Oh yes." It was dark then, perhaps eight in the evening and I said, "Well, I can hear voices just over the top." "They'll be Germans," he replied.

At first light, I saw a few Germans a hundred yards away running from hedge to hedge and I took a few shots. Then, shortly after, we heard a hullabaloo on our left and we learnt that the Germans had broken through the Northamptons; in fact they'd swept right past us and captured the artillery and the headquarters. We'd been ordered not to retire but when we saw the Germans coming round the front of us, our officer did a bunk but only ran straight into the arms of the enemy.

When you join the army, you're not told what to do when you're captured. When I was ordered to climb out of the trench, I still had my rifle and bayonet in my hand and narrowly avoided having a bayonet run through me because I didn't drop my weapon quick enough, very close indeed.

They marched us away from the trenches and put us in lines of five to be counted. I had an unlit pipe in my mouth. An officer was counting us, and when he came to me, his hand came up and tugged at the pipe. "This is my blinking pipe," I thought and I stuck to it.

Corporal Taylor, who was behind me, shouted, "Let go of that bloody pipe, you fool." Good job I did, because as the officer tugged at my pipe with one hand, he was about to screw his revolver round my temple with the other. A moment later, I would have been dead.

Able Seaman Alf Bastin, Hawke Battalion, Royal Naval Volunteer Reserve, 1896-1997

After we were captured, we were put in closed cattle trucks and taken away to Germany. We had nothing to eat for days and we were starving by the time we stopped at Cologne railway station. The Germans had been told that the British Navy had been captured and they wanted to show us off, so they opened up the trucks to public scrutiny. I could see that the platform was crowded with people, mostly women. They just walked along and looked at us, throwing mildewed bread as an insult. This, of course, we were only too glad to eat as we were hungry, and we tore off the bits that weren't so mouldy. We were all bewildered, we'd been on the road for three days, then taken on this train, and we wondered what the hell we were coming to. They were shouting at us in German, "Englische Schweinhund!" spitting and swearing, then out of this tumult, I heard one voice shout out, very distinctly, "Englanders, bloody fucking bastards!"

Private Frank Sumpter, 1st Rifle Brigade, 1897-1999

My platoon went in twenty strong and eleven came out. We'd had nothing to eat since 2 o'clock the day before, so you can bet we were pretty all out tired when we got back to our billet. Sergeant Webb spoke to us. "When the Company Officer is available, we'll get our instructions where to assemble. In the meantime, we'll go into this schoolroom." So we got in to this building and threw down our equipment to get some rest, just as our platoon officer turned up. He'd come out from Sandhurst, about nineteen years of age, brand new and full of discipline. He turned to the Sergeant. "These men will fall asleep, but we can't move until we get orders. What do you suggest,

Sergeant?" "I know, Sir, have a kit inspection." Unbelievable! We'd just come out of action, we were exhausted and now we were to have a war-time kit inspection, each of us laying our kit out in the ordinary barrack-room fashion.

When we'd done this, the lieutenant went along for an inspection until he came to me. He looked at my kit:

"Where is the stopper of your oil bottle?"

"I lost it last night in the attack, sir."

"Fiddlesticks!" he said. "Put him on a charge."

So I was put on a charge for losing, by neglect, an article of equipment; failing to report the loss of equipment; rendering myself an inefficient soldier, and conduct to the prejudice of good order and military discipline.

These were serious charges, and when they went before the Company Commander, the Captain said, "I can't deal with this, he'll have to go in front of the Colonel." So I was marched in front of the Colonel, but when I started to explain what had happened, the Sergeant Major barked, "Speak when you're spoken to!" Nobody spoke to me, so I couldn't speak. The Colonel said, "This is very serious, a very serious charge, I can't do less: a regimental entry, eight days No1 Field Punishment." I didn't mind the punishment but what I didn't like was that a regimental entry goes onto your paybook and onto your records and is assessed when they make up your gratuity when you leave the army. In my case, No1 Field Punishment amounted to nightly jankers, one hour tied to a gun wheel and then carrying ammunition back up to the trenches, taking another risk with your life.

THE CHRISTMAS TRUCE

[Ed. Soldiers in France and Belgium were facing their first Christmas away from home and for a few days trench life had been relatively

quiet. On Christmas Eve, mysterious lights began to appear in the enemy trenches, then Christmas trees, and, out of the dark, carol singing, and calls to Tommy across the trenches to come over. An impromptu Christmas truce began to take place, but it would require an astonishing consensus from both sides to be successful.]

Corporal G B Jameson, 1/1st Northumberland Yeomanry, 1892-1999
On Christmas Eve, we were withdrawn from the line. We thought we had struck it lucky getting out of the trenches for Christmas Day. I landed the job of duty corporal so I couldn't wander away from the billet when some of the ration party heard about this Christmas Truce. Two brothers, Keith and Philip Ridley, came dashing up to me and said, "The Jerries are walking around on the top, singing carols and exchanging cigarettes." I couldn't believe it. He said, "These ration party fellows who I have just been talking to are quite certain they are." "Well," I said, "I'm tied here, but you can go up if you like. Go and find out." So off they went with another fellow, Les Wood, up the front line. Some time after, Keith came back with a Landwehr hat, which I tried on, while Philip had a water bottle and Les a fistful of cigars. "It's marvellous," they told me, "wandering about, and they're dishing out all sorts of things and kicking a football around!"
[Ed. In 1990, G B Jameson returned for a nostalgic visit to the town of his childhood, Newcastle upon Tyne, where he was introduced to 94-year-old Jack Irving, a sergeant in the Gateshead Troop, B Squadron, Northumberland Hussars. Both men had served throughout the campaign in 1914, including the Christmas Truce, and although they served in different squadrons, they vaguely remembered each other. Later that day, G B visited the Northumberland Hussars' Museum where he met the curator. While looking around the museum, he spotted a picture of Keith Ridley. "I mentioned the fact that Keith had come back from the front line with this hat. The curator took me to the other side of the museum and said, "There's your Landvehr hat", and it was, in a case, given to the museum by Keith. I said, "That's damn

funny, the last time I saw that hat, I had it on my head on Christmas morning, 1914."]

Private Frank Sumpter, 1st Rifle Brigade, 1897-1999
We heard the Germans singing "Silent Night, Holy Night," and then they put up a notice, "Merry Christmas." Then they started singing, and our boys said, "We'll join in." So we joined in with a song and when we started singing, they stopped. So we sang on and then we stopped and they sang. The Germans waved their hands, "Happy Noel, Tommy", and we shouted back. One German took a chance and jumped up on top of the trench and shouted out "Happy Christmas, Tommy!" No one fired a shot, which was marvellous, as before then you couldn't put your finger up without it being blown off. Of course our boys said, "If he can do it, we can do it." The Sergeant Major came along and said, "Get down there, get down there." We stuck our two fingers up at him. "It's Christmas!" and with that we all jumped up and the Germans beckoned us forward to the barbed wire and we shook hands. I spoke to one German and he said, "Do you know Islington?" He could speak very good English. "Do you know the Jolly Farmer's pub in Southgate Road?" and I said, "Yes, my uncle has a shoe repairing shop next door, and he said, "That's funny, there's a barber's shop on the other side where I used to work before the war." He must have shaved my uncle at times and yet my bullet might have found him and his me.

The officers didn't join in; they hid themselves. They'd given the order, "No fraternization," and turned their backs on us. Nobody tried to stop it, they knew they couldn't, the boys weren't in the mood. We didn't talk about the war, other than how long it would last, and our families. I stood there about half an hour and then I'd had enough and came back. I was young and wasn't very interested, but most of the boys stayed there the whole day and enjoyed the curiosity of walking about in No Man's Land.

Private Frederick Dixon, No9775, C Company, 2nd Leicestershire Regiment, 26 September 1895-January 1991

What a glorious feeling, to be able to relax, not to hear a shot fired, or to stand in trenches half-full of water. Two days before Christmas, we'd been relieved and marched out of the trenches to a quiet area of civilization. We halted in a disused farmhouse and were billeted so many to a room, squeezing in. It was a lovely house, hardly damaged, fully furnished, with lovely pictures and full length mirrors everywhere, but no beds. The owners had rushed out of the house when the Germans approached and had no time to take anything. On Christmas Eve, we explored. Poultry and pigs had been turned out to fend for themselves in the open. The poultry were roosting in the trees, so we shot them as we wanted. The pigs were finding what food they could in the garden and fields. It seemed too good to be true. We had been living on bully beef and hard biscuits for a long time and here was pork in abundance. So we shot a beautiful porker. Our cooks drew no rations that day, we supplied all their needs and we all mucked in preparing it for cooking. The pig was dressed by us old farm hands, and the poultry plucked, perfect. Then we raided the garden for the necessary vegetables for stuffing. I never did enjoy a dinner quite like it in all my life. Over seventy five years later, I can still taste it.

Then we went and spoilt it. The lads found some wine in the cellar under the house. It was full of bottles, we tried first one then another and soon we were hopelessly drunk. I did not drink much, so kept all right, but some of the lads tried everything including something that turned out to be mentholated spirits and that finished things completely. Several of the lads were very ill and two of them died, so our little celebration eventually became a funeral party.

[Ed. The success of the recruitment drive that drew so many into the army in the first months of the war tailed off by the year's end. Many of those young men who resisted enlisting did so for good reason; often commitments to ill or dependent parents or siblings put paid to

any immediate thought of enlistment. Yet the pressure to appear patriotic was never far away, and when the opportunity finally arose, most young men were not found wanting.]

Sapper Stanley Clayton, No480143, 457th Field Company, Royal Engineers, 62nd Division, 27 October 1894-17 March 2000
On Christmas Eve 1914, I was with my girlfriend and I told her I was going to join the army. "If you are," she said, "we'll make a pact, we'll have our photographs taken and I'll carry your photograph and you carry mine."

You'd be called a scabber if you didn't join up. The girls would say you were frightened. First one lad would volunteer, then another and another, and they'd say, "You're frightened, you are." My brother had been very ill with Bright's Disease, a form of kidney disease, then just after Christmas 1914 he died. We buried him on the 3 January 1915, and my mother was crying and I said, "Look, mother, I'll soon have to join the army in any case, so I might as well go and you might as well cry for two. I'm going to join the army," and all she said between the tears was, "All right, lad, all right."
[Ed. As promised, Stan carried the picture of his girlfriend all through the war, indeed right up until his death in 2000 that same picture remained secreted within his wallet. His marriage to Kate lasted nearly seventy years.]

Private Archibald Lee Richards, No200862, D Company (D7), Heavy Section, Machine Gun Corps, 7 January 1897-10 February 1998
I was scared I might be called up and pushed into something I didn't want, so I came home and had a few days' holiday. Before I enlisted a recruiting agent came to Upton Cross, and he said, "Well, there's a list here of things you can join."

You'd have thought that I wasn't very much for King and Country. I didn't fancy joining the local regiment, the Duke of Cornwall's Light Infantry. I'd heard a little bit about what was going on abroad, that the infantry had been badly cut up and how many were being killed or wounded, and I thought, "I'll plump for the Garrison Artillery, perhaps it'll keep me at home." Not very patriotic, was it? Heavy guns, back out of the way, but it was up to me what I joined and I took hold of that. I'd made a pledge, to serve, and I knew I couldn't back out, so I just resigned myself to it and said, "Well, if I'm lucky I'll come through, if I get killed, I get killed." I would go through with it; I was patriotic enough to do that.

Trooper Albert Elliott 'Smiler' Marshall, No1771, Southend Troop, A Squadron, 1/1st Essex Yeomanry, 15 March 1897- 16 May 2005

I had been working as a groom and I decided to go where my mates were, because all the farmers' sons round where we were joined the Essex Yeomanry. Of course, everybody in the countryside could ride then, the butcher, the baker, the candlestick maker, they all had a pony; cars were almost unheard of. So a little before Christmas 1914, I goes up to Colchester, to the Essex Yeomanry office, and knocks on the door, and the sergeant major called me in. He says, "Good morning," and asks my name, and all the rest of it, you know, were my parents English, and then he asks my age. So I told him I was seventeen. "What year were you born?" I said, "1897." He says, "I think you've made a mistake." "Don't be funny," I said, "course I haven't, see." "Well," he said, "you just go outside that door and think it over and then come back and see me." I goes outside into a passageway and there was a chap from Colchester. I got talking to him, and told him the sergeant major had sent me out for making a mistake with my age. "What did you tell him?" "I told him I was seventeen." "Well, you can't get in until you're eighteen." So I goes back in, as if I'd never been before. "How old are you?" he asks. "Eighteen," I told him. "Oh yes, um" and then he says, "I'll tell you what, it's nearly Christmas, come back here in the New Year and you attest then," and that's what I did, on 5 January 1915.

CHAPTER TWO

1915

VETERANS IN CONTEXT

THE WORLD INTO WHICH THESE MEN WERE BORN and in which they grew up was so different from that of my generation that they seem to belong not only to another time but almost to another culture. Many recalled living in small terraced houses with sometimes two and even four children sharing a bed, with the lavatory at the end of the garden. In large families, each additional child inevitably put a strain on the father's resources, and children were sometimes sent to live with elderly relatives, or temporarily fostered. Vic Cole, the oldest of seven brothers, was 'farmed out' to his paternal grandmother and aunt, in their house in Gypsy Hill, London. Cecil Withers, the youngest of eight children, was sent to live with a foster mother, Mrs Secker, for twelve years, until he was reclaimed by his real family and told to forget all about his foster mother. Yet a family of seven or eight children was hardly unusual; veterans Walter Burdon and Jack Davis, were one of seven and eight children respectively, and many families had considerably more: Robert Renwick was one of 15; Joe Yarwood the eldest of 13 and Alfred Lloyd one of 16 children. Born in 1898, Alfred was the last in a long line of siblings stretching back to his eldest sister, Elizabeth, born in 1876.

Given the size of many families, as well as the prevalence of illnesses such as consumption and smallpox, it was not uncommon for children to lose parents and siblings at a comparatively young age, forcing young sons to grow up quickly or to fend for themselves. Alfred went to live with his sister Elizabeth, after his exhausted mother died in her late forties when he was two, and his father when Alfred was four. Smiler Marshall's mother died when he was four, and his only brother died of spotted fever when he was seventeen, followed four years later by his father when Smiler was coming home for demobilisation, aged just 22. Some soldiers heard of the death of their parents when they were serving in the army: Ted Francis's mother died while he was training, and he heard indirectly of the death of his father (and the loss of his home) while he was serving in France. Richard Hawkins was on the march to Bishop's Stortford, on his way to embarkation for France, when, in his own words, "I got a telegram delivered by a boy on a red bicycle, a post boy, to say that my father had just died." Richard was twenty.

In interviewing veterans, I was always aware of the wide variation in their reasons for enlistment. Some enjoyed their lives and even their work, and enlisted largely as a matter of patriotic duty, mixed, no doubt, with a young man's sense of adventure. Others were more inspired to leave their dead-end jobs in the hope of finding a new challenge and opportunity that did not seem likely to occur if they stayed at home. For youngsters who hated their jobs, such as those in the mines or in heavy industry, it was clear that the war provided an opportunity to escape onerous and sometimes frightening work. Ironically, one lad loathed his job in an engineering company and feared the heavy machinery – "I was always afraid I might get caught up in it" – and gladly exchanged this employment for the prospect of excitement and adventure fighting for his country.

Inevitably, most of the veterans I have been fortunate enough to meet have been the 'young' ones, who were either still in education or had recently started work, often in dull and unrewarding jobs, before they enlisted. In 1914, most children left school at fourteen, and even earlier if they had a good attendance record. In Lancashire, for example, a child could begin to work part-time at the mill when he was just eleven, working either mornings or afternoons. For the majority, leaving school on a Friday meant starting adult work on the Monday, with poor pay, long hours and often dangerous conditions.

For men such as Walter Green, or Arthur Barraclough, both of whom had trained as barbers, or Robert Renwick, who had worked in a grocer's shop, it was not too difficult to return to their previous employment when they later came to leave the army. Some employers kept jobs open for returning soldiers, but this was not always as successful as one might expect. Those who had been apprentices faced particular problems: as former Cameron Highlander Andrew Bowie said, "I went out as a boy and came back as a man" and it was not easy to fit back into the subservient roles they had had before. Norman Collins, himself an apprentice in the drawing office of a Hartlepool shipbuilder, freely admitted that after the best part of five years' service, he had forgotten most of what he had previously known. The idea of returning to his apprenticeship on the wages of a teenager was anathema. Critical time had been lost. Men in their early twenties who had been at war often came back with a strong desire to marry and have a family, yet this was impossible on wages that were proportionately the same as those they had been paid as sixteen-year-old apprentices before the war. These men had been taught how to fight but had not necessarily developed other skills that were particular to their chosen trade.

Vic Cole was in an unusually fortunate position: before the war he had been an apprentice at the Clapham School of Telegraphy, and during his military service, had worked as a wireless operator. The skills that he had learnt enabled him to obtain an apprenticeship at the Marconi Company when he came home and he rapidly became a junior wireless operator in the merchant navy. Arthur Halestrap, who had a similar training during his years of service, also came home to work for Marconi.

Once a former soldier had found a job, he would frequently keep it for the rest of his working life. The society of the 1920s had much less work mobility than later generations, while the scourge of unemployment held such fears for family men that they were unlikely to throw in a safe job and try their hand at something else. It was important to stay in the same geographical area in which they had grown up, surrounded by a mutually-supporting network of family and friends. Stan Clayton lived in Sheffield all his 105-year life; similarly, Ted Francis lived in Birmingham; Cecil Withers remained in the suburbs of southeast London, moving only locally even on his retirement; Clarrie Jarman lived for 100 years in Woking.

Today, we see movement up the property ladder as a natural progression, a choice of lifestyle not necessarily connected with work, or the advent of family life. In contrast, many veterans stayed put all their working lives and often well beyond that. Reginald Spraggins, who lost an arm in 1918, lived all his post-war life in the home built in Norwich for maimed veterans after the Great War. Arthur Daniels lived in the house his parents had bought when he was just a toddler, remaining there for over a hundred years. In Northampton, Fred and Olive Hodges moved into their house after their marriage in 1925, and there they raised a son and daughter. They stayed there for more than seventy-five years, until forced to move by ill-health and the inevitable frailties brought on by great age; they were both aged over 100 at the time. Similarly, Jim Lovell, the last living recipient of a gallantry award of the Great War, lived on in his parents' house from childhood until just days before he died, his tenure lasting from 1899-2004. The door he passed through to collect his pension in 2004 was, as shown by his surviving enlistment papers, the same door he had walked through to join up in 1915. Many stuck tenaciously to their homes, and when finally 'persuaded' to leave, died soon after, unwilling to settle or incapable of making an adjustment to a new home.

These men lived in another world from any that I have known or can fully appreciate. And yet, by their continued existence, they provided a tangible link to the past, to a bygone world that, by proxy, it is exhilarating to touch. When Alfred Anderson talks in 2005 of the Boer War, it is a more distant event today than if he had spoken to someone in his youth about Trafalgar or Waterloo. And that has always been part of the excitement of meeting these men of such great age. The links to the past have proved so extraordinary. As a small boy, Vic Cole told me that he had spotted W G Grace when the great cricketer attended the South London annual school sports day. "He watched the boys racing for a while and then went off to the Bowling Green – I know, for in my fascination I followed him there."

Over the years other veterans, such as William Godfrey, ex-London Regiment have described seeing the former Prime Minister Gladstone lying in state. "I was surprised by how small he was," he said. Jack Rogers, ex-Sherwood Foresters, saw Queen Victoria during her Diamond Jubilee in 1897. In 1912 Arthur Halestrap walked around the *Titanic* when she was docked in Southampton. Many years later, Percy Wilson sat in the waiting room with the famous mutineer Percy Topliss at Tebay train station, just days before Topliss was shot dead by the police. Norman Dillon discovered T E Lawrence in his post-war squad of recruits, taking down his notes in Arabic. In the 1930s, ex-Gordon Highlander Horace Gaffron, while working as an illustrator for *Life* magazine in Chicago, was introduced to Al Capone, who spoke at length to Horace and was most interested in his war service. Other connections were more tenuous but no less fascinating. Edgar Cranmer, born 1891, (and a distant relation of the great Archbishop) recalled his great grandfather, born around 1805, telling him that his great grandfather had met the highwayman Dick Turpin.

1915

Christmas 1914 had been a remarkable interlude in an otherwise monotonous time at the front. War, in terms of actual fighting, had been put on hold. Men stood in the trenches, stomped their feet and patted their bodies to generate heat, and performed the repetitive and menial tasks that formed daily life in the line. Offensive operations were suspended during the winter months: the ground had become so churned up, so water-logged and impassable, that to fight was a waste of energy. It required colossal expenditure of time and money to force the long columns of wagons and trucks, mules and horses, along frost-covered roads to re-supply the men at the front. The regular army had taken on the might of the numerically-superior Germans and fought them to a standstill, but at a heavy cost. The arrival of the first territorial units in September and October 1914 had helped to stabilize the front, but it was time to rebuild and wait and bide one's time until spring, when the weather would be better suited to offensive action.

On the Western Front, the BEF announced the end of the winter hibernation with the launch of its first major offensive. On 10 March, the British Army undertook an operation at Neuve Chapelle, as much a demonstration to the French of the BEF's willingness to fight than an attack of strategic importance. The aim was to seize the high ground which looked across to the German-held town of Lille. In the event, the three-day onslaught met with initial success, but early gains were not exploited owing to problems of coordination and supply. This offensive set the tone for the year, as army commanders wrestled with the increasing scale and complexity of operations while bowing to pressure from France to undertake supporting operations before they were ready. On 9 May, troops were ordered again to attack at Aubers Ridge in a one-day operation which was followed on 15 May by an ill-fated attack near the village of Festubert. Both actions were hastily conceived and poorly executed, and proved very costly at a time when the BEF was engaged in a defensive operation at Ypres, a little further to the north. The fighting in the Ypres Salient was a short-lived affair undertaken by the Germans and as it turned out, it was the last such operation they initiated against the British Army for nearly three years. Deciding to concentrate on operations against the Russians in the east, the German High Command sanctioned only attacks that were limited in scope against the BEF. The offensive around Ypres in April and May was such an endeavour. Nevertheless the German attack used, for the first time, the new weapon of poison gas. In fierce fighting, British and Empire troops were forced back almost to the gates of the city. If it had fallen, it might have opened up the way to the main railheads and vital lines of communication and perhaps eventually the coast itself.

Throughout 1915, the Germans maintained their superiority in ammunition and men, using poison gas and flame throwers. The second attack at Aubers Ridge had thrown into sharp relief the lack of firepower available to British forces, which had had to restrict their preliminary bombardment to just forty minutes. The desperate shortage of ammunition, evident since the first months of the war, caused a political storm back home when it was portrayed by elements of the press as the reason for failure. Britain, it was felt, had to shed the mantle of the amateur and don the clothes of the professional when it came to fighting a European war. In May, a new Ministry of Munitions was established to deal comprehensively with the issue of armaments, while in France troop numbers rose dramatically, the BEF doubling its size from 350,000 in January to more than 800,000 by the end of the year.

In February 1915, a combined Anglo-French bombardment of the Turkish forts in the Dardanelles had signalled the opening moves which in April led to a full-blown invasion of the Gallipoli peninsula, and the opening up of an alternative front to that in France.

The Allied campaign at Gallipoli began with landings at Helles and Anzac Cove on 25 April. Heavy casualties ensued, but a foothold was gained. However, attempts to break out were frustrated by poor planning and dogged enemy defence. Despite opposition from commanders in France, the Gallipoli landings were reinforced by more men from Britain and the Empire, and a second offensive was launched at Suvla Bay further up the coast. The landing itself was almost unopposed but British forces failed to push on and the initial momentum was lost. The campaign ground to a halt once again. Increasingly, the Gallipoli operation was deemed an expensive failure. With offensive operations about to begin in France near Loos, and another front due to be opened in Salonika, there were no more troops available for a failing campaign, indeed, many of the troops required for Salonika would have to be drawn from Gallipoli. There was no alternative to drawing down the forces on the Turkish peninsula.

At home, Kitchener's New Army continued training. Over the winter and spring months, camp life across the country had gradually improved from the appalling conditions suffered by keen volunteers in the late autumn of 1914. Hutted encampments had been erected, and uniforms and equipment issued to most volunteers, now proud to wear khaki and 1914 pattern leather equipment instead of the hotchpotch uniforms of the previous year. The days of broomsticks had also gone, and for the most part even antiquated rifles such as the Boer War vintage Lee Metford and the Japanese Arisaka had been replaced by the highly efficient and superbly-manufactured Short (Rifle) Magazine Lee Enfield No.1 Mk III. The supply of live ammunition was still woefully inadequate, restricting the time and opportunity that men had on the ranges, but most volunteers were fit, healthy and well-trained. By May, the first Kitchener Divisions were deemed ready to sail for active service to support the depleted regular and territorial armies. The 9th, 14th and 15th Divisions were taken into the line around Ypres, while in August the 18th Division sailed for France and went directly to the Somme, a region previously held by the French but taken over in the summer by Britain as part of her expanding commitment to the fighting.

In September, an Allied offensive was launched in what was the first truly concerted effort on the part of British and French troops to break the German line. In the north, in the coalmining district around Loos and Lens, the British were ordered to attack over a seven-mile front, while the French, much further to the south, attacked in the region of Artois. The BEF were to go into action with six divisions of infantry, around 72,000 men. Unlike earlier attacks, this one would be supported by a five-day bombardment, the consequence of improved ammunition supplies. The initial onslaught would be undertaken by regular and territorial units but would be developed by Kitchener Divisions in their first major action.

1915 was a year of radical change for the British Army on the Western Front, finding its way in a new form of siege warfare where open spaces proved lethal and machine guns and artillery forced men to dig trenches. Back in 1914, nobody anticipated how long British forces would have to stay put, or how far the British economy would have to be adapted and re-designed to supply men with all the material they required, not just to prosecute a war but to survive for prolonged periods with little prospect of an early victory. The British entered 1915 wholly unprepared for war on an industrial scale; they ended the year with a radically different outlook.

KITCHENER'S MEN

Trooper Smiler Marshall, 1/1st Essex Yeomanry, 1897-2005
In the Yeomanry you had to ride all different horses, nothing on them, no saddle, no bridle, no nothing. You had to have a stick, a little cane under each arm, and when the riding masters cracked the whip, the horses you were on just stopped. They were trained for that, they were proper cavalry horses and they'd stop dead from a trot, canter, or gallop. You had to sit tight, or else. I never came off because I put my

arms around the horse's neck – but half of them fell off and the sergeant major used to shout, "Who the hell told you to dismount?"

Private George Aquila Louth, No20915, 15th Hampshire Regiment, 27 February 1897-1 April 2000
A lot of men built up anger against the sergeants during training. They would make us square bash for ages and route march with 90lb on our backs, for 20 miles. I had trouble for years with my feet. At 5.30 in the morning, we had a basin of cocoa and a biscuit, then a five mile run, breakfast at eight, then four hours square bashing, then lunch, then another three hours square bashing.

Private David Francis Weston, No4435, 1/5th Bedfordshire Regiment, 11th March 1895-9th March 1998
There were some men who were always going sick if they knew we were going on a route march, the same faces, always. There was a chap there by the name of Rainbow who rarely went on a route march; he used a bit of soap, hidden in a fag packet, and he would shove it up his behind and come down with diarrhoea, and off he'd trot to see the medical officer. He wasn't the only one to pull the trick.

Private Ted Francis, 16th Royal Warwickshire Regiment, 1896-1996
These route marches were sometimes very long, perhaps twenty miles. Of course we had rests of ten minutes every hour, but when you march with a rifle and kit, you get very tired and fed up, and all the time the officers are saying, "Keep in step", and then one says, "Let's have a song, boys, you know, to buck us up", which was often as we were nearing a town or a village. It was to impress the inhabitants but it didn't impress us. We were almost forced to sing. "Sing, you blighters, don't put your heads down, march properly and sing!" At times, in the summer weather, we were very pleased to start our own singing, we'd sing in good voice, but, as I say, we objected very much to being told. But when you're in the army they can order you to do anything, and

you've got to do it smartly, or else.

Lance Corporal Vic Cole, 7th Queen's Own (Royal West Kent Regiment), 1897-1995

We marched from Codford in Wiltshire to a vast open field near Stonehenge. Men with worn clothing were issued with new tunics, trousers and puttees, and we were ordered to carry rags or brushes in our haversacks to clean the dust off our boots before the General, I forget which one, came round. When we eventually arrived, the whole Division appeared to be there, the 18th Division on three sides of an enormous square, Battalions of the West Kents, the Queen's, and the East Surreys, while the supernumeraries were grouped centrally. A senior officer advanced right into the middle on a lovely horse, stood up in his stirrups and shouted "Attention!" We all sprang to attention and were ordered to present arms, and they kept us like that while the General came round with the King. The King was mounted and there were a couple of Generals and other red tabs. King George V with his beard and his little legs came past, and I was in the front rank at the end, and the General said, "West Kent Regiment, Sir." The King said, "Ah, my mother's favourite regiment," but I reckon he said it to every battalion he passed!

Trooper Smiler Marshall, 1/1st Essex Yeomanry, 1897-2005

We were in private billets and I was billeted with a lad who couldn't write. His surname was Flood and his initials were E.L, so his name was Bloody Hell, and of course everybody laughed. Reveillé was at 6.30am and the snow was on the ground; that was my birthday week, in March. For the first hour, we had physical jerks with Sergeant Beavis from Clacton on Sea. He shouted, "Jump forward, bend!" Anyway, I was a bit of a lad. I was in the second row, and I rolled a snowball and threw it and caught the bloke in front of me, up the behind. The sergeant saw this and said, "Ha ha, that's funny isn't it? Well, you might break your mother's heart but you won't break mine.

I'm talking to you." I'm standing there with my lips pursed, trying not to smile, and he says, "I'm talking to you, Smiler". And from the next morning my mates called me Smiler, instead of Albert.

Private Archie Richards, D Company (D7), Heavy Section, Machine Gun Corps, 1897-1998
I joined the Royal Garrison Artillery and did my physical training on the Hoe at Plymouth, where local people lined up and laughed at us as we made mistakes. Then a group of us were sent to Garden Battery, a six-inch battery at Devonport. I didn't like the training, it was like going back to school again, maths, and sights, ranges and velocity, oh no, I didn't like it one bit, and I and others took pains to show it, acting like dumb schoolboys. They in their turn probably believed we'd never make good artillerymen, so they sent a group of us to Bisley to train on the Hotchkiss machine gun. We trained for several months, and then one day they sent us to Thetford in Norfolk, what for we didn't know. We assumed we would be sent to the trenches with machine guns but we couldn't understand why, when there were the Vickers and the Lewis machine guns, we were training so intensively with the Hotchkiss. Then one day they lined us up and said, "Well, here you are, here's this new weapon and all you people are going to crew them." It was the latest secret weapon, what we called armoured crawlers, tanks in other words, and we were the first to train on them.

Private Ted Francis, 16th Royal Warwickshire Regiment, 1896-1996
We enjoyed the training, enjoyed it very much. We had three months' camp in tents in Malvern and it was more like a holiday than training for war. The fact that our troops were having a rough time and actually getting wounded or even killed never entered most of our heads. We thought, "The war isn't here, we want to go to France." I was a soldier, I had a rifle, there was a war on – what more could a young lad want?

The great day came, after five or six months, when we were issued with rifles. We were all waiting for that; some of the boys would rub that rifle, clean it, brush it, worship it, like a mother with her newborn baby, but for me the greater thrill was when we had real bullets to fire at a target. Now that was something.

[Ed. While Kitchener's volunteers continued their training, in Germany the first prisoners of war were settling in to their new surroundings. Few, if any, suspected that they would not see home for another four years.]

Able Seaman Alf Bastin, Hawke Battalion, Royal Naval Volunteer Reserve, 1896-1997
Within five days of capture, we'd arrived at Doberitz prisoner of war camp where I was to spend the first six months of my captivity. In the early days the camp was just tents and large marquees, holding up to 200 men at a time. These were being occupied by lots of Old Contemptibles, regular soldiers who'd been captured at the Battle of Mons and in the subsequent retreat. When they heard our tale of woe, they christened us CIVs, Churchill's Innocent Victims, after all, as First Lord of the Admiralty he had been the one who'd sent us out there.

We had to sleep under canvas that first winter. We were all lice-bound, sleeping on straw sacks, and of course it was freezing cold. There were no proper washing facilities, and it took about a fortnight to clean us up before we were medically examined. When it came to my turn, the German doctor looked at me and said, in English. "How old are you, young Englander?" I said, "Eighteen years, Sir". "Good God," he said, "you ought to be at home grinding your mother's coffee." He marked me up for light duties, helping the officers on duty, cooking food, but that didn't last long. One day we played a game of rugby; the American embassy had fixed us up with boxing gloves and athletics equipment and such like, and the Germans were watching this game. I knew bugger all about rugby but I must have played quite well, because at the next medical parade they marked me up A1 and I was sent out on a working party digging gravel from a pit.

Lance Corporal Joe Armstrong, 1st Loyal North Lancashire Regiment, 1895-1997

We were lying on straw in marquees to well into the New Year, but we'd seen just across the barbed wire that they were building huts with chimneys on, and we thought, "This is going to be nice, we'll be out of these marquees and in to some proper accommodation." Then, in the second week of January, they came and collected all the Irish, particularly the Roman Catholic Irish, and put them in these huts and soon smoke was billowing out of the chimneys. It transpired that the Germans were trying to form an Irish battalion to fight against us. Anyway, after a few days these Irish lads raided the German canteens and, knowing the conditions we were living in, brought the food over to us, and the next day they were back with us in the marquees.

Able Seaman Alf Bastin, Hawke Battalion, Royal Naval Volunteer Reserve, 1896-1997

One of the men at Doberitz was Private Sidney Godley, one of the first Victoria Cross winners of the war, although it was some time before we knew that he'd been awarded the honour, perhaps Christmas time. In those days the Americans weren't in the war and information used to come to the camp through them. One Sunday, a special parade was ordered and we wondered what it was for. It was announced by the American ambassador that Private Godley had been awarded a VC for his courageous work at Mons, when he held up the German advance with fire from a single machine gun. And do you know what? The camp commandant actually came and shook hands with him after the award had been announced, and Godley was given a staff job at the camp. The men made a special fuss of him. Why they called him Mud Godley I don't know, but that was his nickname.

[Ed: Sidney Frank Godley, 1889-1957. His citation reads: On 23 August 1914 at Mons, Belgium, Private Godley took over a machine-

gun on Nimy Bridge when the lieutenant in charge of the section had been mortally wounded. Private Godley held the enemy from the bridge single-handed for two hours under very heavy fire and was wounded twice. His final act was to destroy the gun and throw the pieces into the canal. His gallant action covered the retreat of his comrades, but he was eventually taken prisoner.]

Able Seaman Alf Bastin, Hawke Battalion, Royal Naval Volunteer Reserve, 1896-1997

There were quite a few escape attempts. The first one was a Russian prisoner. We had been moved to Dyrotz POW Camp, and on Ascension Day, 13 May 1915, we woke up to hear moaning. We looked out of the windows and on the parade ground there was a poor old Russian prisoner with his hands above his head tied to a big flag pole. He'd escaped about a fortnight earlier, been captured and brought back to the camp. Once it was realized he was going through agony, and it must have been because he was standing on his tiptoes, one of the senior NCOs went along and cut the fellow down. Oh dear, that created chaos. The Germans rushed out and ordered everybody back to their huts and yanked the Russian prisoner off to the dark cells where he was given eighteen days in the pitch dark with just bread and water. For the next few days, we were only allowed out to line up for our food.

When the Russian came out, he came to the British section of the camp and we found he could speak English. He was a Russian Jew who'd been working in London on a stall on Petticoat Lane, and just before the war he had returned to Russia for a holiday.

Lance Corporal Joe Armstrong, 1st Loyal North Lancashire Regiment, 1895-1997

A lot of us were about two miles from the Kiel Canal, shoving empty tip-up trucks along two-feet-wide tracks to barges on the Canal. On the barges were some other prisoners unloading lime for us to take back. It was March and it was a beautiful sunny day and we were sweating buckets, and I thought, "If it's like this, I'm going to get away. I'm going to dive into the Kiel Canal." I went behind a little cabin on one of the barges and took my clothes off. I was a very good swimmer – before the war I was in the regimental life-saving team – and I could swim three miles easily. I dived in, wow, it was bitterly cold, it took my breath away and that saved my life. If the water had been warm I would have struck out, but as it was so cold I immediately twisted round and swam back, just in time, as I saw the sentry there with his rifle pointed straight at me. If I'd begun to swim, I'd have had a bullet in my back. I was blue by the time they dragged me out and got me on board. Looking back, quite what I would have done on the far bank without any clothes on I don't know, but you don't always think straight.

Able Seaman Alf Bastin, Hawke Battalion, Royal Naval Volunteer Reserve, 1896-1997

Only one chap escaped from our camp and got back to England. He was a tall, lanky chap in the RNVR who was training to be a naval architect, so he knew something about the sea. He made up his mind to escape and got hold of some German books and began to learn the language. He had a pretty good mind, and when he escaped he posed as a German tramp and wandered up to the Baltic coast to a seaside resort where he found some rowing boats. He stole some stores and at night took a boat and rowed out into the sea, where he was picked up two days later by a Danish Red Cross boat, exhausted. He was taken to Copenhagen and handed over to the British authorities, who took him to hospital and looked after him. When he was fit and well, he had his photograph taken on the sands at Copenhagen, sitting in a deck chair, smoking, and he sent a copy of it to the commandant of our camp. We only knew this because he also wrote to a friend in the camp, a man called Mitchell. He sent a letter and it went round the huts. What we didn't know was that he also sent maps and compasses sealed in tins, disguised as food, and Mitchell tried going the same route. He didn't get very far and was quickly recaptured.

[Ed. Alf remained in Germany until the end of the war. Like many other soldiers captured early in the conflict, he was allowed to work on a farm where he was well fed and, in time, learnt passable German. In 1995, Alf lived in a residential home on the outskirts of London. His neighbour was another veteran, 102-year-old Ernest Doran. Eighty years earlier, as Alf had languished in a POW camp, Ernest was on his way from Malta to the Western Front, where he arrived in February 1915.]

Corporal Ernest Doran, 2nd London Regiment (Royal Fusiliers),1893-1996

We stopped outside a farmhouse and a lady came out, waving, and one of our fellows who could speak French quite well asked her if she could make us a cup of tea and she was quite amenable. We all got our tea ration together and got a dixie, which was roughly a foot in length, and gave it to her with all our accumulated tea in the bottom, and off she went. She brought it back and handed it to us and she'd put the whole lot in cold water; she'd never made tea before in her life, this country woman; they only drank coffee in the countryside.

Trooper Ben Clouting, 4th (Royal Irish) Dragoon Guards, 1897-1990

The farmers lived a traditional and, to our minds, a primitive life. The farm where we stayed had an open-air toilet cut into a rising footpath that led up to the barn, barely hidden for privacy by a canvas screen. The pathway was quite wide, into which a circular hole had been dug. In front were two footmarks, to guide the occupant to the perfect 'gun-site' with waste going straight into a pit beneath. All manner of things were put into the pit. I saw some kittens dropped into the midden, while on another occasion I watched an old woman carry a couple of puppies up the pathway before throwing them in. In France animals earned their keep, pulling carts or working treadmills; those that did not, or were surplus to requirements, had harsh and usually short lives.

Corporal Ernest Doran, 2nd London Regiment (Royal Fusiliers), 1893-1996

In February 1915 we occupied some trenches up at Ypres and all we doing was filling sandbags to keep the sides up, because we were up to our thighs in mud and water. They issued us with waders which you had to button to the top of your trousers, but the water came over the top. I was given quite a cushy job. I had to walk from the trenches to Ypres where I dug up floorboards and removed beams and turned them into duckboards for the bottom of the trench. They pulled Ypres to pieces for wood, quite honestly.

Trooper Ben Clouting, 4th (Royal Irish) Dragoon Guards, 1897-1990

The trenches were little more than shallow ditches joined together. There were no neat traverses, no proper firesteps or parapets, there was only a quagmire of shallow holes filled with oozing mud and water, for so shallow was the water table in the Ypres area that it was impossible to dig down more than a couple of feet without hitting water. Trench foot was a major problem. The constant cold and wet affected the blood's circulation to the toes in particular, causing men's feet to swell disgustingly. I deliberately took size eleven boots instead of my usual nine. This way I could pack my boots with lengths of straw to keep my feet warm, just as I had seen French peasants do with their clogs. If straw wasn't available, newspaper would do just as well. When the weather was bad, it was common to see a man with sandbags wrapped around his feet or puttees to protect his legs. Trench waders were issued in just two sizes, with two pieces of string that we held on to if we walked anywhere, for the suction power of the mud was so great that without them our feet would simply have left the boots.

[Ed. The weather gradually improved and offensive operations resumed. On the Western Front, the British Army launched its first offensive of 1915 near the village of Neuve Chapelle. Four divisions, part of General Haig's First Army, attacked along a two-mile front.]

Private Fred Dixon, 2nd Leicestershire Regiment, 1895-1991

I shall never forget the morning of 10 March. After a sleepless night, I was out at the front line. Captain Weir was a few feet away, and I was watching Colonel Gordon with his watch in his hand. He was shaking like a leaf as the minutes ticked away, then he shouted "Charge!" at exactly 8am. "Come on, Dixon," said Captain Weir, and climbed the ladder to get out of the trench. I followed at once, and we scrambled over our own barbed wire entanglements and made for the enemy. We had orders to ignore their main trench, which would later be attacked by support forces, and to advance as far as we could.

There was no opposition as we jumped over that Jerry trench, but I could see a number of Germans crouched in the bottom of the trench; they had had a battering most of the night. I stuck to Captain Weir until we were both tired out. He then said, "I think we will stay here and dig in; pass that down the line." But I said, "There is no line; there is only you and me." I looked round and there was nobody but us two. I saw a partly-dug trench so I pointed it out to him, and we decided to work on that. He then said, "How far do you think we have come?" I said, "Almost a mile." So he said, "Go straight back to Colonel Gordon and say we have advanced about three-quarters to one mile, and we want reinforcements." Then he surprised me by holding out his hand and saying, "Goodbye, Dixon." I shook it, "Goodbye, Sir", then turned round to plot my way back, and that was the last I saw of him.

How different a plot of land looks when you have seen it from one way and then turn round and look at it front to back! At last I spotted the stump of Richebourg St Vaast Church, and knew if I made for that, I could find my old trenches and Colonel Gordon.

There were lots of bullets coming from somewhere as I plodded along in the sludge, and I could not travel very fast under those conditions with my equipment and rifle. However, I kept going, thinking one of these will get me yet; but I was lucky to drop straight into the trench from where I had started out, and I found Colonel Gordon. I gave him the message exactly as Captain Weir had told me and the Colonel said, "Go straight back to Captain Weir and tell him to hold the position at all costs – and we have no reinforcements. Off you go!" The Colonel dived back into his dugout. My thoughts were unprintable.

As I went up that ladder once again and my hands reached the top rungs, a machine gun opened up from the enemy trench we had left alone: they were waiting for me – no doubt they realized I was carrying messages. Something told me I was not going to get back safely this time, and I dropped back into the trench to wait a bit. If there was ever a time when I felt like being a coward, it was just then. I didn't want to go on, but I thought if I don't go, I shall be shot by my own side as a coward, so I may as well go and chance it. So I plucked up courage, and went as fast as I could, even though I was tired out. As I passed that first German trench again, I saw several men together, but one in particular was carefully taking aim at me, the others looking on. I heard the bang as he fired; and felt the bullet go through my knee joint like a red hot needle. My leg just stopped and I fell full length with my face in the sludge. I had gone off unconscious, but I awoke to realize I was being fired on again; a German officer was firing at me from a communication trench. Two bullets hit the ground each side of my head and I kept perfectly still, thinking, "He'll get me next time", but he dare not expose himself too long, and no doubt he thought he had done enough at me, so he went away. I lay there all day until about 6.30pm when I was found by a stretcher-bearer party from a Scottish regiment. *[Ed. Fred believed that Captain Donald Weir DSO, MC, had been killed. In fact he survived the attack and served until the end of the war. He died in 1921 of Cholera whilst serving in India.]*

Private Frank Sumpter, 1st Rifle Brigade, 1897-1999
We went over and took about two fields and a couple of lines of trenches. As soon as they saw us, down went their rifles and up went their hands and we took them prisoner. The Provo Marshal had them all put in a pen with his men round them and he put a German officer in charge to talk to them, to tell them to go one way or another. I saw the German officer standing there and a man came up to him and the officer said something to the man. He can't have received a polite answer, because he slapped him round his face. I was talking to a couple of Germans and said if he did that in the British army, he would be finished as an officer. They said, "Don't talk rot," and I said, "I'm telling you. If a British officer slapped a man in the face he would be cashiered." They couldn't understand it. They said, "But he's an officer!" as though that answered everything.

2nd Lieutenant Norman Dillon, 14th Northumberland Fusiliers, 1896-1997
In spite of the dismal failures at Neuve Chapelle and later at Ypres, the Higher Command still believed we should smash a hole in the German line and get on with the sort of war they seemed to consider the gentlemanly thing to do. Infantry in long lines, attacking under cover of their own fire and their officers cantering up and down shouting "Up and at 'em". It did not work like that and it cost many thousands of lives. As one concession to modern ideas, our swords were no longer worn – a pity! Having sharpened them as in Part I of the mobilisation tables, it would have been nice to have used them.

2nd Lieutenant Richard Hawkins, 11th Royal Fusiliers, 1895-1994
The casualties were enormous. I can't remember the number, it's all been written down. People say that the Generals were wrong in making us go and fight the enemy as we did. Dammit, we couldn't sit there forever. You couldn't sit there in a trench, you might still be there. We'd got to get on with the job and kill the enemy.

GALLIPOLI

[Ed. Killing, or at least neutralising, the enemy would require, according to some, a new, more inventive plan of attack. The decision to assault the Gallipoli Penninsula was taken in the face of heavy opposition from senior commanders in France who felt that the war could be won only on the Western Front. Others disagreed, and a rift was created between those who counselled continued fighting in the west, the so-called "Westerners", and those who sought to expand campaigns elsewhere, the "Easterners". The latter argued that if an Allied force could wrest Turkish control from the Dardanelles Straits, then a passage to the Black Sea could be opened up between Britain and France and their ally Russia. Equally, if Turkey herself could be knocked out of the war, then Germany's strategic position would be greatly undermined without the need for further heavy losses in France and Flanders. The plan, though well conceived, was poorly executed. The campaign lasted from April 1915 until January 1916, when the Penninsula was finally evacuated, a decision that appeared to vindicate the views of the "Westerners".]

Private Robert Richard 'Dick' Barron, No1629, 2nd London Mounted Brigade Field Ambulance, Royal Army Medical Corps, 19 October 1895-14 February 1999

We were on field exercises when one night, practically with no warning, we were entrained with all our equipment. We found ourselves next morning in a drizzling rain at Southampton Docks and there looming above us was the *Aragon*, a Royal Mail Steam Packet Liner which had been converted to a troop ship. Just before we were about to start, something happened which I will never forget. The whole of the ship's company from the top deck right down, including ourselves, suddenly burst into song. "Homeland, homeland, when shall I see you again, land of my birth, dearest place on earth, I'm leaving you, oh it may be for years and it may be forever. Homeland,

homeland." Up to then the whole thing had been most enjoyable, but my heart stood still. I suddenly realised that this was warfare – I might not return.

Able Seaman Walter Burdon, ZT90, B Company, Nelson Battalion, Royal Naval Division, 26 June 1895-May 1992
Because I was a signaller, I had access to a telescope and a pair of glasses. We weren't due to land on Gallipoli until the 26 April, the second day of the assault, so instead I watched the first landings from our ship. Looking through the telescope, I could see the Australians in action. There were people running all over the place, while others appeared to be lying down, stationary, as one of our big ships, the *Queen Elizabeth*, bombarded the shore. "I hope we'll be getting some of that," I said to a man next to me. You don't realize at the time that you might be going to your death.

Soon after that, we got orders to get ready to disembark, ready for landing. We got onto a destroyer and we went in as far as we could, towing about a dozen rowing boats behind us. The destroyer stopped and we climbed into the boats. That was the most terrifying moment for me because we had to descend a rope ladder trailing down the stern of the ship. The stern curved away, and as we clambered down with rifle and ammunition, the ship rose and fell in the water. It was clear to all that if you slipped you would not come up again, you'd sink like a stone.

As we rowed into shore, I could see the hull of another ship, the *Majestic*, upside-down in the bay. At this time we were under fire but not a great deal and we were certainly not as badly off as the Australians, who had got mowed down the previous day. When we came ashore, I was carrying two three-foot flags and a six-foot flag: the smaller flags were for semaphore and the larger for morse. I saw the Australians lying there, and I was sitting beside them, when one said, "You're a flag man, are you? Then take those two flags off that boy's back." He pointed to this lad who was dead with a pack on his back, attached to which were two much smaller flags. "Yours are no good, they are too big. You stand up to use those, you'll never live, throw them away." I took his advice.

Private Dick Barron, 2nd London Mounted Brigade Field Ambulance, Royal Army Medical Corps, 1895-1999
We knew nothing at all about what was going on. We had spoken to the wounded coming from Gallipoli, but we still had romantic notions until we got to see the place for ourselves. When we landed at Suvla Bay. I was in a state of nervousness, I had too much imagination, I could imagine myself all lacerated. However, I saw a couple of old sweats who had served in the Boer War and they were sitting down smoking, as calm as anything, and I took strength from them.

Private Adolphus Arthur James Price, No1751, A Company, 1/8th Hampshire Regiment, 13 November 1893-November1993
On the way back from a dressing station, we saw this fellow from my own town of Shanklin on the Isle of Wight. I knew him as being a bit simple, we used to call him Dotty Fred. I don't think he'd done any work in civilian life, but he'd got into the army all right and gone to Gallipoli. He was laid there, dead, and his mouth was wide open and it was black with flies. Many years after, and to my great shock, I saw Dotty Fred back in Shanklin. He told me he had been suffering from typhoid, so he must only have been asleep when I saw him.

Private David Weston, 1/5th Bedfordshire Regiment, 1895-1998
These Gurkhas had been lying out for three weeks and we were detailed for the job of burying them. We went out at night. I say bury them, but you couldn't dig a hole; the ground was so hard you couldn't bury bodies, you had to cover them over with stones. So we did the best we could, but you needed a drill to penetrate the ground. There were twenty or thirty dead on this ridge, dried-up corpses coloured deep brown. We had to cut off their identification discs and all the

time we were doing this the stench was awful. The next day, as the weather got hotter I actually saw the legs of these Gurkhas coming out of the ground, bodies we'd buried under stones. The heat of the sun had made them swell and rise up into the air only to sink back down again at night. I said to the sergeant major, "If you put me on a job like that again, I will refuse to do it," and I would have done, too, it was a wicked job. I smelt of those dead Gurkhas for weeks after that.

Private Dick Barron, 2nd London Mounted Brigade Field Ambulance, Royal Army Medical Corps, 1895-1999
The London Yeomanry were crossing the salt lake at Suvla Bay in waves. I was attached to a medical officer and more or less followed him. We were attacked by shrapnel bursting all over the place. Casualties were falling, and I was staggering forward, bewildered more than anything else. The first casualty I dealt with was my old friend 'Gally' Lee; he got hit right next to me. We didn't have steel helmets then and I was shaken by the burst that caught my friend; he was hit in the head and his brains were more or less hanging out. He was unconscious and I looked at him and I could see his brains on the top of his skull and all I could do was to push them back and put a bandage on, a first field dressing. I knew he'd had it but you can't imagine seeing your mate like that, I don't think you're in a normal state. That evening the shrub on the dry salt lake caught fire and there were wounded out there, so we had to try and rescue those we could. You get into a state of mind where you just behave like an automaton.

Able Seaman Walter Burdon, Nelson Battalion, Royal Naval Division, 1895 1992
My platoon had occasion to move forward during the night; we moved so many yards and stopped. When dawn came, to my horror I was a matter of yards from the Turkish trenches. I could see their bayonets sticking straight up in the air, all the way round, hundreds of them. How we'd got there without being noticed, I don't know. I looked back

to our trenches a hundred yards away where the Australians were, and I saw a man, he'd a real heart because he must have seen the predicament we were in, jump up on top of the parapet and pepper the Turkish line with machine gun fire to cover us.

If we'd had a few grenades we could have cleared that trench, but we had nothing to help us, so I said to the fellow next to me, "We have no chance, I'm getting out of it." By this time a Turkish machine gun had opened up. I waited until the gun paused and then I was off, up and away like hell across the valley. The machine gun began again so I got down behind a little hillock, and I could hear the bullets whistling overhead. When a machine gun stops, it takes about half a minute to put a new belt on. You get to know when a belt has been used up, intuition. I scrambled up again and ran, weaving about, in full view of the enemy, towards the Australian trenches, and I jumped down, my bayonet going right between the legs of an Australian who was sitting at the bottom. I asked for a periscope and just got it above the trench to see one of our fellows running along the gully down which I'd just come. I don't know if he made it because the periscope was shot out of my hand.

A fellow beside us, a New Zealand machine gunner, threw his gun over the top and jumped over. He wanted to cover those who were left out there but he was killed straight away, his body being left on the parapet as a sandbag. That's the way things were. There were two lads crouching there, just below the parapet, young fellows and one's bayonet was red with blood, and he had a bandage round his head, and he was saying, "Come on, come on, let's get at the bastards, come on!" They were not a very disciplined lot, the Australians, but they were fighters, fine fellows.

Private Dick Barron, 2nd London Mounted Brigade Field Ambulance, Royal Army Medical Corps, 1895-1999
We were carrying a man down and could not get him round a trench as it was too narrow, and after a while I said, "I must have a rest, my

arms are coming out of their sockets." Men get very heavy when you carry them on a stretcher. There were a few spent bullets buzzing around but not many. Anyway, we lay down under some cover when all of a sudden a bit of shrapnel flew past us and this man leapt off the stretcher and ran down and lay beside us. I looked at him in amazement. "You can bloody well walk the rest of the way," I told him. I saw the MO and said he was as fit as we were.

Able Seaman Walter Burdon, Nelson Battalion, Royal Naval Division, 1895-1992

We moved down to Cape Hellas and on 5 June I was shot in the head. We were told to advance so far and dig in. We'd got down about eighteen inches when an officer joined us and said, "Prepare, prepare, enemy right". We lifted up our rifles and pointed them and just as I was about to fire, something caught my attention and made me turn and I got a terrific whack at the side of the head. A bullet or a piece of shrapnel had hit my rifle and disintegrated into small pieces of metal. When I came round, I was bleeding like a sheep. I said to these fellows, "Can I get out, can I get past?" but they said, "We're not getting out, we're not standing up, we'll get killed." I had blood pouring down my face and bullets flying about, so I couldn't blame them. I said, "Would you lie down and I'll crawl over you." This was to get to the end of the trench where the parapet was a little higher. I crawled over them to a sort of seat, sat down and passed out. When I came round, there was a right melée going on, they were in a real battle. My own officer, Sub Lieutenant Bookless, was killed just then. I woke to see him standing with two mills bombs in his hand, shouting "Get that machine gun!" but the machine gun got him, and I watched as his batman carried his body away.

While I was unconscious, my hand must have been protecting my face because when I put my hand down, blood poured out in a torrent from my sleeve. A first aid man came over. "You've been peppered this time, mister," he said, and got me down to the first aid shelter for further treatment before I was eventually taken down to the beach for evacuation.

I was in hospital for months while they removed the metal fragments from my head. My nerves were also bad and I was eventually deemed no longer fit for service. During the time I was in hospital, I dropped a line to the family of Sub Lieutenant Bookless to tell them I'd seen him shot. I got no answer. He was a member of a wealthy fruit family and they must have thought I was on the scrounge, but I wasn't. I was just letting them know that someone had seen him killed.

As for my rifle, I spoke to a man afterwards and he said he'd never seen owt like it, my rifle, it was just bits.

[Ed. Not all the metal could be removed from Walter's head. Even in 1992, when Walter was aged 97, he still had two fragments embedded in his skull, one to the side of the head and the other on the crown.]

GOING TO FRANCE

[Ed. By May 1915, with the expedition well under way at Gallipoli and with losses spiralling on the Western Front, the first Kitchener Divisions were required to embark for France, and take their place in the field, much earlier than Lord Kitchener had foreseen. That month the 9th Scottish, followed shortly after by the 14th Light Division, landed in France, to be joined throughout the summer months by more New Army Divisions as they were required.]

Lance Corporal Vic Cole, 7th Queen's Own (Royal West Kent Regiment), 1897-1995
We went to France, embarking at Southampton aboard the cross-Channel packet Mona's Queen, of the Isle of Man Steam Packet Company. It was a good trip as far as I recall, nine hours in all. We

were buoyed up by the spirit of adventure, which helped those of us who suffered a bout of sea-sickness on the way, packed as we were like sardines below deck. We arrived in excellent morale at Le Havre and were observed with great curiosity by stolid German prisoners working on the roads under the watchful eyes of French sentries. French reservists also patrolled the railway lines, occupying sentry boxes every two or three miles up the track. As we passed, one of these gents saluted us in baggy red trousers and a blue frock coat and wearing a Kepi rather rakishly, I felt.

Private Jack Davis, 6th Duke of Cornwall's Light Infantry, 1895-2003
We didn't know where we were going or how long we would be on the train, and as most of the lads had been drinking before they got into the carriages, they soon needed the toilet. Anyway, those who were further up the train, where I was, just opened the window and urinated. When we eventually stopped, some of the lads further down who had stuck their heads out of the window were saying, "Oh, you could feel the steam from the engine", but it wasn't that at all!

Lance Corporal Vic Cole, 7th Queen's Own (Royal West Kent Regiment), 1897-1995
After forty-eight hours of incarceration in cattle trucks, we were detrained at Amiens. A short rest here and then we took to the roads. French roads were mostly cobbled across the crown, leaving four or five feet of soft going on either side. When marching in fours and keeping to the right of the road, two men of each four would be on the cobbles, number three would have one foot on cobbles and one foot on soft ground and number four would be altogether on the soft going. A halt was called at the end of every hour and a change-over made: the outside man went to the inside and the others moved up one place.

At night the western skyline was lit continuously by flickering star-shells and the glow of Very lights, while the intermittent thunder of guns became louder and louder. The sector we were heading for was held by the Regiment's First Battalion, and we, the Seventh, were to go in with them for instruction in trench warfare. For the first time, I began to realise what I had let myself in for.

Private Jack Davis, 6th Duke of Cornwall's Light Infantry, 1895-2003
On 12 August 1915, we were going to take up our forward positions ready to occupy the front line. There were four companies, and one was to occupy each of various points just behind the line: the Ramparts, Salicourt Bridge, the reserve line and the cellars of St Martin's Cathedral. I was in D Company and it was a toss-up between C and D who occupied the Cathedral down below in the cloisters. I had a charmed life. C Company went in and they'd only been there, settling in, for about ten minutes when the Germans shelled the place. They had a 17-inch gun on a railway line at Dickiebusch, what we called the Dickiebusch Express, which was shunted up into position. There was a direct hit on the Cathedral and our boys were underneath, tons of masonry falling on top of them. Working parties were immediately sent from various battalions as well as our own regiment, trying to get these boys out. We had ten minutes to get to them before the next shell came. This went on all through the night. We couldn't reach them, couldn't move the mass of masonry, blocks of stone weighing several hundredweight, and we had only our hands, no other means. I don't think we got many out and much of the company was killed, including the second in command, Major Barnett, and many more wounded. Their bodies were not recovered until after the war.

Private John Rea Laister, No1222, 2nd King's Royal Rifle Corps, 14 May 1897-September 1999
We were ready to go into the trenches and the order came to go up the communication trench. We go down into thick slimy mud, it goes into your boots, creeps up your legs, goes around your privates, gets to about waist high. We're relieving the French, who were noted for burying their dead in the side of the trench instead of removing them.

So anyway, we're in this mud with no gumboots and you had to keep pulling your leg up, all the way along, and the snow is coming down, and all of a sudden an arm hits you in the face, buried in the side of the trench. You pass the word along, "Arm 'ere", you go a few more yards, you see a head hanging out, "Head 'ere", until you reach the front line. When you were out there a week, you forgot all thoughts of ever coming out, a week in those trenches, a week, and you're never coming home again, you took it for granted, and from then on you didn't care a damn. That was the feeling and it stayed with me all through the war.

Private Ted Francis, 16th Warwickshire Regiment, 1896-1996
The news flashed around in the first line of trenches, this fellow had been killed coming up a communication trench carrying food and water. Parts of the trench had been knocked down by shellfire and he was a bit careless. Instead of bobbing down, he'd walked by standing tall and a sniper had got him in the head. We were in the front line and the news was flashed round the whole battalion very quickly. It sobered us up and kind of put a doubt in our minds about this soldier business. We were not playing at soldiers now and people were getting killed.

2nd Lieutenant Norman Dillon, 14th Northumberland Fusiliers, 1896-1997
I was full of curiosity and the foolishness of youth. I was about to put my head above the parapet to have a look, when an old hand pulled me down. "We've lost several doing that," he said. "Use a periscope." So I did and hardly had I put it up when a bullet came through it.

Private Jack Davis, 6th Duke of Cornwall's Light Infantry, 1895-2003
There was a sergeant and his brother in the same company as me. The Germans had a fixed rifle centred on part of the our trench and every now and again they'd fire this, which kept making a hole in the

sandbag parapet and it had to be built up every night. At Stand To the next morning, this brother of the sergeant said he'd spotted the sniper and he got up on the parapet and put his rifle up to fire but the sniper got him first. The bullet hit his thumb and went through his mouth and out again without hitting his teeth. How lucky can you be? Anyway, we stuck a cigarette in his mouth and off he went down the line.

Lance Corporal Vic Cole, 7th Queen's Own (Royal West Kent Regiment), 1897-1995
As a signaller, I had a leather frog with a pair of wire cutters on my belt as well as a little bag full of wire prongs for fixing the wire to the side of the trench. When you laid a new telephone cable, you laid it along the side of the trench and held it with the prongs knocked into the back wall about ten yards apart. It was my job each day to check they were all right.

Along the trench were other wires placed for the Royal Engineers' Signal Company. They always had superior, thicker cable than ours, and another wire was dug in for the artillery spotters. So there were three wires: our thin black D3 cable, and below that a thicker red cable for the artillery observation post, and below that a thick black cable of the Royal Engineers' Signal Company.

I carried a D3 telephone with me and if the wire was broken, I could put the bare end round the terminal and turn a little handle and try to get through to make sure the rest of the line was intact before fixing the break. However, sometimes when we got into the line I found that the first chap to lay the wire had done it at night and instead of going round the trench, he had gone over the top. This meant that if the line was broken I might have to climb up and look round. Zzzzp, a bullet, so back down I'd go again, cut a new piece of wire, strip off about two inches of insulation at the end of a wire, tie a reef knot, put a bit of insulation tape round and peg it round the trench instead of the line going over the top.

I enjoyed signalling. All the time I could go where I wanted, but the infantry, the poor buggers, couldn't move. Instead, they made little niches in the side of the trench to avoid the shrapnel, while those who weren't resting were on the firestep for hour after hour, I felt really sorry for them.

Trooper Smiler Marshall, 1/1st Essex Yeomanry, 1897-2005
Their sap and our sap were about eighteen yards apart and between was an old communication trench which was full of barbed wire and jam tins that would rattle when anyone approached. One day, the Germans sent a stick grenade over, to which they had tied a couple of cigarettes. After a bit I went to the bomb, and my mates Sunny Caines and Stil Pride were saying, "For God's sake, don't touch it." They thought the bomb would go off and blow me up. But I went and smoked one of the cigarettes and it was all right, so we actually sent back the same stick bomb with a whole packet attached. I hope they enjoyed them.

Second Lieutenant Richard Hawkins, 11th Royal Fusiliers, 1895-1994
I went round with the rum bottle every morning at dawn, and the tot was an eighth of a pint. You could feel that rum going down into your boots, which were probably full of icy water, drying up the water and coming up to you and saying, "Now, where's that ruddy Hun?" It saved lives. It was old navy rum, until supplies ran out; and then we got ordinary rum, and by Jove, there was a difference.

Trooper Smiler Marshall, 1/1st Essex Yeomanry, 1897-2005
There were plenty of lads who'd give me their rum ration for one or two cigarettes, and so my water bottle was always a third or a quarter full of neat rum. When we were in the front line, the orderly officer and orderly sergeant used to come round twice during the night, once just before twelve and once between five and six in the morning, to see things were all right. When they'd gone past, I knew they'd got a good distance to go along the front line. So, quick as lightning, I unwrapped

my puttee and took my boot and sock off and poured some rum into my hand, taking a little lick myself, then rubbed it into my toes for five minutes and then put my boot and puttee back on. When they went by next time, I did the same to the other one and my feet were as good as anything. You are not allowed to take off any clothes of any description in the front line, but I managed to do that for all three days we were there.

Private John Richard 'Dick' Trafford, No2356, 1/9th King's Liverpool Regiment, 12 December 1898-March 1999
You were walking in several inches of mud and sludge such a lot of the time, your feet wet and cold, turning to frost bite. In time your feet felt dead, no feeling in them whatsoever, and they'd swell like balloons. To protect your feet, the stretcher bearers were detailed to massage your ankles and feet in whale oil, in the reserve trenches, even in the front line, which was never supposed to happen, but our feet got that bad they had to do something.

Coming out of the line, you'd have a job to lift one foot up after another, but it's a pleasure to get out and walk on hard ground to feel the blood circulating once again. Out on rest, you took your boots and socks off and your feet were a lightish grey, with no feeling in them at all. If your feet were really bad and you took your boots off, you'd never get them back on again. Those who did, you could tell, because they'd be walking or attempting to walk about with sacks round their feet because they couldn't get their boots on, or walking along using walking-sticks, their feet were that sore.

Lance Corporal Vic Cole, 7th Queen's Own (Royal West Kent Regiment), 1897-1995
The cooks would bring the food so far up the line then dump it, to be collected by orderlies sent down from the regiment. The food was carried in large dixies, about half a yard long, and you had to carry these one in each hand, and heavy they were, too, as you edged along

the communication trench. The problem was that the cooking had been done on wood or coal fires and consequently these dixies were covered with black soot, so everywhere it touched your trousers or your uniform you got a great big black mark and you got into trouble for having a filthy uniform. So you tumbled to it, got a couple of sandbags and tied them round your legs. Once the food arrived, the corporal from each section would call for the mess tins and they'd all be put down in a line and he'd dish it out. It was typically soup with little bits of meat floating in it, a dumpling each, until the dixie was empty, plus half a loaf of bread per man per day, carried up in a sandbag. The men who brought the dixies then cleaned them and took them back to the cooks. The orderly man was named for the whole period in the line or perhaps just for the day, and he would hide the sacking for the next time.

Private Jack Davis, 6th Duke of Cornwall's Light Infantry, 1895-2003
I was our company officer's servant, and so when it was our turn to take over the front line I was sent up in advance of the 6th Battalion to take over the officers' dugout and headquarters. I walked from the Menin Gate up to the front line. At that time you couldn't use the communication trench because it was full of water, and you had to scramble over the top. Walking up, perhaps a mile, to the line, you had to dodge in between shell holes, and the place was like a cemetery, the smell of death everywhere. I got up to within fifteen yards of the front line and got the usual challenge "Halt, who goes there?" and suddenly I thought, "I know that voice." "Bob, it's your brother Jack." And there was not just Bob but my other brother Bill on a double sentry, up to their thighs in water, both wearing waders. Bill was looking through the periscope over the parapet. They were wearing greatcoats, but they'd used their razors to cut the bottom of their coats off because they were dangling in water – they were both charged with damaging government property for that! Bill and Bob were both in the 9th Rifle Brigade, and they were in the front line while we were in support.

Only a few months before, Bob had been rejected medically unfit and Bill too as being under age and that was the last thing I knew. What strings they'd had to pull to get out there I've no idea, but I had no inkling that either was even in France. It was such a strange coincidence and a never-to-be-forgotten reunion before I had to leave.

[Ed. No Man's Land had become too difficult and dangerous to occupy or cross and alternative approaches to conducting hostilities had to be found. The war underground was every bit as vicious as that conducted across the trench lines above. It grew from what had almost been a cottage industry in 1914 to a sophisticated weapon of war employing thousands of men, working in cramped, airless conditions to mine under enemy positions in order to blow them up.]

2nd Lieutenant Norman Dillon, 14th Northumberland Fusiliers, 1896-1997
I made friends with a Royal Engineers Tunnelling Company officer who was mining under the German front line positions. This was difficult work, because the water table was high and the workings had to be kept clear by constant pumping. One advantage of mining in the clay was that it was almost soundless, so much so that we broke into a German tunnel, which was found to be partially flooded. As we listened, the noise of a pump could be heard. This was a great opportunity for a bit of fun, and as the River Lys flowed close by, it was easy to put a large hose from the river into this gallery. The water flowed by gravity and the Germans spent some weeks pumping the river through their mine, until they realized what had been done.

Private Harry Norman Edwards, No2912, 1/6th Gloucestershire Regiment, 13 January 1894-21 September 1999
In front of Ploegsteert Wood it was reasonably quiet, when all of a sudden there was a most enormous blast and our Sergeant, Bertie Harris, a schoolmaster from Manchester, poked his head out of the

dugout. He hadn't got his trousers on because he was having a sleep, although he shouldn't have taken any clothes off in the front line trenches. "What's to do, lads?" he asked and I said, "As far as I can make out, a mine's been blown under the Hampshire Tee Trench down the road." "Oh blimey," he said, "any of our men on duty there?" I thought there was, but by this time there was such an uproar, with all the guns going and shelling, I'm not sure he heard me. After a while the furore gradually died down and we were able to go along with a trench periscope to have a look. The Germans had mined out to this isolated part of the trench system, and had blown a hole twenty feet deep and thirty feet across. Fortunately from our point of view, they'd been out in their reckoning and instead of blowing up the Tee, we could look over the trench wall with the periscope and right down into this great hole. We'd been lucky and suffered no casualties but our trench was now right on the lip of the crater.

2nd Lieutenant Richard Hawkins, 11th Royal Fusiliers, 1895-1994
You never knew when you might be blown up by a mine, and that knowledge put a tremendous strain on the nervous system. When we were down at la Bassée, the Germans were forever driving tunnels under our lines and blowing us up. We of course tried to counter-mine, or blow up their trenches too. We had an Australian mining engineer posted to us and he used to come round at 4 o'clock in the afternoon to let us know what was happening. "Are you in charge of this section?" "Yes." "Well, um, a mine's going up here tonight, probably about two in the morning, not quite sure. I should clear these trenches, if I were you. The mine's been overcharged and the whole thing is going to go up and there won't be a lip. Good afternoon and have a good evening," and off he'd potter. Wonderful. That night I was writing, sitting in the dugout on a little stool, 2am, situation normal, then woosh, the ground absolutely rocked backwards and I'm sent crashing to the floor. Anyway, he'd stopped the Germans mining out to us for a while, that was for sure. Damn clever chap, that Australian.

Trooper Smiler Marshall, 1/1st Essex Yeomanry, 1897-2005

Our intelligence could tell that the Germans were ready to blow a mine and we were told to evacuate the line but we didn't go far enough. They made a bloody great crater, hundreds of tons of dirt blew up into the air. Two of our fellows were almost completely buried, another was caught up to his legs, and I had my feet trapped. The weight was so great, I tried to pull myself out but couldn't. One chap had just his head sticking out of the earth and a message was passed round from this man, "Is Smiler all right?" That came round to me and I said, "Yes, but I can't move, I'll have to wait until our lads come to dig us out." "Well, for Christ's sake will you sing "Nearer, my God, to thee."" My Sunday school teacher went down on the *Titanic* and we had grown up hearing that was the hymn they sang in great peril, and when in trouble I have always sung it. So I sang this hymn until they dug us out:

Nearer, my God, to thee
Nearer to thee
Just like the wanderer
When the sun goes down
Darkness comes over me
When my rest was a stone
Yet in my dreams I'll be
Nearer, my God, to thee
Nearer, my God, to thee
Nearer to thee.

LOOS

Private Dick Trafford, 1/9th Kings Liverpool Regiment, 1898-1999
We were going up the communications trenches in the early hours of the morning to get ready to go over the top. There was a bit of a step at the trench bottom and in the darkness I slipped and fell onto the

man in front of me and this feller started lashing out. Of course I lashed out back, and we had a good set-to in the trench before the sergeant came along and grabbing both of us said, "Come on, it's the bloody Germans you've got to fight, not each other." We were parted, at least for the time being.

It was still dark and we passed through a battery of guns just as it opened up to start the final bombardment for the attack. I was near one of the guns and as it fired, the noise burst my eardrum, blood squirting out of it, and I was deaf straightaway. The sergeant took one of the dressings we always carried in case we were wounded and packed my ear with cotton wool to plug it, and of course we were expecting to go over the top in an hour or two, so I would have to go with my ear already wounded. I wasn't allowed to turn back. There was only one way – forward.

You feel like in a race, you're waiting to start, waiting for the signal, then the sergeant would shout, "Right, lads," and you're over the top. It wasn't always nice getting out of a trench because you didn't have footholds or any steps, you got over the best way you could and then you ran like hell to get to the German trenches. I remember thinking that if my time came I hoped it was a bullet and that it would be sudden; I never wanted to be a cripple or robbed of my senses.

In a sense you relied on the Germans to give you orders. It was a case of hide and seek: you drop in what we call the prone position, you're on your face, then when the German machine guns stop firing for a moment you're up and as fast as you can go towards the wire. If a man dropped, he dropped, that was it, whether they were killed or not you were not allowed to stop. You could hear men calling, "I'm wounded, I'm wounded, will you come over here?" It was the stretcher-bearers' job to come along and pick them up, but there were some horrible sights all the same, men with their arms hanging half off, some with their legs badly wounded.

When we got to the German line, the whole lot gave themselves up – they came over with their hands up. They were marched down together with one or two of our fellows, as they might have done on parade in their own regiment.

2nd Lieutenant Norman Dillon, 14th Northumberland Fusiliers, 1896-1997

When we moved up, there was a scene of the utmost chaos. I was sent up with my platoon and I arrived in what used to be the front line. It was a dreadful sight. There in front of the German trench were rows and rows of dead men all lying down close together, facing the uncut barbed wire and extending as far as one could see. Many were in such good and tidy order that my chaps thought they were asleep, they looked so peaceful, and they tried to wake them. "Wake up, wake up, you don't want to be sleeping here." They had been killed as they lay in front of the impenetrable wire. There were, of course, some bodies that had been killed by shellfire and were not a pretty sight.

As we buried the dead, the Germans began to shell us. I was very young and inexperienced and I didn't know whether I had to be brave and go on burying the dead in the midst of a rain of shells, or hold back until the shellfire had finished. Luckily, the Germans packed up and we got on with the task in hand. My job was to collect the identity discs and personal wallets from the dead, put them in a sandbag and label them, while the men got on with the grisly job of burial. They quickly got quite callous about it. I remember standing next to two chaps who were burying several in a grave, and a great head came rolling along like a football. "Get hold of it and see if it fits any of yours," the bowler said.

Private Dick Trafford, 1/9th King's Liverpool Regiment, 1898-1999

The Germans counter-attacked the day after, when it was dusk. We couldn't see them until they were almost on top of us. We only had one machine gun per company and this was positioned to kill as many Germans as possible. I knew the little gunner, Bob Grantham, he came from Ormskirk and he was in what we called the power pit, in the trench, and he had the machine gun trained to swing over and catch the Germans as they came over the Loos-Hulluch road. When they crossed the road, the machine gun got most of them, but of course Bob couldn't watch the road all of the time. I suddenly looked up and this German was stood on the top of the trench ready to jump down with his bayonet, which would have gone well into me, but Bob must have opened fire on him and instead of falling into the trench he fell the other way. He was a big man with a beard, a Bavarian Guard, I was told.

Not long after, one of the chaps shouted, "Hey, Dick, will you come over here and reach me a cigarette?" I went over and saw that half of his shoulder was missing; he'd no arm left. He couldn't get to his cigarettes so I got them from his pocket, looked for some matches, and lit one for him and put it in his mouth. A wounded man would always crave a cigarette and he'd had what he wanted to help ease the pain. But he hadn't two puffs on it when he conked out – he died there and then because the loss of blood must have been terrible.

2nd Lieutenant Norman Dillon, 14th Northumberland Fusiliers, 1896-1997
My memory is dim of this time. There may have been a German counter-attack, but at all events, we were sent up to provide a reserve to the front line. The scene beggars description: disordered units mixed up and nobody in charge and no information as to what was happening.

In the dark, the pandemonium was worse. One of my brother officers, of my own age, was seized by an elderly Staff Officer who said to him, "Now, my boy, here is your chance. Rally all these men and do a service to your country." He might have replied, "Rally them yourself," but discretion was the better part of valour and he said, "Yes, Sir" and disappeared into the crowd.

Private Dick Trafford, 1/9th Kings Liverpool Regiment, 1898-1999

We came out of the trenches and by stages we were marched to the town of Poperinge where I saw this big building like a big barn and all our fellows stood outside. "Come on we're waiting for you," and here this bloke was standing there, the one I'd fought with. He was stripped off, with boxing gloves on, waiting to give me a bloody good hiding. A lot of lads in the same company knew me because I belonged to a boxing family.

There was no question of backing out and we got stuck into it and knocked hell out of each other. I had toothache and my face was all swollen and he caught me once on my jaw, and that made me a bit bad tempered, and I knocked hell out of him for a while. Anyway, the sergeant stopped it, he said, "I'll have to call this a draw, you've been at it long enough."

2nd Lieutenant Norman Dillon, 14th Northumberland Fusiliers, 1896-1997

In due course all the inexperienced divisions were taken out and sent to quiet parts of the Front. One unfortunate episode occurred during our withdrawal. The Divisional Staff had drawn up the usual march table, so that the various units should take their allocated places in the column. Those that were coming back from the front near the village of Vermelles started first and others should have joined in. We were about one and a half miles back and should have waited our turn. However, the march table specified our route, which involved a one and a half mile march forwards and then a return over the same route. This was sheer lunacy and I protested, but was told by a staff officer that I must do it as it was there in the orders. We set off on our circular tour of the frontal area. As we were passing through a derelict row of houses at Vermelles, I saw a large board erected. It read, "Do not halt here – this road is shelled every afternoon at 2.30pm". It was then 2.25pm and, as the column was passing this noticeboard, to the minute several shells struck. We lost a number of men killed and one officer as well as many more wounded. Fortunately, it was a routine affair and there were no more shells. Shortly after, we passed our old bivouac area where we should have begun our march. We received an apology for our disaster, but this did not help those who had been smitten so uselessly. There was already a feeling against staff officers, who were commonly thought of as being idle. There was a saying that the soldiers had bread but life on the staff was one long loaf.

[Ed. The Battalion Diary states that D Company went into rest on 27 September; when shrapnel burst overhead, 2nd Lieutenant Barra and five other ranks were killed, two officers and twenty-four other ranks wounded.]

[Ed. On 25 September, Jack Davis' Brigade had made a diversionary attack in front of Ypres as the major offensive at Loos got under way. The 9th Rifle Brigade, including Jack's brothers, were in the forefront of the fighting while the 6th DCLI was held in reserve. In the event, the Rifle Brigade suffered heavy casualties with only four officers and 140 other ranks left unwounded to return to camp. For the next three weeks, Jack had no idea what had happened to his brothers, even if they were still alive. Then, in mid-October, he heard that the 9th Rifle Brigade were in billets at Houtkerque, five kilometres away.]

Private Jack Davis, 6th Duke of Cornwall's Light Infantry, 1895-2003
We were in a hop field under bivouacs made of our groundsheets, and it was teeming down with rain. I was at a pretty low ebb: my thoughts were with my brothers. I'd got to find out what had happened to them, and in the conditions which we had to endure, I thought to myself, "Well, rather than putting up with it here, I might just as well try and see if I can find Bill and Bob." After a lot of enquiries, I learned that their battalion had been sent back and housed in a field in bell tents at a place called Houtkerque. I set off about 10pm. In between them and us was an international frontier with a Belgian and French checkpoint, so I had to make a detour all the way around to avoid the guards, scrambling over ploughed fields until I reached a road again but it was

the early hours before I found the 9th Rifle Brigade.

I looked around the tents until I found one in which a group of men were clustered round a table on which were a number of parcels and letters. There I found my younger brother, Bill. Of course it was very emotional, and seeing the state he was in, all the more so. He'd lost half of his equipment, all he'd got when I saw him was a balaclava and of course his rifle and bayonet. We were like a couple of kids, I suppose, falling over each other. He was lucky to survive. Bill told me that my elder brother Bob had been wounded and sent back to a CCS [Casualty Clearing Station] but was doing well.

While I was there, Bill used a brazier to brew up a cup of tea and he made us a snack. We shared a letter and we chatted for about an hour. At one point a sergeant looked in and saw me, and my cap badge. He may have heard what was happening; anyway, he made it obvious he didn't want to know, so he pushed off and left us. Dawn was breaking and I'd got to get back for rifle inspection at eight in the morning or be pronounced absent without leave. I was exhausted by the time I got back. I'd missed roll call and was arrested and put under guard before being sent before the Colonel, Thomas Stokoe. I explained what had happened and, no doubt about it, he took a lenient view. He told me, "You can have a court martial or accept my punishment," so I said, "I'd rather take your punishment, Sir", which I did, three days' pay stopped. I thanked him and left, my emotions almost overwhelming me.

[Ed. Bob later transferred to the Royal Flying Corps, while Bill remained with the Rifle Brigade. All three brothers would survive the war, although Bill was badly wounded in the head and taken prisoner on the Somme in 1918. His life was saved by pioneering treatment by a German surgeon. Bill lived to be 95.]

Private Fred Dixon, 2nd Leicestershire Regiment, 1895-1991
One day, after a stint in the front line, we were marched down to a disused brewery for a hot bath. Beer vats were used, but most had no

more than a few inches of hot water. We stripped and waited in line. Twelve men were ordered in at a time and when it came to my turn the water was stone cold and filthy. The change of underclothing we were given was no better than what I'd been wearing for months. I felt lice moving around my body as soon as I got it on; some were the size of ladybirds. However, it was a case of take it or leave it.

I found being lousy one of the worst trials of the war. I had been brought up in a very clean home but in France I had no option but to grin and bear it.

Private Clarence Walter Harry Jarman, No1644, 7th Queen's (Royal West Surrey Regiment), 9 May 1896-9 November1996
We had to go for a bath when we came out of the trenches. We'd been in the line for 14 days and we were filthy and lousy. There were big barrels cut in half, and we'd have a bath and a change of clothes and we'd fall-in in two lines outside the wash house and you could see the man in front with lice still crawling up his neck. We used to say, "I'll give you two little ones for one big one."

Lance Corporal Vic Cole, 7th Queen's Own (Royal West Kent Regiment), 1897-1995
Out of the line, out on rest, men used to gamble and Crown and Anchor was the game to play. I had a board made of card that I folded and kept in my haversack and anywhere you could lay it out you used to get chaps crowding round and the money used to come down, French coins and English pennies and half-pennies and farthings, and filthy little French notes, indescribably dirty, muddy, torn and stuck together.

There was a patter you learnt, but you said anything really, just to attract players.

"Over here, the name of the game, lads

Crown and Anchor

The more you put down, the more you pick up

Who says the lucky old die
Come here in rags, leave in riches
Crown and anchor, put your money down
Come on, another one for the Anchor
Crown, who's coming on the Crown?"

The board had six squares, in each of which was a symbol: a diamond, heart, club, spade, crown or anchor. There were three dice too, each with the six symbols. Once I'd got a crowd I'd shake the three dice and let them fall. If they came up two diamonds and one spade, you pay double on the diamond and one on the spade, and took the rest for yourself.

You paid out on the winnings on each square, it was nothing to do with whose money it was. Then it was up to the men to pick it up and they could fight it out amongst themselves if there was a problem. There would be arguments at times, but it was nothing to do with me. I'll tell you what, though. It used to be a quick money maker for the banker.

The army stopped it after a while because it was getting out of hand. When we were out at rest, you might see six of these boards being worked at any one time.

THE PRESSURE TO ENLIST

[Ed. Recruitment into the British Army had dropped alarmingly since the heady days of 1914. By mid-1915, it was barely half of what it had been, and the authorities were forced to accept that conscription was the only alternative to voluntary enlistment. Meanwhile, as newspapers published columns of the latest casualties, those who had so far failed to enlist were increasingly pressured into doing so whether they were old enough or not.]

Private Harold Leonard Judd, No516997, D Company, 2/14th London Regiment (London Scottish), 30 July 1898-November 1998

My occupation was reserved, being on the railway in the operating department. I was walking down Euston Road and these two bright ladies, or whatever you'd like to call them, presented me with a white feather. "Do you want one of these?" and they tried to slip it in my top pocket, but I stopped them. They were saying I was a coward even though I had a badge in my lapel saying I was in a reserved occupation. It was plain damn silly, presenting white feathers to people. I tried not to let it bother me, as I had other things to think about. I wanted to volunteer, regardless of what other people said or did.

I thought the kilt was a wonderful thing, far better than trousers, with the white spats and the Glengarry, so I went down to Buckingham Gate, the headquarters then, signed on for the London Scottish and was given the King's shilling. When I got back to the office and told them I'd joined, they sacked me because my job was reserved. It wasn't until I was serving abroad that I got a letter to say that I'd been reinstated. My superannuation would be carried on and paid as if I was there, they told me, and the job was open when I came back.

Private Percy Johnson, 21st London Regiment, 1899-2002

I was working in a munitions factory when one day, as I came to work, a group of girls approached and gave me some white feathers. I was a bit annoyed and threw them away. Two days later they came up again and gave me more feathers, so I said, "So you think I need these, do you? Well, you go home and tell my mother that she ought to be ashamed of herself for letting me stop in England, when her husband and three sons are already in France. I'm not seventeen yet and I'm looking after my mother and the children and allotments." Anyway, they won. I lost my temper, walked straight up Mill Hill and joined up, and let my mother down.

Private James Alfred Hudson, No23132, C Company, 8th (Queen's Own) Royal West Kent Regiment, 10 March 1898-11 June 2001

I joined the Royal Naval Volunteer Reserve at 112 The Strand. I was taken first to Scotland Yard where we were examined by Sir Thomas Barlow, the physician of that period. We were stripped naked, two ranks of us, and he walked along and threw out people by just looking at them. There were eight of us left, and we were sent around to chief petty officers, who took chest measurements and expansion, height and weight, after which I went back and signed a form. I was given a day's pay and sent home to await my call-up. Three weeks later, I hadn't heard a thing and I went up again, this time to join the signals section of the RNVR. I forgot about the paperwork, the last question of which was, "Have you before ever served or attested in any of His Majesty's armed forces?" I said to the Chief Petty Officer, "I don't have to sign this, do I?" Well he tore me off one hell of a strip and told me to bugger off home and wait until I was called up.

Lord Derby had a scheme by which you could join the army to be called up when needed, so I attested for this instead and was given a khaki band with a red crown on it, which we wore with great pride to save us from being given a white feather. I'd joined the army a little under age, and wasn't called up until the following year when I joined the Royal West Kents and went abroad. I had already gone over the top and I was in the Ypres Salient when I received a letter from my mother, saying, "I've had a letter from the Royal Naval Volunteer Reserve asking you to report to Crystal Palace, at such and such a date. What should I do?" What could I do but write back and tell her to get in contact with the RNVR and say they'd lost a good chap.

Private Alfred 'Fred' Charles Lloyd, No33467, Army Veterinary Corps, 23 February 1898-28 April 2005

I tried to enlist at seventeen, but I went up the Town Hall at the wrong time. I worked as a gardener on an estate, and Mr Streatfield, whom I worked for, was sitting on the recruiting committee. He said, "What do you want, Fred?" It was all Christian names then, we were more like a family really, because we were all born locally. "What are you doing up here?" I expect he thought I ought to be at work, and I said, "I want to join up, Sir." "What? Join up? What are you talking about? You're only seventeen. You go back and get on with your work." He was very short and sweet. "I'll tell you when you can join up." There were probably a dozen off the estate who had enlisted, and two had already been killed, one lad from the stables, and a footman, and another, Joe Gilmour, he'd lost an arm. In the end quite a few lads were knocked off.

Private Cecil Withers, 7th East Surrey Regiment, 1898-2005
I worked in the general manager's office in the accounting house of WH Smith, and people used to look at me. "When the bloody hell are you going?" and the pressure and the denigration got so great, I got fed up, so on the last day of November 1915, I thought, "Blow it!" I drew my month's salary in gold and went straight out of the office and said "Goodbye". I walked along the Strand and Fleet Street. I didn't know where to go or where to stay the night, so I asked a policeman, who mentioned Rowton House, a real low-down place for sixpence a night. You went through a turnstile to get in and were given just an old bed and a red blanket. I was warned to hide anything valuable, so I put my wages in my boots and went to bed. In the morning, I had a cup of tea with a roll and butter, then I got the tram to Tooting, and I walked along the high street to Tooting Broadway, where I met a sergeant who came up to me and asked if I wanted to enlist.

There's two pulls of loyalty: there was one to the country and one to the family. You got two tugs of war, and I gave way to the country, the country come first, that's the way I looked at it. You'd see a propaganda picture of soldiers marching by outside a window, and a woman there bending over a table and two little children with a spoon having breakfast, and underneath, these words, "Aren't they worth fighting for?" The words were like a magnet. The woman there with two nice little children, looking at their mum, it touched you, touched your heart. It was so impressive that you never thought about lies; you were fighting for them, going to war for people like that. They were good people and that's how it was. Of course, I felt a bit shame-faced telling a lie, but it was a patriotic lie, I suppose.

If you enlisted under the age of eighteen, your parents could apply for your return, because you were under age. I knew that. I didn't want to be humiliated and dragged out like a naughty boy, so when they asked my name I said George Harrison, who was then a big noise in the newspaper business.

Nobody questioned it, besides, how would they verify it? They couldn't phone, only a very few people were on the phone. Anyway they didn't want to question your age, they didn't want to find out because they wanted as many as they could get; they agitated for more and more, not less.

They asked me where they should send my civilian clothes and I said, "Oh, 124 Old Kent Road", any old address. I was given a brown piece of paper, string, and I took my old jacket and trousers off, bundled them up with my shoes, tied the string round and sent it all off to the Old Kent Road. Whoever lived there must have had a surprise.

It was only after I had done my training that I thought, "I'd better tell my parents, else mother will worry about me, wondering where I've got to, been drowned or jumped ship for New Zealand." All these ideas entered my mind, so I had to get it straight. I wrote and posted the letter in London when I got a pass out of the barracks, to make it look like I was in the Capital. I told them to advertise in *The Times*, to say that they wouldn't apply for my discharge, and then I would give my real name to the army. Anyway, I did this and when I went the next day to answer the roll call, the sergeant called out, "Withers! Harrison yesterday, Withers today, when was the bloody wedding?"

[Ed. After the Battle of Loos, the British army settled down for the

winter, indeed, the British Army would not again be engaged in a major military offensive for almost nine months. The failures of 1915 brought a change at the top, when the British Commander-in-Chief, Sir John French, was replaced by General Sir Douglas Haig, hitherto Commander of First Army. The expected victory of 1915 had not materialised; 1916, it was hoped, would be different. In the meantime there was Christmas to contend with, and strict orders were issued that there would be no repetition of the previous year's truce: there was to be no further fraternization with the enemy.]

Private James Wilson, 7th Leicestershire Regiment, 1896-fl.1998
We were taken out of the line early on Christmas morning, before my company, A Company, were sent back up as a working party. The fighting had stopped, how that happened I don't know, but something had been arranged, and the men were being allowed to go over the top and move around in the open. The Germans did the same but we were ordered not to go any further than our front line wire, and we had to be back in our trenches by midnight.

There was no calling to the Germans and shaking hands, no swapping of gifts, and with nowhere to go, most were back in the trench well before it got dark. I didn't go out, mind you, I didn't go up on top.

During Christmas Day, it became misty and foggy long before it got dark. Next day there was a roll call, to check everyone had turned up, but unfortunately one was missing. We looked round and we found him, poor devil. His name was Lance Corporal Armstrong; we found him spread-eagled on their wire. He had gone the wrong way and he'd been shot, and we could see him through our periscopes. There was no attempt to fetch him in.

[Ed. The Battalion Diary noted: "The enemy made no attempt at friendliness or in any way put out feelers for a truce opposite this sector. Had he done so, both by orders and inclination there would have been no response.]

Private Dick Trafford, 1/9th King's Liverpool Regiment, 1898-1999
It was Christmas morning, still dark, and this Bob Taylor from Skelmsdale shouted, "Dick, Dick, come here quickly." I ran over. "Shall I shoot?" I looked to where he was pointing and there was a German, all on his own, trying to crawl under our barbed wire. I couldn't understand what he was up to, so I asked Bob, "Has he got a rifle or anything?" "I can't see anything but he's sure to have a bomb or two in his pocket," Bob replied. I couldn't understand what was going on. "I'll tell you what, I'll go out, but if he moves to attack me in any way, then shoot him." I was covering myself. I got onto the parapet and went out to our wire, and the German stopped and he got hold of my hand, and shook it, "Happy Christmas," or words to that effect, and he appeared to pray in his tin-pot way. I shook his hand and said, "Right, Happy Christmas, now bugger off," which he did.

We waited a while and kept peeping over the top of the trench. It was daylight by this time and after a while we saw a hand come up, waving. I assume it was his.

Private Clarrie Jarman, 7th Queen's (Royal West Surrey Regiment), 1896-1996
At Christmas 1915, we had orders that any man fraternizing with the enemy would be severely dealt with. Well, the Germans on Christmas morning started to sing and to the left of us somebody opened fire on them. And talk about peace on earth, the Germans retaliated, giving us a real bashing all day long and pretty well all Boxing Day too, for firing at them.

Private Ted Francis, 16th Warwickshire Regiment, 1896-1996
On Christmas morning, we were out of the trenches and we were trying to put a festive dinner together when a sergeant major put his head round the door. "Ted, I've got a job for you. Headquarters of such and such a battalion half a mile away has been hit by two shells, and there's twenty lying dead and wounded, and bits of people too, mainly

bits. I want you and few others to gather it all up." Before we went, we were given half a glass of rum. You'd do the silliest and the bravest of things after a good tot, you felt nothing could hurt you and, of course, it had the desired effect. We had a good long drink and said, "Right, where are they?"

That was my Christmas morning, two or three hours to gather these people up into some sort of order so that they could be taken away for burial, after which I was expected to come back for Christmas dinner and enjoy it.

CHAPTER THREE

1916

GOING BACK TO FRANCE

ARTHUR HALESTRAP, WHO DIED IN 2004, increasingly regarded his war experiences as a mechanism for reminding us all that we should not forget the sacrifices made ninety years ago; he saw himself as one of the last representatives of his generation. He undertook annual trips to France and Belgium and gave the exhortation under the Menin Gate in the presence of thousands of people, not because he was happy to do so, but because he felt he must.

Jack Davis, who frequently travelled with Arthur, felt a similar sense of duty. "When I speak those words of the exhortation at the Menin Gate, it is a sacred duty I have to fulfil because it means so much to me, knowing so many of my comrades did not return. Although it is very emotional, it is something I cannot fail to do." He performed this duty until shortly before his death at 108 years old.

In some instances, it was the families that held back veterans who wanted to go to France. Understandably, they worried about the stress on frail bodies and emotions. In fact, there have, to my knowledge, been no deaths of veterans on official tours, but a few, such as Harold Judd, died within days of getting back; whether their visits and their deaths were connected, it is impossible to say.

Norman Collins, on the other hand, was asked to go back by his son, keen to see where his father had served. Norman himself said that he had had no intention of ever returning to the battlefields; he lived in the present, and rarely dwelt in the past. Nevertheless, when he did go back, in 1989, the irony of the situation did not escape him.

"I would consider it amusing, if I were able to, if I died 73 years after the battle, on the same spot where I should have passed on at 19 years of age. I'm sure I would be greeted by cries of "Late on parade, Sir?"

"I have a greater chance of living a week at the age of 92 than I did when I was 19.

"When I went to France 73 years ago, there was nothing but brick dust blown into the soil. I am going to see the real France, the villages of which, when I was out there before, there was nothing left. Then, I could only see them from the trenches with a periscope, but now I will be able to walk about freely on the battlefield and it will be an amazing sensation. Before, I only had a rat's view, a worm's view of the French countryside."

Harry Patch returned to Belgium for what was almost certainly the last time in late September 2004. Seemingly he has no wish to make the trip again. He is likely to be the last veteran to visit the Western Front, the last member of the British Expeditionary Force to leave, and the last of the many tens of thousands of veterans who have visited the battlefields regularly since the early 1920s. Harry's trip was the final stage in a subconscious pilgrimage to settle the war in his own mind and to come to terms with the loss of close friends. From the age of 100, Harry has changed much from the man who had refused for over eighty years to talk about the conflict, or even to watch a war film. In the seven years since, he has made a remarkable transition. He said he would never return to the Western Front; he would never return to Pilkem Ridge where he was wounded and lost his friends to a shellburst. And the idea that he would meet a German soldier, let alone an artilleryman, was incomprehensible. Yet he has done all those things since his hundredth birthday, and as a result the war sits much more gently on his shoulders.

Two years ago, he laid a wreath on his Divisional memorial on Pilkem Ridge, just months after he had been unable to leave the coach because memories overwhelmed him. Then, last year, he went to Belgium again, to meet German veteran Charles Kuentz. They shook hands and toasted each other, exchanged gifts, affirmed and even toasted their friendship. Together, they laid a wreath in Langemark German Cemetery. It was interesting to watch how each of these men, through translators, reassured the other that, at least as far as their war was concerned, nothing was personal: Harry, a machine gunner, shot at the legs, Charles merely fired shells in the general direction of the enemy; there was no hatred, only orders.

One of the earliest veterans to go back was James Hudson, of the 8th Queen's Own (Royal West Kent Regiment).

"It was 1923. A travel agency sent me a brochure about trips to the battlefields and on the spur of the moment, I thought I would go. This was on the Monday and I travelled on Friday.

"There was only one other old soldier on the coach. We got to know each other and together we walked into the cemetery at Passchendaele, Tyne Cot. It was a lovely summer day, quiet and peaceful, and at the back of the cemetery was a young Belgian fellow with a single plough drawn by a mule, one of ours, for it had an arrow stamped on its backside. The peace, the quiet, the scene had both of us damn nearly in tears. We parted and we were left alone for some time before we could pull ourselves together a bit. It brought back so much, to think of these chaps."

Vic Cole returned to the battlefields in 1962 on a cycling tour. He visited Bécourt Château where he had helped set up a brigade wireless station just prior to the Somme Battle. Behind the château in 1916 were two French graves, on one of which hung a rosary. Vic had taken the rosary and had worn it for the rest of the war; he felt it might bring him the good luck denied the French soldier. Forty-six years later, Vic felt it appropriate to return the rosary and placed it in the small chapel rebuilt at the side of the château. He told me about it, that it hung from a nail to the left of a small altar, and I promised on my next visit to see if it was still there. It was, only the chain had broken and the beads lay scattered across the floor. I took a picture. "Did you pick up a bead?" Vic asked. I had not, and I could see he was momentarily disappointed; he would have like to have made a physical attachment. The chain hung on the wall until a couple of years ago. I discovered only last year that the chapel, long used as a storage room, had been cleared, and inevitably the chain had been thrown away along with the beads, which presumably were swept up and discarded.

In the nineteen fifties and sixties, the veterans made their own way over, either together with their mates or, like Vic Cole, on their own. In the seventies and into the eighties, more returned, frequently brought to France by their children, who were curious to see where their fathers had fought. As late as 1987, a few veterans made their own way over. That year Tom Bromley, a 90-year-old veteran, went to France, armed with a small travel bag and passable French learnt while soldiering seventy years earlier. His technique for smoothing out the vagaries of travelling alone involved an envelope of twenty-franc notes that were distributed with largesse in exchange for a minute or two of help onto a train or up a flight of hotel stairs. He had visited France for decades, seeing the descendents of a farming family he had befriended in 1916, and visiting Dantzig Alley Cemetery where lay his three mates, killed in a single shell explosion, which miraculously left him untouched. His independent travel became harder as he grew older, until he finally gave up hope of revisiting France in 1991, the 75th anniversary of the Somme Battle.

On the wreath he sent to be laid at the Thiepval Memorial to the Missing, he wrote:

"I wanted so much to attend this 75th anniversary, but sadly at 94 my legs and wind have failed me. I will not see this place again but my comrades resting on this battlefield for these many years will never be forgotten until I, at last, join them once again. Tom R. Bromley, Dulas Court, Hereford."

Tom, Uncle Tom as he liked to be called, died in February 1992 shortly after his 95th birthday.

Latterly, veterans have joined the coach tours that have become such a feature of life in northeast France and Belgium. In May 1990, soldiers of the regular army known as the Old Contemptibles made their final trip abroad, their average age was a little over ninety-five years.

Since then, numbers have dwindled: of the estimated 150-200 Old Contemptibles alive then, only one remains, Alfred Anderson.

In 1986, for the seventieth anniversary of the Battle of the Somme, dozens of veterans joined coach parties, and not only were there British veterans, but French and German too. By 1996, this figure had shrunk to fourteen.

A similar number made the trip in 1998 for the eightieth anniversary of the Armistice, but since 2000, veterans have appeared in France in numbers of four or fewer, and 2005 will be the first year since 1918 that no veteran will visit the former battlefields.

The trips to France were ostensibly to allow veterans to remember their friends, but all those who went with them knew that it was as much about allowing these old men to enjoy the company of others, to talk and be feted. Stan Clayton interrupted his routine in 2000 in the expectation of going back to France. He stopped going out, fearful of having a fall, or some other accident that would incapacitate him. Everything was directed towards five days on the Somme in July and in the end, before he could go, he tripped over the carpet in his house and broke his leg. He died just a couple of weeks later.

1916

On the Western Front, 1 January 1916 was a cold, wet day. Elsewhere, the British forces began the final stages of their evacuation of the Gallipoli peninsula after more than eight months' hard slog. Leaving the peninsula proved a spectacular success, in stark contrast to the original landings, which had been so costly. Leaving was the final act in a campaign that had, in the end, proved a misadventure. As the troops filtered down to the lighters that took them to their ships, the stores that were left behind were torched, lighting up the night sky. The Allies had escaped from under the very noses of the enemy, who until the morning were unaware that they had departed.

On 21 February, the Germans launched their massive campaign against the French at Verdun. Early success pushed the French back almost to the gates of the city, while French reserves were brought forward remorselessly to stabilize the line. The campaign became a bloodbath for both sides. For the French, the defence of Verdun came to symbolize the defence of France as a whole. 'They shall not pass' were the words uttered by Marshal Petain to instill in French troops a sense that the continued existence of a nation depended on the maintenance of national honour. The city had to be held, no matter what.

For all the evident determination to hold Verdun, behind the scenes the French urgently appealed for Britain to launch an offensive in order to draw off the enemy's reserves. The attacks against Verdun were threatening to bleed the French army dry, an expressed aim of the enemy. After talks with the British High Command and the new Commander in Chief, Douglas Haig, it was agreed that the two allies would launch a joint offensive, and the region chosen was the Somme, a relative backwater of the war. The date set, after much wrangling, was late June. Standing shoulder to shoulder, the British and French troops would attack over an extended front, smashing through the enemy's deep defences and allowing the cavalry to wreak havoc behind the German lines. This would be the Big Push, starting an advance that would begin the wider drive to retake northern France and push the enemy back to her national borders.

As the build-up began, fresh British divisions arrived in France, swelling the number of troops from one to one and a half million. New divisions, such as the 31st Division, had been training abroad in the heat of the Egyptian desert; others, such as the 34th, had been on Salisbury Plain, enjoying the comforts of country living in Wiltshire and Somerset. To guarantee future troop requirements, conscription had been introduced in January, bringing into the army whole swathes of men previously employed in civil industry. These would fill the barracks left empty by the recent batch of Kitchener's Divisions to leave for overseas service.

The 34th Division had left Somerset for France in January 1916, including Tom Dewing, an affable and gentle boy, the son of a draper and sub-postmaster from Norfolk. Another on the move was Joe Yarwood, a gangly, intelligent lad, the eldest of thirteen children from Walworth, south London. He was serving as a stretcher bearer with the Royal Army Medical Corps attached to the 31st Division. They made the move from Egypt to the Somme in March.

Detailed preparations for the push continued in earnest. The Allies needed a positive campaign as, since the Battle of Loos, little had been going right for the British abroad. Three months after the evacuation of Gallipoli came British setbacks in the Middle East when a force sent to relieve the besieged town of Kut failed to break the Turkish defences and had to withdraw, leaving 15,000 British and Indian soldiers to face inevitable starvation and disease. Hard on the heels of this reversal came the Easter Uprising in Dublin, which stunned the British authorities, as a small number of Nationalists declared Irish independence. Furious at such treachery, the Government sent forces to the city and in street battles lasting several days, control was wrested from the nationalists and the ringleaders arrested. Then, while the embers of burnt-out buildings still flickered in Dublin, news came from the besieged town of Kut that the British forces had surrendered to the Turks. The British and Indian soldiers marched into captivity; most would not live to see the end of the war.

In June came the inconclusive naval engagement at Jutland. The Germans proclaimed a victory, for more ships of the Royal Navy were sunk than were lost by the enemy's High Seas Fleet. In fact strategically, Britain's control of the vital North Sea remained unbroken, but a hard-to-discern 'success' was not what the press and public had hoped for and there was much disappointment at the outcome of the battle.

A week later, Britain's great icon, Lord Kitchener, was drowned when, on a visit to Russia, his ship HMS *Hampshire* hit a mine and sank. The nation was deeply shaken just as its military forces prepared for the largest offensive of the war.

As far as the British were concerned, the rest of 1916 would be dominated by the offensive on the Somme. The logistics in preparing such a battle were enormous, culminating in a round-the-clock bombardment of the enemy lines, intended to last five days but, owing to poor weather, extended to seven. The enemy trenches, it was assumed, would be smashed before the infantry attacked on 1 July. Then, just prior to zero hour, a series of mines dug under German strongpoints would be detonated before the infantry went over the top. In all, around 120,000 infantrymen would advance on what turned out to be a glorious hot sunny day.

The German infantry, secreted in dugouts forty feet below ground, were far from obliterated, and when the British barrage lifted, they swarmed up and cut down the advancing troops. Around 50% of the men deployed that day were either killed or wounded. Only in the southern sector of the front did British soldiers meet with any visible success.

A battle of attrition ensued and continued for four and a half months, as the Germans fell back to defend new lines constructed little more than a mile behind those they had been forced to give up. As individual woods and villages were contested one by one, the losses on both sides mounted. The British adapted, deploying new battle tactics and weapons to break the stalemate. Their introduction met with varying success, most notably the introduction of the first tanks in September. However, the hoped-for breakthrough that would return the war to one of movement remained elusive, and the offensive bogged down in the winter mud just six miles from where the troops had started, back in July.

Neither side could claim a victory, although the British commanders had learnt much from the onslaught, with tactics revised and honed for the next offensive. After suffering appalling loses at Verdun, the Germans could ill afford the protracted Somme campaign, which cost the German nation so many of its best fighting troops. The tide of war, if yet indiscernible, had begun to gradually turn in the Allies' favour.

THE BIG PUSH

Private Thomas 'Tom' Alfred Dewing, No85196, 2 Section, 34th Divisional Signal Company, Royal Engineers, attd. 101 Brigade, 21 April 1896-1 February 2001
On the first day of January 1916, the first sections of our Company embarked for France and we were sad to see them go. Then the next day we left, and cheered like mad as we made for Southampton. But no, it wasn't an adventure.

I think by the time we actually embarked for France, we were all feeling a bit sad – it's hard to say after all this time, but yes, I would say that we were definitely feeling sad, and as we went down the Solent we all stood and watched the shores of England fading into the darkness.

Private George Louth, 15th Hampshire Regiment, 1897-2000
Just before we went to France, a Lieutenant, a new one, got us round in a ring. "Now then," he said, "we are going to France. Get rid of all your animosity to each other. You may say, 'I'll shoot the bastard when I get out there,' but you won't do it, you'll all be friends."

Rifleman Robert Renwick, No18700, A Company, 16th King's Royal Rifle Corps, 7 June 1896-3 October 1997
I got draft leave and went home. We knew we were going overseas when we got back to the Regiment, and my mother was a bit upset. My father walked me to the station five miles away, Corbridge Station. I never thought he'd turn back. "Robert, I know you'll do your duty but will you promise me you won't take any undue risks?" I couldn't find an answer to that one.

When I arrived, the Company Commander, Captain Crockford, was going around the troops, checking we'd all got our overseas boots on and giving the men a little training on how to look after them. And he came across a fellow called Petty.

"Why haven't you got your overseas boots on, Petty?"

"I haven't got my teeth yet, Sir." He had been going on about his need for false teeth for a while.

Crockford says, "Your teeth? You're not going out to eat them, you're going out there to fight them, man."

Private Tom Dewing, 34th Divisional Royal Engineers Signal Company, 1896-2001
We landed at Le Havre on 7 January 1916 and we got a shock when we saw the train that was to take us inland. It consisted of cattle trucks labelled in French, HOMMES 40 CHEVAUX 8, which left one wondering if it meant 40 men and 8 horses. One of these vans was allotted to our section and we were not unduly crowded. Each van had double doors on each side and we opened them wide and watched the hedgeless countryside as the train slowly made its way through France until we disembarked at St Omer.

Private Ernest William Ford, No7260, 3 Platoon, A Company, 10th Queen's (Royal West Surrey Regiment), 13 July1896-June1995

After the usual messing around, we were eventually stowed into cattle trucks, 'Tommies' Pullmans' bearing the trade-mark, Hommes 40 Chevaux 8, from which we inferred that a horse was worth five men. Whoever was responsible for this sign must have been a very optimistic person. I doubt whether it would have been possible to put 40 men, with all their impediments, into one cattle truck without making two layers of them. Anyhow, there were 28 in my truck and there was not sufficient floor-space for us all to lie flat. We piled our legs down the middle of the truck and endured a 19-hour journey followed by a nine-mile march into billets.

Private Tom Dewing, 34th Divisional Royal Engineers Signal Company, 1896-2001

Our accommodated consisted of wooden huts with pitched roofs of tarred felt. Each hut had a door at one end and a slow combustion stove at the other. There was a battery of field guns nearby and it was an interesting experience when we heard the first shells. One morning the Germans started shelling the battery and we all rushed out to watch. A shell burst fairly near the huts and a piece of shell whirred past us. We followed the sound with our eyes. Presently a second piece went through the roof of an empty hut and we all rushed to find this bit of shell. I found it and I carried it in my haversack for months.

Private Charles Douglas Gerald 'Tommy' Thomson, No6562, 2nd Battalion Honourable Artillery Company, 25 June 1898-11 August 2003

The first man I saw killed was very soon after we got to France. We were in a quiet sector and this chap had put his head over the top to have a look, and a sniper shot him clean through the head. He'd just arrived in the line, at Ploegsteert. When they examined him they found that his adoring mother had given him a body shield that she had purchased and lovingly sent to France to protect his life.

Private Andrew Bowie, No22693, D Company, 1st Cameron Highlanders, 3 October 1897-26 August 2002

I had an uncle who happened to be an agent for bullet-proof vests that looked similar to a thickly padded waistcoat. Now these vests would, in theory, stop a bullet, so my sister purchased one and sent it to me. I wore it under my tunic. There was a sergeant major, who was a rather cowardly type. He knew about my bullet-proof vest and he used to say to me, "When you get killed, I'll have that vest." We were out on rest once, and he said, "Come on, we'll try your vest out." So we draped it around a sandbag, went about fifty yards away and fired shots at it. They went right through the padding, after which his eager claim dropped a bit.

Private Tom Dewing, 34th Division Royal Engineers Signal Company, 1896-2001

I had been on night duty, and was lying down hoping to get some sleep when there was a sudden burst of anti-aircraft fire. The other men all went out of the hut to see what was going but I decided to stay where I was. However, their exclamations became so excited that I got up and joined them.

A German observation plane was on its way home and puffs of smoke from bursting anti-aircraft shells seemed to surround it. Perhaps he was beyond their range, for he went on and presumably returned home unharmed. When we went back to the hut, I saw that there was a hole in the roof above my bed and I found a round shrapnel bullet lying where my head had been.

Lance Corporal Vic Cole, 7th Queen's Own (Royal West Kent Regiment), 1897-1995

In the trenches around Bécourt Château, there had been a German attack in the early days of 1914, and a lot of French had been killed. It meant that when we dug new trenches we came across these bodies, including, I recall, a ghostly hand sticking out where some earth had given way. Yet we just went on, thinking that was the way it had to be. It didn't worry me, seeing bodies that had turned black, you took no notice because it didn't matter, because very soon you yourself would be like that.

Battalion HQ was situated in the very extensive cellars of the Château. The building had been much knocked about but part of the roof was intact, and from there I could just see the 'hanging virgin' crowning the ruined basilica in Albert.

The Château was still habitable on the ground floor, where there was a salon and an old piano. This was played now and again to the accompaniment of machine gun bullets and shells passing overhead. One shell burst in the small library, scattering books. They were torn and dusty but one could see amongst them the beautiful bindings of old volumes mostly inscribed on the fly-leaf or cover with the name 'Comte de Varicourt'.

In the cellar, there were one or two tables and a telephone switchboard into which we plugged the various wires we were using; the plug was the bullet out of a 303 cartridge, the wires were wrapped or soldered onto the cartridge, and the bullet was put head first into whatever cartridge you wanted, to make a connection. It was all very ingenious.

To exit the cellars, we dug a door in the back that brought us out onto a path that led into a wood and down to the communication trenches. In front of the Château, there had been a garden with a well, which we were told had been poisoned. There was a wall each side and iron gates, and we called the square in front of the Château 'Piccadilly Circus'. Out of the iron gates, the communication trench, Dufferin Avenue, led down a slope to a sunken road where our water cart was, and from there up to the support line.

We were well behind the line here but that did not mean we were safe. Death or injury could happen at the most unexpected moments. I nipped down one night to the water cart to fill my bottle just as a machine gun opened up and a shower of bullets smacked into the ground all around the cart. A man beside me groaned and fell. A stretcher bearer came up at the run and we found that a bullet had entered the poor bloke's back in the lumber region and had come out just above his left knee. When bandaged, he seemed to be all right and went off on a stretcher, smoking a cigarette.

Private Smiler Marshall, 1/1st Essex Yeomanry, 1897-2005

My mate Lenny Passiful was in a different troop from me. I was in the Ardley Troop; he was in the Colchester Troop, but he asked his sergeant if he could come and join me in the same bay of the trench. A German had been using a sniper's shield and we reckoned there was a chance of getting him because when he shot there was a tell-tale flame from the barrel of his rifle. So what we'd try and do is get ready and concentrate, waiting for the next time he fired.

I'd had five or six shots when my mate Lenny said, "Let me have a go, Smiler," and he jumped up on to the fire step. Now I'm down in the trench watching and he had a shot or two when the German fired and I suddenly saw Lenny collapse. I put my arm out and broke his fall.

He lay at the bottom of the trench and I spoke to him. "Never mind, Lenny, you've got your blighty one. What more do you want?" He coughed up a little blood, but he managed to smile and say "Ta ta, Smiler." I wanted to take him down to the chalk pit, to the first dressing station. "Please, he's my best pal, I'd love to take him, so that I know the RAMC have got him." But Sergeant Geoffrey Weir said he'd take him and as he went along the communication trench, a German mortar came right over and blew the parapet down, blocking the way. He had to take Lenny over the top, so for a couple of minutes he was exposed to the Germans, who opened fire with their machine guns. He got a medal for that.

Lance Corporal Vic Cole, 7th Queen's Own (Royal West Kent Regiment), 1897-1995

You could look over the top but you had to be very careful. Sandbags lined the length of the parapet so we'd sew a sandbag onto our tin hats and peer over, just your eyes, so that you were practically invisible to the enemy. Then you'd just rest your arm next to your rifle and you'd be quite comfortable for a while. Then you might see a puff of something over there and wonder for a moment what it was, ch ch ch ch, the sound, you know. "Trench mortar coming over!" And we'd all dive down the dugouts, and it would come, ch ch ch ch, like a train, a large tin canister turning over in the air, CRAAAASH, and then we'd all come out again.

Lieutenant Richard Hawkins, 11th Royal Fusiliers, 1895-1994

We all had great fun really, tremendous fun. I personally enjoyed the ruddy war, I don't know why. Of course, it wasn't very pleasant when Minenwerfers were being thrown in the air, great big five-gallon oil drums, filled with rusty metal, you could see them turning over – where's that going to drop? Now, which way should we run?

Lance Corporal Vic Cole, 7th Queen's Own (Royal West Kent Regiment), 1897-1995

You weren't having a battle but it was a game of wits all the time. Up near Fricourt, there was a German machine gun we nicknamed Banjo Willie; he used to open up every night at 8 o'clock. "Oh, there's Banjo Willie," and he would fire 'tat, tat, tat, tat tat….tat tat' from two different places, then quickly swing his gun round and loose off two extra shots. It was his signature.

We learnt to spot the snipers too. You'd put up a large turnip on the end of your bayonet with a tin hat on it, and so attract the sniper who might fire. If he did, we'd take the turnip down very carefully and take a bearing through the hole that the bullet had made, then do it again further up the trench and get a cross bearing. We didn't fire at him ourselves, rather we would ask the trench mortar people to drop one on him.

Private Smiler Marshall, 1/1st Essex Yeomanry, 1897-2005
I wrote to Lenny's mum after he was shot. "Expect Lenny home within weeks, he'll be back in England, he's been shot." About four or five weeks later, I got a letter back. "Dear Smiler, you'll be very sad to hear that he only lived three days." They buried him in Béthune Town Cemetery. In his paybook there was about £3 or £4, and they stopped £1 for the blanket he was buried in. What do you think about that? A soldier wounded in the front line, and the army took a pound for the blanket, unbelievable, but that's as true as I'm here.

Private Andrew Bowie, 1st Cameron Highlanders, 1897-2002
When we were in the line, the mail from home was vital to morale and wasn't censored. Mail going home was read by an officer, to see that you hadn't said where you were fighting. If you did, then a big black pencil would go through the offending words. Many people had an understanding with home, a code, so, for example each paragraph would start with a letter which, added up to the opening letters of every other paragraph, would spell a word. "You are in my constant thoughts, "Y". "Present days are very tiring," "P". "Received your letter with great pleasure, "R"…and so on "E" and then "S"…Ypres. So you'd tell your friends at home you were at Ypres.

Trooper Ben Clouting, 4th (Royal Irish) Dragoon Guards, 1897-1990
One of the quickest ways of sending a message home was on a printed Field Postcard, on which the soldier was only allowed to scrub out the official words, "I am well/not well", "I have/have not heard from you lately", that sort of thing. The soldier was only meant to date and sign it at the bottom, though some added the odd caustic word or two if they had not heard for a while, one man, I recall, writing "never" when he came to, "I have received your parcel dated…"

Private Andrew Bowie, 1st Cameron Highlanders, 1897-2002
There was no toilet paper in the trenches, no privacy either, well, you
didn't think about privacy. So you used your last love letter from your
dearest friend, that's where all the good love letters went. You used to
see men reading them for the last time before they came to a sticky
end. If you had a sense of humour, it helped a bit; you can imagine a
lovely delicate lady doing her best to write a lovely letter, and that is
how it ended up.

Private Ted Francis, 16th Warwickshire Regiment, 1896-1996
I'd written three letters to my father, telling him about the war, and I'd
had no replies. I couldn't understand it. Of course, leave was out of the
question. Then one day, a letter came for me from a strange hand. It
was from a gentleman who had taken over my father's pub and he said,
"I've opened a letter you sent and it's obvious to me you don't know
that your father is dead – he died six weeks ago from cancer." That
knocked me over. He told me that my eldest brother, who was twelve
years older than me, had had what he liked of the home and put all the
rest to auction, and therefore I'd no home.

When I got leave, I had to find my brother and beg to stay at his
place. He wasn't too keen, but his wife said that I could give them a
hand and that there was a spare room, so I got lodgings. I had no
money at all and I had to rely on my brother and his wife to give me
half a crown to go up town and go the pictures or theatre. That was a
miserable ten days for me and in a way I was glad to be back in France.
That was my only leave in three years.

*Lieutenant Norman Dillon, 14th Northumberland Fusiliers, 1896-
1997*
In 1916 we were issued with steel helmets for the first time. They were
uncomfortable because they didn't fit; they sat on one's hair, but they
worked. I sent home for a liner which fitted like a bowler hat and was
comfortable, but most annoyingly it was stolen. The maker was

Lincoln & Bennett of St James. It was interesting how one could order London-made goods in the middle of a war, and what is more, receive them.

Lieutenant Richard Hawkins, 11th Royal Fusiliers, 1895-1994
One of my fellow officers by the name of Lewis wrote to Dunhill and said, "Dear Mr Dunhill, please send us a pipe," and this parcel was delivered by the post office to us in the dugout, the night before an attack. Lewis opened the parcel and there inside were twelve pipes, each in a little box, with a tin of ointment and a spare aluminium tube. Beautiful French Briar, famous they were, and there was a letter, "Dear Mr Lewis, thank you very much for your letter. We don't know what size or shape you prefer, so we are sending a dozen for you to choose from. When you've made your choice, please at your convenience return the remainder, unless of course any of your brother officers would like to buy one." Well, I fell for it, fourteen and sixpence, but it was beautiful.

2nd Lieutenant Norman Collins, 1/6th Seaforth Highlanders, 1897-1998
To ease the pressure we smoked; almost every man seemed to smoke. Cigarettes were a great comfort and, at the right time, worked wonders. Most of the cigarettes were terrible and were hardly worth smoking. The cheap cigarette was a Woodbine. The Players and Goldflake were quite good, sixpence for twenty or fivepence ha'penny for Players. Although I might smoke up to 40 or 45 cigarettes a day, I never inhaled, so I can't say that I was a great addict, but some men would take the end of a cigarette and relight it and, even though it was saturated in tar and nicotine, they'd enjoy it. Smoking was all part of the camaraderie and of course it relieved stress, no doubt about it.

Trooper Smiler Marshall, 1/1st Essex Yeomanry, 1897-2005
Most men smoked cigarettes to help relieve the pressure, but I didn't.

Instead I would start to sing, to help morale, break the ice, so to speak. It was better than standing there twiddling your thumbs. If you can start singing, you're all right. It stopped the fear, stopped you being mopey or worrying. If everything was quiet and a machine gunner began sweeping your parapet and then the shells, trench mortars and rifle grenades started bursting, and everybody is sitting there, nobody speaking, it doesn't matter what it is, start singing. Everybody will look up, and the whole place will be more lively.

In the front line, we used to sing all sorts of songs, and I made one up about the food we used to eat.

James William Maconochie
Made a monarchy
On his own
Beans mixed up with turnips and carrots
And all sorts of things.
The troops all did a funny 'un
When an onion came to light
But the troops didn't mind
That the man who got fat
Was JWM

Private Jack Davis, 1st Duke of Cornwall's Light Infantry, 1895-2003
At La Bassée we had no recognized front line. We were operating from saps, dug in the ground, Suffolk Sap, Machine Gun Sap, and Lunatic Sap, which speaks for itself. I had to do a tour of duty with my company officer to supply the other saps along the front with a rum ration. So we were out for more or less three to four hours supplying the ration, after which we came back for a rest until Stand To. One day a young officer joined the regiment, and I was told to take him out and show him the route we took to the other saps. So the first night, all right, no problem. But, being an officer, he was taught to lead, while other ranks were taught to follow. So he said, "All right, I'll lead tonight," and he did, and took us onto the German wire. I was furious

because he was insistent. He had only been over this ground once, and I had made regular tours with my Company Officer. What can you say? You don't say, "You're going the wrong way." You don't argue, you've got to follow.

The machine guns opened up all along our front. Self-preservation took over, and I got into a shell hole for cover and I called him and he came in. The Germans traversed their machine gun, and we waited until they passed us and made a dash for it, it was just a few yards to a bombing post, and we got back safely.

The next night he was still not satisfied, he wanted to lead, so he said, "Make sure we take Corporal Hubbard with us." He was in charge of the machine gun, and the same thing happened, we ended up on the German wire. Once again we jumped into a shell hole but the Corporal lost his head. He was running up and down the German wire while they were machine gunning. The officer and I got back, but we couldn't leave the Corporal out there and so I went out again with another man and got into a shell hole. We shouted out for him to join us, which he did, and all three of us ran back to the bombing post. However, as Hubbard bent over to get into the post he got a machine gun bullet right across his back, a flesh wound. He was the luckiest man alive, for it was within an eighth of an inch of his spine.

Trooper Smiler Marshall, 1/1st Essex Yeomanry, 1897-2005

A corporal and some men were going up the line to mend the trenches that had been blown in by a trench mortar. We were selected for the working party, but two lads, John Eade and Harry Jowers, they had the wind-up terrific. They had sweat dripping off their chins. Eade had the wind-up because he had numbered off as 13, so I tapped him on the back and said, "Change places with me. I'll number off 13, I'm not superstitious." We changed places, but they both died. Next morning they were buried a mile or so behind the lines. We'd had leather jerkins issued that night, so they wore them for the first time, and then they were buried in them. They were best mates, close as anything, and would have been together when they were hit.

Every night on the working party the padre used to come up and say a little prayer, and he used to say that it doesn't matter how near you are to death, there's always somebody nearer, so that's what you've got to try and think. Don't think that you might be the next one.

[Ed. The Regimental Diary notes that Eade was killed outright and Jowers was wounded and died a few hours later.]

Rifleman Robert Renwick, 16th King's Royal Rifle Corps, 1896-1997
Corporal Hiddins had gone to the company office and come back fuming, so I asked him what the matter was. He said, "What's the matter? I have to take a man with me and get a sample of German barbed wire." I said, "What are you waiting for?" "Are you volunteering?" he asked. "Yes, and I have a set of wire cutters." So off we went over the top. I then suggested that there was plenty of wire about without going anywhere near the enemy line. I picked up a length and cut each end clean, and of course we spent a bit of time sitting in a shell hole. The wire was accepted as being German and I thought we were fully justified in dodging the order.

Private Andrew Bowie, 1st Cameron Highlanders, 1897-2002
A captain, who had been the adjutant in Invergordon, came out to the battalion and went out on patrol, as ordered, from his part of the trench. Another patrol under a young lieutenant called Stephenson went out as well, and they were supposed to go along No Man's Land and meet and come back again. Stephenson came in and said he had not met the captain, but the captain said he had gone right along there as ordered but hadn't seen Stephenson. The captain had told a deliberate lie, because the men who had been with him told the truth and said, "He never did that, we were with him and we just went over into No Man's Land and we all sat down and came back in again. He never did his patrol." That was very serious, of course, he could have been court martialled. The other men backed Stephenson, that he'd

gone along all right but nothing had been seen of the captain. He was a pure coward and the men had a nasty feeling about him.

2nd Lieutenant Herbert Ernest Brighton, 10th South Wales Borderers, 20 November 1896-29 September 1997
We'd lie flat out in No Man's Land when the Very lights went up, then we'd move. We took rifles and fixed bayonets. I always wore an other rank's uniform with just the pips on my shoulder to show my rank. Whenever I was out on patrol I took a man called Davenport, a reliable man. It was his manner, if we got close enough to the enemy trench, to always spend a penny on their barbed wire entanglements. He was a brave and a grand man. Just to show his contempt for the Germans, that's what he said.

Private Jack Davis, 1st Duke of Cornwall's Light Infantry, 1895-2003
My Company, A Company, were to take part in a bombing raid so we were taken out of the line to a field a couple of miles away. There they had a plan of the German line all mapped out in tapes, and we practised attacking the line for 10 days before the raid took place. I was made bayonet man, which meant I was on the extreme left of the line when we went over. I personally carried six mills bombs, a bandolier of ammunition, rifle and bayonet, two four-pound tins of high explosive amanol to blow up the German wire and two stokes bombs with two five-second fuses to bomb the dugouts.

To give the signal for our advance, the light artillery opened fire on the German wire, but in the event they fired short. We had to take evasive action and I found myself right on top of a Lewis Gun team that was meant to give us cover. My first instinct was to get rid of some of this arsenal, to avoid being blown sky-high, but the guns lifted and we made for the German line.

On reaching the enemy trench, the section commander got up on the top of the parapet, brandishing his revolver. As soon as the Germans knew we were going to attack, they panicked and rushed their machine gun down into their dugout. This was stupid, because a stokes shell went down after them and blew the whole lot up. We took a prisoner at this point: he was the fellow who had operated the machine gun, and as he'd tried to make a getaway, our officer shouted and the German was so terrified that he stopped. They collared his rifle and stuck it up the side of the trench, and they sent him back with two men to our lines for questioning at headquarters.

At this point, we still occupied only a small portion of the front line so we spread out, bombing all the dugouts and if possible capturing anything of any use. As bayonet man, I went to the head of their communication trench that led straight out under the la Bassée road. Covering me were three men with mills bombs, which they had to lob from behind me towards the enemy who were now trying to advance.

The raid lasted twenty-five minutes before the signal to retire, which was a Very light fired from the back of our lines. By this time I'd got no support, as the bombers had all been injured, and I was entirely on my own. It was extremely cold that night but I was sweating like a pig. The Germans must have sensed that the raid was ending and tried to rush the communication trench where I was now the only bloke to stop them. Fortunately they'd difficulty getting round a corner of the trench while I kept up a rapid fire. I was very excited, knowing this was a case of self-preservation. I was fortunate. The Germans' fire suddenly subsided and I knew they'd given up.

Before we left, the stretcher bearers had to move in to evacuate the wounded. I had to stop until all the raiding party had got out. When I was ready to go, my section officer stopped me and said he wanted the German rifle that was stuck on the top of the trench, and then he said, "Oh, and pick up all the unused bombs that are left there." There was nobody else now, I was the only one in the German front line. I had to get out quick so I grabbed what I could, then scrambled over, tearing my uniform on the wire as I went. We'd lost 26 men on the raid.

Private Joe Yarwood, 94th Field Ambulance, Royal Army Medical Corps, 1896-1995

As a rule we didn't go in the front line, we were left in the second line at what was known as a Relay Post. It was a monotonous job, and there were long periods when there was nothing happening and you were bored to the pants. Very often the regimental men were the people who administered first aid to their wounded before we'd pick them up. The first case I ever took out of the line was a man shot through the head. We were at a place called Cheerio Dugout.

We dashed down and the poor devil was lying up on top behind the parados. He'd been concentrating on a sniper and he'd been shot through the head. The regimental stretcher bearers had dressed him before we lifted him off the parados with the nasty feeling we were going to get bumped off any moment.

We found we couldn't carry the stretcher down the trench as it was frightfully narrow; it had been dug by the French and they hadn't done the job properly, so we carried that poor devil out with great difficulty, holding the stretcher in the crook of our elbows, as the trench narrowed. One fellow walked behind, hanging on to the casualty's wrists, for we found there was a tendency for them to grab at their bandages. At one point where the trench widened, we stopped for a moment and put him down, and as we did so, sure enough, he snatched the bandages off and his brains and blood went all over my tunic. He then vomited. What a mess! I had felt sorry for the poor fellow and put my tunic under him.

When I got back to headquarters, I had to indent for a new tunic, and when the colonel heard, he told me I was a bloody fool and that if I did it again I would have to pay. My paybook was bloodstained all round the edges and yet I carried that through the war.

The poor fellow was called Corporal Hazeldine of the East Yorks. I heard from others that he survived with a metal plate in his head but I find it hard to believe.

THE BATTLE OF THE SOMME

Private Tom Dewing, 34th Divisional Royal Engineers Signal Company, 1896-2001

We realized that we were in for a battle, no doubt about that. Everything was building up to such a vast scale that we were all convinced that this was the push, the 'Big Push' that was to end the war.

We had a Norfolk sergeant with us, Sergeant Britcher, an old soldier, and he wasn't so keen. He said, "I ain't a-going to be in no big push, I'm going back to England."

To us that seemed extremely unlikely, but Britcher had it all worked out. So he claimed to the doctor that a tumour on his face, which he had had for years, was making him deaf. The doctor said it could not possibly be the case but Britcher persisted and it became increasingly difficult to hold a conversation with him.

The officer knew perfectly well he was swinging the lead, so did we all, and he knew that we knew. One evening we were in an estaminet and one of the lads went quietly up behind him. "Would you like a drink, Sergeant?" Britcher glanced round to see nobody was watching, "It ain't no good you saying would you like a drink, 'cos I can't hear you."

In the end he managed to convince the authorities that he was deaf, even though the doctor was adamant he was shamming, and Britcher was sent back to England to train other troops.

Lance Corporal Vic Cole, 7th Queen's Own (Royal West Kent Regiment), 1897-1995

If you didn't want to do something, or you got fed up, you went sick, or tried to go sick. If the medical officers knew you'd had a rough time they were lenient with you, but if you were trying to swing the lead, as they called it, they would just give you a No.9 pill, a mild laxative, and send you back up the line.

I was on my way back to the battalion after a short leave. The battalion was due to attack on 1 July, and the bombardment was on. I was in the village of Meaulte, just behind the lines, when about midnight I was wrenched into wakefulness by the roar of an explosion. Extricating myself through clouds of dust and debris, I discovered that my trousers were wet with blood from a gash above the hip-bone. I was packed into an ambulance and sent to a convalescence camp. I had an idea that they didn't want to send me home, but rather to a hospital around Amiens. Anyway, I had been told that if you chewed a piece of cordite it would give you all the symptoms of a heart attack. I had some strips of cordite because I had been opening brass cartridges to make a telephone switchboard in the cellars of Bécourt Château. So there I was lying in bed, and I cut off a quarter of an inch – I didn't want to cut off too much just in case it blew my head off – and chewed away. I quickly frothed a bit at the mouth, and my heart started racing. The nurse, she'd just come out from home, and she said, "Whatever's the matter?" I said I felt terrible and she called for a doctor, saying, "Look at him!" She persuaded him that I should be sent down the line instead of Amiens Hospital, and I got all the way back to England just as the offensive got into full swing.

Lieutenant Richard Hawkins, 11th Royal Fusiliers, 1895-1994
One of our objectives for the 1 July was to take some German guns close to a wood, I forget the name now. We were practising for the attack near the village of Maricourt and my dear friend Adie was with his platoon, lying out in a field, when General Maxse rode up. Adie should have been going for those guns, but for some reason he'd failed to do so. I don't remember the whole story, but it ended up with words I'll never forget. "Lieutenant, write home to tell your mother you made General Maxse cry."

Lieutenant Norman Dillon, 14th Northumberland Fusiliers, attd 178 Tunnelling Company, Royal Engineers, 1896-1997
Our job, as officers, was to keep underground watch with primitive

sound detectors, some form of electrified earphones, and note what was going on. It was not possible to keep the mining silent. In the chalk, sounds were bound to be made.

So long as one heard digging, one could be moderately sure that it would continue in one place, indicating the formation of a chamber, and later there would be the sound of dragging sacks of explosive. This was a signal for a possible blow, and the staff were informed so that precautions could be taken against the usual surface attack subsequent to the blowing of a mine. It was a very nerve-wracking business, sitting fifty feet down in the chalk and wondering if the filling of the chamber had been completed or whether one would never know at all.

We worked in shifts round the clock, two to three hours each in tunnels three feet high and two feet wide. However, digging in chalk required very little support as regards props and so forth. The chalk was carried out in sandbags to maintain silence while bellows and pipes were used to provide ventilation. It wasn't very pleasant and we had a very high casualty rate.

While I was on relief duty, the Germans blew a camouflet, a small explosion designed to eliminate the enemy and his tunnel but not to destroy the trenches above. It killed an officer and two other men, but that was part of the accepted risk. You tried to refrain from blowing such a counter-mine because you blew your own tunnel same as the enemy's. We only did it when absolutely necessary.

Private Joe Yarwood, 94th Field Ambulance, Royal Army Medical Corps, 1896-1995
We were in the line several days before the attack on 1 July, and everyone was optimistic. I was sent up on 28 June to join the three squads who would deal with the wounded. I took the place of a man who had gone sick. He had been in the Boer War, and was old enough to be our father. He went sick and poor old Joe had to take his place, which I wasn't happy about, as I had to endure the bombardment. You

can take it from me, it was hell. The lads had blankets there in which to sew up the dead, and when I arrived they said, "You, you long bugger, you'll need more than one blanket," and they were actually measuring me up to see whether two blankets would be sufficient, as a joke, of course, they were being funny, but it wasn't particularly funny to me.

Close to where we were, was a place called Euston Dump and nearby there was a battery of guns that were going night and day for the whole period, only stopping to let the guns cool. Every so often, I would pass through the guns just as they opened up again, wooossh!, and my tin helmet would fall over my face with the shock. The only relief we had was the knowledge that the Germans were going through hell over there, and that made it easier for us.

1 JULY

Lieutenant Norman Dillon, 14th Northumberland Fusiliers, 1896-1997

I had heard that my battalion was going to take part in the attack and I wanted to be in it as we believed this was the big one. I couldn't see any future to tunnelling if open warfare was going to resume and we were on the move, as I hoped we would be. So I put in a request to go back to my unit and they had no grounds to refuse it.

The 14th Northumberland Fusiliers, being pioneers, had to follow the leading troops at some distance, the object being to help consolidate the newly-won positions, but on the day it was all badly managed. We were to enlarge scrapes in the ground or turn captured German trenches round to face the other way, so that the parados became the parapet, and then put out barbed wire.

On the morning of 1 July I was half a mile away when these huge mines were exploded, and the ground shook under my feet. The first waves went over the top and made some progress. I saw a field gun battery galloping up and putting its guns into position and firing just behind what had been our front line. Those guns soon had to limber up and gallop off again because they came under fire; they were too close. I went forward with my company about half a mile, and found one of the junior subalterns, Second Lieutenant Walker, had been needlessly killed after being brought up, then doing nothing, before he was hit by desultory bursts of machine gun firing on our flanks. The truth is we hadn't much idea what we were to do that day because everybody expected to be miles ahead.

Private Tom Dewing, 34th Division, Royal Engineers Signal Company, 1896-2001

On 30 June, the day before the attack, two of us were sent to an observation post called Smiths Redoubt. This was a small dugout with a slot that enabled us to look over the German lines. There we were joined by the Brigade Intelligence Officer, Lieutenant 'Blanco' White, and various runners. We were also connected to Brigade Headquarters by telephone, and had a powerful telescope that could be mounted on a tripod.

Shortly before 7.30am on 1 July we felt the ground heave from the explosion of the mine at La Boisselle but we could see nothing. In the first place, there was a certain amount of mist and then when you add to that the enormous amount of smoke from the barrage, a great deal was hidden. Then when the mist and smoke cleared, we were able to see the infantry going forward in open formation as if on parade ground. In many cases the men didn't get very far, they were just wiped out. One of the officers in our dugout had some field glasses which he allowed us to use from time to time, and looking into the crater we could sometimes see a German getting up, raising his rifle and firing. During the attack, Corporal Bone and one or two other men followed the infantry to their first objective.

They set up a heliograph, as the weather was ideal for its use, and we waited anxiously for the first flash. When it came, we were thrilled; they had reached their objective. They sent our call sign, 'ZJA, ZJA'. Z stood for Brigade, J was the tenth letter of the alphabet, A the first, so we got 101st Brigade. We waited for the message that was to follow but it never came. The enemy had seen the flashing and opened up with a machine gun.

Sergeant Walter James Popple, No14134, 15 Platoon, D Company, 8th King's Own Yorkshire Light Infantry, 16 January 1896-circa 1990
1 July promised to be a beautiful day. The sun had risen high in the sky and we could hear the birds singing. I stood on the firestep and scanned the scene. Jerry had been pounded for a week and would be decimated. What few were left would not be able to offer any real resistance. I recall wondering if that was true as a shell burst in the trench 40 yards away, and an officer and three men were killed outright.

A loud blast on a whistle and the first wave began the attack, as the barrage moved forward. Then it was time for my platoon to go. A line had been cut in the barbed wire the night before, through which to advance, but as I did so I could scarcely believe my eyes.

The first three lines were being mown down. I walked forward in a daze. Near the crest of the slope, I saw the reason for the carnage: Jerry had manned every single post. As I neared the enemy wire, I felt a sharp thud accompanied by a pain in my chest and I fell.

Private Clarrie Jarman, 7th Queen's (Royal West Surrey Regiment), 1896-1996
That morning we turned out our pockets, dumping postcards of naked French girls to ensure they weren't sent home with any personal effects should we be killed. Then the trench ladders were put into place and on the blast of whistles, and after wishing our chums the best of luck, over we went. It was like a dream, lots of the lads were shot down just going over the parapet.

We advanced, each platoon forming a star. Only when we got close to the German line would we move into extended order. But of course it was just a shambles; it was every man for himself.

I was a bomber. I was staggering along with 250 rounds of small arms ammunition, a rifle and a fixed bayonet, seven mills bombs on my chest and seven on my back and a pick and shovel, going along in a dream-like state. All the while you could hear the machine guns, tak, tak, tak, tak, tak.

Lieutenant Haggard had taken us over, one of two brothers in the battalion. The last I saw of him, he was bending over a local chap, Arthur Spooner, who had lost an eye, and shortly after, about half way across, I got hit.

I went down straightaway and crawled into a deep shell hole, dumping all my equipment. I had a look round the battleground and as far as I could see, there were our lads lying out dead, wounded and dying. There were some lads in a shell hole near me and when they saw me looking over, they said, "Get your head down" and I did and didn't know any more. The shrapnel had shattered the bottom part of my right leg and for much of the time I was unconscious with the loss of blood. There was no pain and I lay there all that day, about fourteen hours.

It was getting dusk when a lad from the RAMC happened to come my way looking for wounded, and in a very faint voice I called to him and he heard my call. I was lucky to be picked up.

Lieutenant Richard Hawkins, 11th Royal Fusiliers, 1895-1994
We moved up into our front line trench, and in the early hours every man was given a good breakfast and packet of woodbines, stupid thing to say, but I went over smoking an Abdullah cigarette. It was a lovely morning and over the top we went at zero hour. We had a marvellous day, and got right into their first and second line trenches. The Manchesters to our left were held up and the battalions were held up on our right too, otherwise, someone said, we could have walked

through to Berlin.

I was keen to get on and beat the enemy. I didn't really think I might be hit at any moment. My batman, named Good, followed me over and he was hit early on; we were great friends, damn good chap. He slumped to the ground and appeared to have been shot through the lungs. I thought he was dying, but I had to leave him, I'd got to get on with the war.

You hadn't time to mourn the dead, sorry old thing, very sorry, poor old so-and-so being killed, damned bad luck, never mind, let's get on boys, let's get on with the job. People were being killed all day long.

Private Joe Yarwood, 94th Field Ambulance, Royal Army Medical Corps, 1896-1995

We were taking the wounded from a relay post at the end of the communication trench across Euston Dump to the main road, where the dugouts were. Some of the injured had blighty wounds and you could almost see the satisfaction on their faces. The machine gun bullets were flying all around, all the time. If a chap was able to walk, it was much better for him to walk than to occupy a stretcher, and where we could, we would carry his equipment and escort him down. I met one poor devil injured in the face. He had been a walking wounded case and he was an elderly man, too, and I felt very sorry for him. His face was bandaged but his wound was still bleeding, and the whole of his chest was covered with a thick mat of congealed blood. I thought he would go down any minute with loss of blood. I couldn't help him because I'd already got a case with me, but I got him carried out on a stretcher because, had he collapsed, he might well have died. And that's what I was doing, all day long, simply going backwards and forwards like an automaton, you didn't think much. If we'd been winning, that might have been some consolation, but we hadn't even got that.

There were so many more lying out in No Man's Land, but we couldn't reach them. We talked about it. One team tried to clamber out over the top, but one of the lads was shot straightaway, a bullet smashing his thigh, and the rest of the team scrambled back in. We were amazed that Jerry was able to survive the bombardment.

Sergeant Walter Popple, 8th King's Own Yorkshire Light Infantry, 1896-1990

Running footsteps to my rear seemed to bring me back to reality. Then came the sound of a falling body, and with it the certain knowledge that a sniper was about. A German was firing from an advanced post, picking off anyone he saw, including the wounded. As I glanced upwards, he saw me. He fired, a bullet taking the heel off my boot. My rifle was somewhere around but my shoulder was so stiff that I couldn't handle it. Then there were the two grenades in my tunic pockets but I couldn't throw them that distance. All these thoughts flashed through my mind with the ugly realisation that any pot shots might easily set off the grenades.

I came to the terrible decision that it was better to get it over with quickly and die, rather than to be picked off piece by piece so I raised my head and pushed myself upwards, almost kneeling to look straight down into the muzzle of his rifle. A sharp crack, and my helmet flew off and my neck stiffened. I sank to the ground. Utter silence. The hours passed by. At first there was a buzzing sensation in my head and then sharp piercing darts of pain. Had I been killed as I first thought? I dared not lift my head and there I remained through the heat of the day, wondering if in fact part of my head had been blown away. Night came, and I cautiously turned over and began to take stock. I gently lowered the bandolier full of ammunition from my shoulders, and the two hand grenades. Moving on my hands and knees, I crept to a large shell hole and despite the bodies around it, began to make myself comfortable. The bullet, I realized, had hit flush on the front of my helmet but instead of killing me outright it must have ricocheted upwards with such force that it ripped the straps from the flanges on my shrapnel helmet, sending it spinning into the air. The Germans, of course, would have assumed that I was dead.

All through the night, incessant calls were being made for stretcher bearers interspersed by rifle and machine gun fire.

The next day followed the same pattern except that we were shelling Jerry's front line trenches with high explosive shrapnel that at times crossed the shell hole where I was sheltering, wounding me in the right leg and shoulders, some seven more wounds in all.

Lieutenant Richard Hawkins, 11th Royal Fusiliers, 1895-1994
General Maxse came to see us afterwards. He was about five foot six tall and, rather stupidly, we thought, he had a guardsman as his aide-de-camp, Captain Montague, who was about six foot three.

Maxse spoke to us: "Morning, gentlemen, damn good show, thank you very much, you did very well, marvellous. Tell me, where would you expect to find a group of officers congregated together in the middle of the biggest battle there has ever been?" "Ooh," we thought, "now, wait a minute." "I'll tell you," he said. "walking about on the skyline looking for souvenirs! I saw them through my field glasses." Well, there wasn't anything else to do, all was peace and quietness where we were and I managed to pick up a marvellous German pickelhaube.

We had a good day on 1st July, no doubt about it. As for my batman Good, he was picked up later in the day and the wound was nothing like as bad as I'd feared. He wrote to me from hospital about my new batman, a Northerner. "I hear you've got Green doing for you now, Sir, he's a good lad but it's a pity he don't speak our language." Marvellous fellow. Became a police sergeant on the other side of London somewhere.

[Ed. The 11th Royal Fusiliers were one of the more fortunate battalions in action that day. Casualties were relatively light and German resistance in the trenches attacked by the Fusiliers was less determined than on other parts of the front.]

Henry John Patch
29095 C Company
7 Batt DCLI
20 Div
fever Gunner Ypres 1917
June 17. 1898

Alfred Anderson
1643 - 240222
1/5th Black Watch
Born 25th June 1896

Harold Lawton (centre) serving as a teenager in the Rhyl County School Cadet Force before he was called up in 1917.

Below: Private Ted Francis training with the 16th Warwickshire Regiment. His idealistic view of war was shattered by his experiences. He served for three years in France and was wounded only shortly before the Armistice.

Above: France 1917. Lieutenant G B Jameson, MC, serving in the Royal Field Artillery. He survived over four years' fighting in France.

Alfred Finnigan (*left*) served as a driver in France between 1917-1918. He was the last surviving veteran of the Royal Field Artillery. Alfred died in 2005.

Above: A portrait of Lieutenant Richard Hawkins, MC. His air of calm belies the fact that, after living for nineteen months under shellfire and going over the top on at least three occasions, his nerves were shattered and he had recurrent stomach problems.

Above: An officer serving with the 11th Royal Fusiliers is snapped looking over the top with an expandable form of trench periscope.

Below: Lieutenant Richard Hawkins (left) in a billet close to the line in 1916. The other officer is believed to be Captain Richard Vaughan-Thompson, killed during the successful attack to take Thiepval Ridge in September 1916.

Richard Hawkins in a trench on the Somme in 1916. He was, as he later recalled, in a very bad mood when this picture was taken on his VPK (Vest Pocket Kodak).

Bill Hall, above right, with
friends. These pictures were
taken near Ochey in France
where the squadron was
based in 1917 and 1918.

Bill Hall sitting in the bomb aimer's position at the front of a Handley Page Bomber. During raids, he stood here, 5,000 feet in the air and fully exposed to the wind, as he dropped bombs on strategically-important railway depots, bridges and factories.

Left and above: Archie Richards, then aged 100. Serving in tank D7, he took part in the first attack by this new weapon of war. He was later mistakenly reported killed in action during fighting in August 1918. D7 ditched during the fighting at Flers on 15 September 1916, the day of the first tank attack. The crew and other survivors take shelter behind the tank. This picture, taken by an official war photographer, includes Archie Richards standing far left.

Below: The exhaustion on the faces of these men is clear to see. They are returning to their battalion after collecting rations from the limbers, February 1918. Courtesy of the Imperial War Museum (Q10685)

21 August 1915: The attack by five brigades of the 2nd Mounted Division across the Salt Lake at Suvla. Dick Barron is one of the ant-like figures photographed above. Courtesy of the Imperial War Museum (Q70704)

23 September 1917: This shell burst fell within ten yards of the photographer during an attack near Zonnebeke in the Ypres Salient. Towards the bottom of the image a soldier is seen advancing. This picture was taken just twenty-four hours after Harry Patch was wounded by shrapnel during fighting nearby. Courtesy of the Imperial War Museum (Q2890)

Far right: Norman Collins has his leg heavily strapped after he was wounded on the Somme in December 1916. He took the other images on his Vest Pocket Kodak, against regulations.

A WELCOME HALT AT S····· S⸬ M···

The 11th Royal Fusiliers during training in 1915. Richard Hawkins can be seen partially obscured by the officer lying down in front.

Ted Francis, left, with his brother, Harry, right. In the centre is their close friend who was mortally wounded by a shell burst.

Above: Harry Slater, MM, Arthur Barraclough
best friend who was killed in action in 1918.

Above: Arthur Barraclough who
died in 2004, aged 106.

Left: Arthur Barraclough's medals
including the Légion d' Honneur, far left,
awarded by the French Government to all
surviving Great War veterans in 1998.
Around 350 were issued.

Right: Harry Patch
receives his Légion d'
Honneur in 1999.

chael Lally

nk Sumpter

3 Jameson

Photographer Roderick Field

Alfred Anderson

The Last Old Contemptibles. Michael Lally served with the Manchester Regiment, Frank Sumpter served with the Rifle Brigade, and G B Jameson with the Northumberland Hussars. All three died in 1999, aged 105, 102 and 106 respectively. Alfred Anderson is the last surviving veteran to have seen action in 1914.

Top left: Alfred Anderson be[...] he left for France. He was se[...] home badly wounded in the [...] in early 1916 and was judge[d] unfit for further service overseas. Today he is 109 yea[rs] old.

Above: Joe Yarwood as a priv[...] in the Royal Army Medical Corps. At first he was rejecte[d] as unfit for the army.

Left: Alfred Henn wearing th[e] blue chevrons on his left cuf[f] signalling three years' servic[e] the Western Front. On his ar[m] he wears the triangular cloth badge of the 29th Division.

Above left and right: Norman Edwards as a young private in the 1/6th Gloucestershire Regiment. After he was wounded, he was comissioned and served as an instructor in the Tank Corps behind the lines.

Below: Jack Davis, photographed shortly before he went to France in July 1915. His remarkable meeting in the trenches with his two brothers, Bill and Bob, was an unforgettable moment in a war that otherwise rendered Jack permanently depressed.

Bottom Left: Robert Renwick, MM, prior to going overseas in July 1916. Within weeks of arriving in France, he went over the top at Delville Wood and afterwards buried the dead from his own battalion.

1917: After being wounded at Boom Ravine in January, Richard Hawkins relaxes with other converlescent officers.

Richard Hawkins spent six months in hospital after his injury on the Somme. Here he is sitting on the ground second from the left.

Private Tom Dewing, 34th Division Royal Engineers Signal Company, 1896-2001

We didn't realize what had happened until afterwards, until the next church parade. At Brigade Headquarters we had regular church parades, and on this occasion, instead of the troops coming along as they usually did, there was just a handful out of each battalion. We felt sick. The colonels were sitting in front of what was left of their men, sobbing. The service was taken by Padre Black, who later became Dr James Black, Moderator of the Church of Scotland. He was a man we all respected; he was more likely to found in the trenches than in the officers' mess. Before the attack started, he had said that he would go over the top with the stretcher bearers but the message through our signal office said, "If Padre Black goes over the top, he is to be arrested and sent down the line for a court martial." Instead, he did the next best thing. He stayed at the first field dressing station.

How he managed to take that service, I don't know. His text was "I will restore unto you the years that the locusts have eaten". He meant every word of his sermon, and we knew it. There were so few, so few men left. How can you describe a mere handful of men where you used to see about a battalion? It must have been a great ordeal for him to conduct that service. It is an occasion that I shall always remember.

Lieutenant Richard Hawkins, 11th Royal Fusiliers, 1895-1994

I was lying out on the night of the 1st of July in the dark, half asleep, happy and with nothing to do, and a voice in the dark said, "Hello, had a good day?" "Oh," I said "yes." "Do you know where the 12th Middlesex are?" I said, "I don't know where the hell they are, somewhere on the right, I think." "Oh," he said, "I'm Colonel Maxwell and I've come to take over the 12th Middlesex." He'd come up in the middle of the night to see where the battalion was. Oops, in the dark I didn't realize he was a Colonel. He couldn't wait until his battalion came out of the line, he had to come up and join it, not because he had to, but because he could not keep out of the battle.

Private Joe Yarwood, 94th Field Ambulance, Royal Army Medical Corps, 1896-1995

The next day the wounded were still waiting to be moved away, but we were lacking convoys. All these elephant dugouts had been turned into aid posts. There were piles of wounded lying on stretchers waiting for ambulances to move them.

I had just left the dressing station when we were shelled, but they landed with a pop not an explosion, and then I got a whiff of it, it was tear gas. I rushed back to lend a hand in getting as many under cover as I could. They couldn't get their gas masks on, so for an hour or so it was pandemonium trying to get these poor devils out of harm's way.

Our Colonel, an Irishman by the name of Stewart, was a bit of a martinet and inclined to shout and bark and call you a bloody fool. He was very ambitious, a doctor in civilian life, and he held the DSO and MC and you don't get those for nothing. A brilliant officer, no doubt, but he was, to my mind, a little conceited, haughty even, you get it with some officers who take a large size in hats. Anyway, when we were leaving the trenches, he sounded like a benevolent father, pleased and very pleasant for once because we'd broken all records with the number of wounded we'd shifted, although he couldn't quite show his gratitude.

We were told to clear out because our lot was decimated. I saw a battalion leaving and there was a band in front and then about three or four ranks of soldiers, and that was all that was left of a thousand: thirty or forty men.

Just around there I recall one poor devil who had been buried in the bottom of the trench, but not deep enough, with the result that the top of his skull was exposed just level with the top of the trench floor. There was a bald patch right down the centre of the poor fellow's skull where troops had marched and worn the hair off his head. My God, what would his relatives at home think if they knew that had happened?

Sergeant Walter Popple, 8th King's Own Yorkshire Light Infantry, 1896-1990

The third day I was exhausted, and it was on this day that a thunderstorm broke the terrific heat. By this time all the bodies around me had turned black. One of them had a waterproof sheet protruding at the back of his pack. I formed a ridge and the water trickled down into my mouth. The fourth day was relatively quiet but I realised time was getting short and unless help arrived soon, I was finished. I made up my mind that, whatever happened, I must reach my lines by morning. Crawling throughout the night, I got to within a few yards of our trenches by daybreak. By a sustained effort, I rose to my feet and hopped the necessary distance. Machine guns opened out, but I held my course and was lucky to enter one of the lanes cut for the attack. A sentry shouted, "Who's there?" I croaked "KOYLI." To hear my own tongue being spoken was nectar. "And yours?" "Middlesex" came the reply, "anyone else out there?" I told him no.

[Ed. Walter arrived back in the front line on the morning of 5 July, and must have been one of the very last men wounded on 1 July to have remained on the battlefield unattended. The bullet that hit him in the shoulder was removed and he kept it as a souvenir. However, the psychological effect on Walter's health was devastating. He lost weight and looked gaunt, and although he recovered from his wounds medically, he was in no fit state to return to active service. In 1917 he was removed from a parade of men due to return to France, as he was clearly in distress. He never returned to the firing line. The memory of those days haunted Walter, before in 1986, aged ninety, he finally returned to France and the Somme battlefield.]

Corporal Norman Edwards, 1/6th Gloucestershire Regiment, 1894-1999

We took over the sector behind the village of Serre on 5 July from the 94th Brigade and at night time, when I looked out, the flares were all going up, and between the lines, in No Man's Land, there were twinkling lights everywhere. I thought, twinkling lights, what could it be? I found out afterwards the Pals Battalions of 31st Division had arranged that every man would carry a triangular piece of tin on the back of his pack so that when he was crawling forward, attacking, our own airmen looking down could see the depth of the advance. All those twinkling lights were literally hundreds of men who had been killed on that morning, before breakfast, awful slaughter. You can understand what a man felt like to see that. I just thanked God we hadn't been ordered to attack, although had we been ordered to do so we would have done our duty, I would think, because we'd got to win the war.

[Ed. After a brief respite, fighting resumed on the southern sector of the Somme battlefield, where the attacks on 1 July had seen a modicum of success, two villages, Montauban and Mametz, having fallen that first day. On 2 July, the Germans abandoned another village, Fricourt, and a day later fresh attacks resulted in the talking of La Boisselle. Assaults of a limited nature continued, before a major night attack was conducted on the 14th on the German second line with positive results; a further phase of the Somme campaign was opened up on the 23 July.]

Trooper Smiler Marshall, 1/1st Essex Yeomanry, 1897-2005

The Ox and Bucks arrived between five and six in the afternoon and were billeted close to where we were, in broken-down houses in Mametz Village. They were to attack the next day. Zero hour was 6.30am and their objective was not far from Mametz Wood.

It was the worst place I ever saw; there was more dead laid there than I ever saw anywhere, and we buried them. The Ox and Bucks went over the next morning at 6.30am and by 8am there was hardly one left. The next night we were sent up as a working party to help bury them, one, two and three in a shell hole. I didn't go through their pockets, that wasn't my job, but one of these dead chaps, he had pictures of his girlfriend and his mother, letters with his address, and these were all sticking out of his pocket or lying on the ground by his body, because shrapnel or machine gun bullets had ripped it open. I took his new boots off and put him in a shell hole, and threw my old boots in the shell hole with him, and took his. A while later I wrote to his mother in High Wycombe, Turner, I think the name was, and I got a nice letter from her. She said he had been reported missing in action. I said that I was on a burying party and told her he was killed near Mametz Wood and that we buried him in No Man's Land. Blimey, it was a rough job, poor buggers, but you just had to get on with it and not think.

We were taken on working parties for several nights and I got hit through the hand, because the bullets and shrapnel were flying around, battle or no battle. You don't know what caused it until you see the blood running onto the ground. I was sent down to the casualty clearing station, walked down. There must have been some dirt as well because my whole hand turned to poison, and it got worse and worse and ached all up my arm. Eventually I got sent to Rouen and then back to England and Newcastle. I nearly lost my arm.

[Ed. Between 25 and 31 July, a large number of men from the 3rd Cavalry Division were sent to help dig trenches between Mametz Wood and the village of Contalmaison. These included around 80 men from the Essex Yeomanry. Nearby, the 1/4th Oxfordshire and Buckinghamshire Light Infantry had made an attack on 23 July, losing a large number of men, including two bearing the name of Turner.]

Rifleman Robert Renwick, MM, 16th King's Royal Rifle Corps, 1896-1997
All the woods round the Somme were hard fought for, Mametz Wood, High Wood. It was after my battalion had attacked High Wood and lost a lot of men, that I was sent to France on a draft just in time for an attack on Delville Wood, or Devil's Wood as it was called, and for good reason.

We were due to go over at a specific time but our bombardment fell short onto our lines so the officer said, "I'll be damned if I'll see my own men knocked out by our artillery," and he took us out and led us into shell holes. We waited for the barrage to lift and we advanced. The wood was just a mess, there was no undergrowth at all. A number of men were falling and I looked around to see a man hiding his corporal's stripes. I think he thought he wouldn't be targetted by the Germans without them. Then, as we dodged about from shell hole to shell hole I had a strange vision. I saw myself back at school and our schoolmaster was coming down his garden path to the wicket to call us in and line us up. I said to myself, "I think if ever you see that place again, you'll be lucky."

After the battle, we were sent back to bury the dead. Being sent back to bury your own pals, I think they did that to harden us up a little bit, but I thought it was rough. It was mainly men from the new draft who were sent to do it, but I thought men from a labour platoon should have done it. We took the dog tags off, and buried the men in their groundsheets.

One of the dead was a lad who had a web belt and a purse with a golden sovereign in it. He'd showed it to us a few times but I couldn't bring myself to take it out. That lad was buried with the sovereign. Later in the war, I would have taken it out, but not then.

A curious incident happened after this. There was a lad who got home wounded and he wrote to my parents explaining how I'd been killed. During the attack he had shouted to me that so-and-so had been injured and was in his shell hole, and he told my parents that I'd come across to see if there was anything I could do. Then he shouted back to my mates, "Renwick's been killed now", and he wrote all this in a note to my mother and father. I don't know how that happened. Perhaps there was another lad of the same name.

I remember the incident but I certainly wasn't killed. My father read the note first and then handed it to my mother, and she got a terrific shock. Then he said, "Look, we've had a field card since this date, so this cannot be right." It was a mystery, that one.

[Ed. The only other Rifleman Renwick killed while serving with the 16th Kings Royal Rifle Corps died of wounds on 15 July, following the attack on High Wood, which is close to Delville Wood. His name was Joseph Renwick, and he came from Gateshead.]

Private Dick Trafford, 1/9th King's Liverpool Regiment, 1898-1999

The rations were being dished out when the sergeant came up with a loaf of bread and some jam. The loaf was divided up and we held our mess tin lids out for our jam ration just as a shrapnel shell burst overhead. One bit of shrapnel went through the jam and my mess tin lid, another chunk cut part of my thumb off, and I had three other wounds on the same hand. The man next to me got a piece through his back, which killed him outright. Another chap was shocked but all right, but the fourth lad, Joe Shaw, he jumped up on top of the road and ran off towards the end of our line, shouting and bawling, waving his arms. We couldn't really make out what he was saying because he was shell-shocked, but this was right in front of the German lines and that was the last we heard of him. We thought naturally that the Germans would get him; he made a good target for any machine gunner.

About three months later, I was on leave in Ormskirk and I was walking down the road, just as a chap in a postman's uniform crossed in front of me, all smiles. "Hello, Dick, don't you know me?" I says, "I know the voice," and it was this Joe Shaw. I said, "I thought you were dead."

During the fighting, the army had a little place in a wood about three miles back from the trenches, where they could put these sorts of cases temporarily, to see if they could recover. However, Joe was sent down to the dressing station, but there were that many wounded, he was bundled in with the others onto a train and sent down the line to hospital. He was shell-shocked, there was no doubt about it, and in the end he was considered of no further use for the army and was demobilized.

Private Ted Francis, 16th Warwickshire Regiment, 1896-1996
On the Somme I saw lots of people in attacks, where you had to go from one shell hole to another towards the enemy, and you'd find people stopping where they were and not attempting to move and giving the officers and NCOs the idea that they were shell shocked – that was common – and an officer or an NCO would almost kick them out of the hole and tell them to go forward with the other chaps. Everyone was afraid, but as a matter of fact my brother Harry and I, seeing other people who couldn't stand it made us a little bit braver, we felt good that they couldn't stand this sort of thing but we could.

Lieutenant Richard Hawkins, 11th Royal Fusiliers, 1895-1994
After the battle of Thiepval, we were withdrawn to a cellar in a château. I spent the night there with Colonel Maxwell, commanding the 12th Middlesex. He was, as ever, passionately fond of war and fighting, and couldn't really understand those who weren't.

While we were there, one of the boys had a bit of shell-shock and kept running across the road, and Colonel Maxwell said to me, "Give him a damn good kick up the backside as he passes you, he'll be all right," so I did, and he was, he was all right.

Maxwell had got a Victoria Cross in some obscure war and had been ADC to Kitchener in India. That evening, he told me he'd been serving in India when war broke out and immediately had asked to be sent to France. When he was told to wait until orders, he said, "If you don't make arrangements for me to go, I shall desert." So they allowed him to go and in the end he was given command of the Middlesex.

In that attack on Thiepval, I'd had a shell land literally at my feet, but it didn't go off and that caused me to be a bit muzzy myself for a time. But Maxwell, he didn't understand the word fear at all. I heard him once say to my commanding officer. "You know, Carr, I don't think you really enjoy this war, do you?" Carr said, "My God, I do not, I think it is a dreadful business." "No?" Maxwell said, "I thoroughly enjoy it."

He was killed in 1917 when, holding the rank of Brigadier General, he was hit walking over the top where he shouldn't have been; he just could not keep out of it.

[Ed. Francis Aylmer Maxwell won his Victoria Cross during the conflict in South Africa. In March 1900, the then Lieutenant Maxwell attempted to retrieve a battery of guns and a number of limbers under enemy fire. On five occasions he went back, helping to save two guns and three limbers.]

Private Edward Albion Leonard White, No12265, C Company, 10th King's Royal Rifle Corps, 16 October 1897-February 1999

I really broke lose when my mate Bobby was killed, that hurt me more than anything. He was one of a draft sent out to the company, just as I'd been in 1915, and he tacked on to me. "On your own? Want company?" and that was it, mates. The bullet that got him must have shot across my breast and stopped with him. That was at Ypres. They carried him off on a stretcher. After I lost my pal, I did swear that I would kill, kill, kill and believe me, I did what I intended to do.

Guillemont, 3 September 1916: two minutes to zero, the whistle blew and I was going to do what I intended to do. I ran and we stormed their lines, we went right through before the Germans even knew we were coming. I killed two. "Sprechen sie Deutsch?" One chap shouted out "Ja". He stood up and I set my rifle and I fired twice and he screamed and went down. I saw another. "Sprechen sie Deutsch? Sprechen sie Deutsch?" A long time before I got an answer, "Ja wohl", and he got up, blimey he was as big as a house. I pulled the trigger. I had a look round, nothing moving, they must have been on their own. "Sprechen sie Deutsch?" I was still carrying on. I got right in amongst them, I had my rifle and I was firing. Put another clip in, my God, you never heard such screaming in all your life.

I did not see someone was behind me, I didn't know, I was young you know, very, very young. Somebody came up on my left shoulder,

I looked, I couldn't do anything, he was too far on top of me, and he just opened up. He blew me, he really, truly, he blew me in the air. I can remember my rifle going one way and I was going the other, straight down, face first into a shell hole. I lay there and turned on my back. Three wounded Germans were down there, and one put his hand out to me.

Nobody came to help me for a long time and then all of a sudden somebody slid down this shell hole. "Need any help, chum?" I can remember his words. I said, "My arm." He had a red cross on his sleeve. "He's only a boy," that's what I heard. I got on my feet, I scratched my way up to the top.

As I walked back, someone spoke to me. Really and truly, I was in such a daze, I wasn't interested in anything. He was a sergeant, and he had a bullet through his neck, lucky bugger, it must have missed his windpipe, so I tagged along with him. A truck came along and he pulled up. "Come on, lads, you can't walk all that way. I'll give you a lift in the back." He helped me up and we started to roll. I was moaning with the pain, and I was told to shut up.

The lorry rolled and rolled and stopped. The driver came round the back. "Come on, lads, this is as far as we go." I've never been so surprised in all my life. Huts, lines of huts from here to kingdom come. A girl came up to me, and said, "Would you like some bread and dripping, Tommy, and a nice cup of tea?"

[Ed. Clearly still very disturbed by his experiences, Edward talked about this incident as though he was back there. It was a very uncanny experience to listen to him talk in such a way, and he was the only veteran I ever met to do so.]

Private Dick Trafford, 1/9th King's Liverpool Regiment, 1898-1999
We were due to attack Guillemont, and I had orders that I must place my machine gun on top of the trench to cover the attack. I objected as much as I dared to the officer, that I preferred to go over the top and

lie in a shell hole because I had a better chance of covering the men. I could sweep the German parapet with the machine gun and keep their heads down while our bombers lobbed grenades in to the trench. But he wouldn't have it, no, that won't do, instead I must fire over the men's heads all the time. Well, obviously he was in charge. The attack started and I opened fire, carrying out his instructions, and a German sniper must have seen the flashes from the gun because he fired and hit the gun and the bullet ricocheted off and caught me in the throat flat ways, knocking me out. It stopped my breath, I didn't know where I was for some time afterwards. The bullet had slammed into my windpipe and for years and years I had trouble swallowing in fact, even today, [1998] I find I sometimes choke.

I found out afterwards that our men took the trench, but the bombers, the men I'd wanted to cover, were wiped out.

THE FIRST TANKS

[Ed. On 15 September, a completely new weapon of war was introduced to the battlefield: the tank. It was used in what was designated the third phase of the Somme Battle, a major attack on a six-mile front during which 49 tanks of C and D Companies, Heavy Section, Machine Gun Corps were used to spearhead the last concerted effort to break the German line in 1916. However, owing to mechanical problems, only 32 tanks reached the start line that day and of these only nine can be said to have inflicted heavy casualties on the Germans.]

Lieutenant Norman Dillon, 14th Northumberland Fusiliers, 1896-1997

Our Division was staging an attack and we were in reserve near the village of Flers. It was a stinking night. The Germans were putting over everything they had, including a lot of gas shells. My sergeant and I were sitting by the roadside when we heard a shell "woo wooing" down very close and a gas shell hit a couple of yards behind us. At the same time, a queer object crawled over the mud and there it was. The first tank in action.

Private Robbie Burns, 7th Cameron Highlanders, 1895-2000
The gunfire was terrific but then I heard this brrrrr, and I thought, what on earth is that noise? It got louder and louder, so I stood on the firestep and saw something moving. I said, "Look!" and we all started to peer over. An attack was going in and at that moment some of the men got up on the parapet to look, and the Germans too were up on the parapet to see what was happening. Behind these tanks were five or six soldiers crowded together with bayonets fixed, taking cover. We could see more than one of these tanks, one would disappear and wouldn't seem to come back up, then another fell onto its side, and all the time we could hear this gentle brrrr of the engines. We didn't know what they were for, perhaps for taking down barbed wire, we thought.

Private Archie Richards, D Company (D7), Heavy Section, Machine Gun Corps, attd. 41st Division, 1897-1998
It was a hot September that year, and the stink – oh – the smell was terrible, terrible. Arms and legs were sticking out of trenches, and rotting bodies. The Canadians, Australians, the British and the Colonial regiments had all taken part in attacks long before the tanks put in their appearance, and they were lying about, the Scottish in their kilts, and there were stretcher bearers, scores of them, picking up the dead. We were moving up for this first attack, and we had to go over the old trenches, and bodies and everything else. I expected war to be dreadful, but I was seeing it in the raw. I felt grateful that we had the tank to cover us a bit; that gave us hope.

On 15 September, all hell broke loose. At about six o'clock in the morning, our barrage opened up. You couldn't hear yourself speak, shells flying everywhere, and the Germans were retaliating. We were scared, really scared, but we just resigned ourselves to putting up with it. We had orders to move down to a village and onto the first main road, a hard cobbled road. The Germans had not shelled it because they had brought up supplies on it previously, and we did not want to shell it now because we were using it for the same reason, so the road remained quite sound, just a shell hole here and there.

Private Ernest Ford, 10th Queen's (Royal West Surrey Regiment), 1896-1995
We found ourselves in front of Delville Wood, at least it was a wood once! Now it was a scanty collection of black scaffold poles, set in a wilderness of churned up earth, roots of trees, and splintered wood. Our trench was merely a hastily dug ditch. In front of us was a stretch of land, a mass of shell holes terminated by a ridge about 250 yards away. It was along this ridge and behind it that our shells were falling in a continuous stream.

At 6am on the 15th September our artillery opened rapid fire, putting a barrage or belt of fire along the German lines and 20 minutes later we were 'over the top and the best of luck'. We simply walked over, keeping just out of range of our own barrage which slowly moved forward over the German positions. A Company was in the first wave to go over and we hadn't gone far before the Germans opened fire with machine guns and shrapnel. It was like hell with the lid off and the noise was deafening. I had gone about 150 yards when I had the impression that a horse had kicked me in the back. I got into a shell hole and investigated and was surprised to find it was a shrapnel ball, one of our own bursting short. It had neatly perforated my clothes but had stopped on meeting my sinewy dorsal muscles.

Private Archie Richards, D Company, Heavy Section, Machine Gun Corps, 1897-1998
Our officer sat at the front with the driver and signalled what he

wanted, and the tank would swing round to face the target. The tank would turn on its own in a wide circle, but with two gear changers you could turn it in its own length. The engine was quite powerful and vibrated the machine somewhat, but it was the movement that was worse, up and down, this way and that. I had a job sometimes to set on my target to shoot. I'd just get set and ready to fire, and bang, the tank would lurch somewhere, throw me right off. The targets were the trenches, anywhere we thought there'd be machine gun posts.

There was no choice but to drive over the dead, you couldn't pick your way through. If they fell in your way, you had to go over them. We never deviated the tanks for anything except targets. When we went into action, the infantry kept tucked in, clustered behind our tanks for shelter, then as soon as we captured a trench, they took over, going along the line and ferreting the Germans out. I only saw Germans when we got right on the trench, with our guns laid on each side. They had never seen anything like the tank before, and when they saw we were armed with small guns and machine guns, they gave up straightaway. A few of their machine gunners got away and we could see them silhouetted against the sky with their guns on their shoulders, going like hell back to their third lines.

Private Ernest Ford, 10th Queen's (Royal West Surrey Regiment), 1896-1995
During the attack, we were assisted by what to us looked like armour-plated cars with caterpillar tracks, 'tanks', as we later discovered. They could easily cross shell holes and trenches and proved useful in riding down machine gun emplacements. But they had the disadvantage of moving at a very slow speed and the infantry got far ahead of them.

All the while that the tanks crept forward, our aeroplanes, dozens of them, were flying to and fro, often descending within 100 feet of the ground whereas I do not recall seeing a single German plane. I also counted nineteen of our observation balloons to the Germans' three, and two of these were brought down.

I went over the German first line and had nearly reached their second when there was a crash somewhere close in front and I collected small pieces of shrapnel, three in my hand and three in the chest. I dived into a shell hole and bandaged myself as best I could. Deciding that a chap with a damaged hand and a stiff back would not be much further use, I made my way back to our trenches.

[Ed. A small piece of shrapnel that had embedded itself in Ernest's left hand was never removed and well into the 1990s it could be seen as a dark centimetre square smudge at the bottom of his palm.]

Private Archie Richards, D Company, Heavy Section, Machine Gun Corps, 1897-1998
As soon as we were out of action, we could open the tank traps. Oh, you would never believe the relief. You took long breaths of lovely fresh air, you gulped it in. There was freedom – freedom all round. Freedom of limbs, freedom of arms, freedom of breath, freedom of mind.

Private Walter Eustace Rushby, No3021, 1/4th Royal Berkshire Regiment, 7 August 1896-March 1996
In October 1916, we were close to the Butte de Warlencourt, a white chalk mound that dominated the surrounding area. In daylight there was some indication where you were, but in darkness it was hopeless, there was no continuity of trenches, the country being totally desolate. One night, a German machine gun team had gone out to relieve another team and got lost and walked straight into our lines, such as they were. There were five of them and they were totally exposed. We challenged them and they saw there was no point in resisting.

One of the Germans had been out in America when war broke out. He was a reservist and made his way back to Germany to join the army. He had been a porter in New York in the Waldorf Hotel and one thing he said to me I never forgot, "You British will win the war, the

French will fight to the last Britisher and you will need one boat to take you home," and as he turned out, he was about right.

2nd Lieutenant Norman Collins, 1/6th Seaforth Highlanders, 1897-1998

In the hours before the attack at Beaumont Hamel, I recall speaking with two fellow officers, Lieutenants Smith and Mclean. We chatted and joked, and then I remember Lieutenant Smith telling me one curious thing, that he was going to go sick but not until after the attack, if he survived. He had developed a severe rupture and he wanted the hernia attended to in hospital, but he wouldn't go sick beforehand as he had been nominated for the attack and his absence would seem cowardly. I thought that was very brave of him because he could have gone sick and saved his life. In the event both he and Mclean were killed.

Private Dick Trafford, 1/9th King's Liverpool Regiment, 1898-1999

Our Sergeant came round the traverse in the trench, "Would you come here, chaps, I want to ask you a favour. I want you to swear that you won't repeat what I'm going to say to you." He looked at me and I said, "All right, Sergeant, what is it?" He said, "When we go over the top tomorrow I want to go over first." I was surprised. "You'll be needed Sergeant, that's ridiculous." He said, "No, I want to get killed first." So we said, "You'll have to give us a reason, because if you're going first, you're going to get a bullet before us." He told us he'd been with a French woman, and he was sure he'd got VD. He said, "Now then, if this is so, and it's found out, my wife is going to suffer and my family, whereas if the Germans kill me, my wife's going to get a pension and a pension for my family, and she's going to get that pension for life. It's either that, my wife and family are going to get looked after, or they're going to get nothing."

"Enough said, Sergeant." The next morning he was killed, right away. He was a nice fellow, a Welshman.

W.J. Popple

Sgt. 8th Batt. K.O.Y.L.I.
16.1.1896.
July 1st 1916 –
Battle of the Somme.

Above: Walter Popple holds the German bullet removed from his shoulder after the attack on the Somme. Bullets and shrapnel were frequently offered as post operative souvenirs.

Left: Sergeant Walter Popple, 8th King's Own Yorkshire Light Infantry, who, after 1 July 1916, miraculously survived four days lying wounded in No Man's Land.

W.J. Popple

Above and inset: Arthur Barraclough, sitting middle row far left, after recuperating from wounds received at the Battle of Cambrai in November 1917. Note the two wound stripes on his left arm.

Right: The 'burnt records' held at the National Archives. These original enlistment papers belonged to Arthur Barraclough and were produced for a special display to mark the veterans' final reunion held there in April 2004. Nine veterans attended of whom three are still alive today.

Below: Vic Cole aged 39, working as a Chief Radio Officer aboard SS *Barjora* in the Persian Gulf.

Left: The rosary chain that Vic Cole took from a French grave behind Bécourt Château in 1915. He returned the chain to the little chapel attached to the Château, where it hung from 1962 until very recently when the room was cleared. At some point the chain had broken and beads lay scattered on the floor.

Below left: Vic Cole, then aged 95, photographed outside his home.

Above: Richard Hawkins' marriage. He was troubled for many years by post-war stress, and was often unable to go to bed until three or four in the morning. Despite this, he became a director of the gas cooker company, Bellings.

Above: Joe Yarwood's marriage in the 1920s. After coming home from France, he found that Britain did not welcome back its fighting troops and for a long time he had only periodic employment.

Left: Henry Allingham with his girlfriend, Dorothy, whom he married during the war. Henry, who enlisted in 1915, is Britain's oldest man, aged 109. When he was asked where he would like to serve, he asked for East Africa but was given the East Coast near Great Yarmouth. He later served on the Western Front.

Left: John Laister with the violin he played after the war to eke out a living. He remained unemployed for three years after leaving the army.

Below: Alfred Anderson commanding the local Home Guard during the Second World War. Few of even the young men in this picture are still alive!

Above: Smiler Marshall holds the crucifix taken from amongst the debris of Albert Basilica on the Somme. It was beside his bed for over eighty five years until his death earlier this year (2005).

Smiler Marshall, above rig
sitting on the horse. Smiler was the last cavalrym
from the Great War and the last veteran to have served on the Somme in 19

Below right: A card sent home by Alf Bastin (above and right) from Doberitz POW camp. On the front it features Private Frank Godley, VC, the first private soldier to win a Victoria Cross in the Great War.

Below left: The rear of the card: Godley received notification of his award in a special presentation in front of other prisoners. Notably, the German commandant stepped forward to congratulate him.

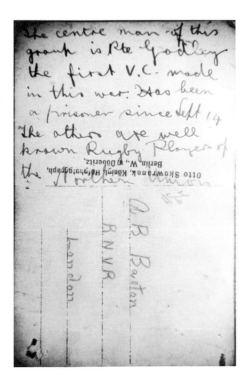

Left and below: Harold Lawton. He is wearing the c[...] badge of the Manchester Regiment. A conscript, Har[...] was called up in 1917. He w[...] moved three times from one[...] regiment to another before eventually being sent to the East Yorkshire Regiment, w[...] whom he was captured.

Right: Arthur Halestrap visits Tyne Cot Cemetery near Ypres. He visited the battlefields almost until his death in 2004, feeling that he had a duty to remember the fallen and to remind younger generations of their sacrifices.

Left: Eighty-seven years later. Jack Davis, then aged 107, is interviewed by ITN News outside the Cloth Hall in Ypres, November 2002. In the cloisters of St Martin's Cathedral nearby, a large number of his comrades in the 6th Duke of Cornwall's Light Infantry were buried by masonry when a German 15 inch gun opened fire in August 1915.

Below: Going home on the ferry from France, November 2002, Harry Patch reads about himself in that day's *Daily Mail*. The three heroes in the picture on the right are sitting under the Menin Gate in Ypres. They are Harry, Jack Davis and Arthur Halestrap. The Menin Gate records the names of nearly 55,000 British and Commonwealth men who died in the salient between 1914 and August 1917 and who have no known grave.

The Old Contemptibles' final pilgrimage to Belgium, May 1990. Standing, from the left, are Bill Thompson, Ben Clouting, Fred Dixon, Frank Sumpter, Tom Sharpe, Johnny Morris, Joe Armstrong, Victor Holden and Basil Farrer. Sitting are G B Jameson, Bill Humphrey, and Archie Stanley. Rear centre is Brigadier GMS Sprake, the then Honorary Secretary of the Old Contemptibles Association and to the right is Laura Parke, widow of Old Contemptible Charlie Parke.

The Autographs of all the veterans on the tour.

Above: Former Royal Engineer Arthur Halestrap, then aged 103, visits The Trench just before filming for the BBC's landmark series.

Above: The Imperial War Museum, 1998. Jack Davis, aged 103, visits the Museum's Trench Experience, walking along the trench duckboards.

Right: Stan Clayton, also then aged 103, sitting on the firestep next to a dixie used for carrying food into the front line.

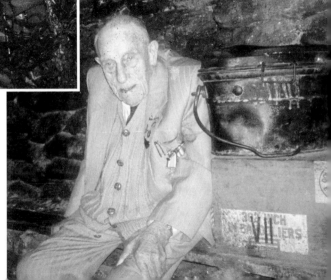

Above: Alfred Hudson, holding a picture of himself sketched in 1917. Five years after the war, Alfred took a bus tour to the battlefields and visited Tyne Cot Cemetery. The peace and quiet he found proved almost too much to bear.

Above: Norman Collins, former Lieutenant in the Seaforth Highlanders, stands under a picture of himself after he was commissioned in 1916. He later served on the Somme and at Arras. He was twice wounded and suffered discomfort from his injuries all his life.

Above and left: Allen Short, who served on the Western Front in 1918 and was twice wounded. He wore this uniform in France and he kept it in a wardrobe for over eighty years.

Above: Former Corporal G B Jameson (right) meets former Sergeant Jack Irving in Newcastle upon Tyne. Both served in the Northumberland Hussars and went overseas in 1914. Although they were in different squadrons, G B and Jack remembered each other.

Below: Ninety years after the outbreak of war, former Lewis gunner Harry Patch, then aged 106, meets former German artilleryman Charles Kuentz, then 107, on top of Mount Kemmel on 21 September 2004. This was almost certainly the last occasion when a soldier of the Great War will revisit the battlefields of Northern France and Belgium.

I cordially invite you to join me at a luncheon to celebrate my 109th Birthday

To be held at the Hydro Hotel, Mount Rd, Eastbourne

On Monday 6th June 2005

12:30 for 1:00 lunch & To Be Followed by Afternnon Tea In The Conservatory

Henry Allingham

HENRY ALLINGHAM

**BORN 6TH JUNE 1896
ROYAL NAVAL AIR SERVICES
WORLD WAR ONE 1915 – 1919**

Above: The birthday invitation to celebrate the 109th birthday of Henry Allingham.

Left and below: Henry Allingham, born 6 June 1896, receives a card from Thomas born 6 June 1996. Thomas was attending the birthday celebrations with friends from Ardingly College Junior School, West Sussex.

Above left and right: 24 May 2005: An honour guard dressed in the uniforms of the Essex Yeomanry and the Machine Gun Corps prepares for Smiler Marshall's coffin. The Surrey town came to a respectful standstill as the funeral cortege made its way down the high street.

Cecil Withers (right) shortly before he died. Below: The Order of Service at Cecil's funeral. His 82-year-old son Raymond, in a moving address, told how his father had worked tirelessly to support his family after the war, holding down two jobs to make ends meet.

Welcome to a Service of
Remembrance and Thanksgiving
at
Days Lane Baptist Church
28th April 2005

We give thanks for the life of

Cecil Clarence Withers

9th June 1898 - 17th April 2005

Jesus said,
"I am the resurrection and the life,
He who believes in Me will live,
even though he dies,
and whosoever believes in Me will never die"
John 11 v25

Photographer Roderick Field

Private Robert Renwick, MM, 16th King's Royal Rifle Corps, 1896-1997

On 3 November, we went up to the front line, and found no dugouts of any description, so a group of us were sent out to look for sandbags and duckboards to make a bit of a shelter for the next night. Well we got them from a dump, which of course weren't supposed to do without permission. Then as we were making off, the sergeant-major in charge returned and in the heat of the moment he fired his revolver as we scattered. A sergeant we were with ran and tried to jump a little trench and fell and broke his ankle, and in the end he got all the way back to Blighty.

The Somme battle was, by this time, nearly at a standstill. Men and horses were sinking in mud, many being shot. On 5 November we were ordered into an attack at a place called Le Transloy. In the whole war, I never saw as many unburied dead as I did round there.

There were fourteen of us in this slit trench just before we went over, and we got two shells, one in front and one behind, direct hits, and six were killed on the left of me, and seven wounded on the right. We were partially buried by collapsing earth but I crawled out without a scratch to help free the wounded. Soon after mid-day we went over the top, dodging as always from one shell hole to another as our protective artillery barrage lifted. I was with another lad when we became pinned down by a sniper. He had us taped but we couldn't spot him, and I must have eased up a little bit out of the mud and water as he put a bullet through the top of my steel helmet. I have a natural bump on my head and the helmet never fitted me very well, and that made a little space through which the bullet passed.

I remember seeing two badly wounded men of the Scottish Rifles crawling around, taking biscuits from dead men's haversacks and water from their bottles. How long they'd been out there, I don't know but they couldn't get back to their own lines. They had a fearful appearance, blue in the face, and I could only hope that our stretcher bearers would find them and pick them up. We over-ran Jerry's front line and dug in at dusk, and I can always remember one or two men, the shovels fell out of their hands and they dropped flat on their faces, asleep. We were relieved that night and we came out to some hutments. The next morning, the men were just lying about, mud up to their eyes, their overcoats soaking with mud and water. About mid-day, Brigadier Penny came in and the men started to get up to salute and he said, "Lie still, men, I am proud of you." He was a man who could either blast you or praise you.

[Ed. Robert Renwick was later awarded the Military Medal for digging his friends out.]

[Ed. The Somme offensive was officially closed down on 18 November on a damp, cold day. The severe weather throughout much of October and November meant that the battlefield was a quagmire and there was little point in continuing hostilities. Once more, both armies battened down the hatches for winter. In the meantime, divisions in need of rest were withdrawn to billets behind the lines and brought up to strength with new drafts.]

Private Cecil Withers, A Company, 7th East Surrey Regiment, 1898-2005
I arrived in France on 22 December and after spending just a few hours at the Base Camp at Etaples was sent with a draft to join the Battalion. We arrived on Christmas Eve and found them billeted in the village of Grand Rullecourt. Christmas lunch was *Daily Mail* Christmas pudding which came in two-pound flat round tins and I've never know how they did it but there was not a pip or a bit of stalk in it; it must have been picked over with the utmost love and care. Wonderful puddings. It was a bloody awful place though; we were in a shed and we were lying on straw and it was full of vermin.

Gunner Alfred Ambrose Henn, No614469, 3rd Battery, Warwickshire Royal Horse Artillery, 3 December1897-24 March 2000
At Christmas 1916, I had a parcel from my mother. I opened it, and

there was a whole chicken, cooked, and what was once a tin of cocoa, which had split open and smothered the chicken. Me and my mate sat down and ate chicken and cocoa for an afternoon's Christmas dinner.

Private Joe Yarwood, 94th Field Ambulance, Royal Army Medical Corps, 1896-1995

We were at Couin, a Corps Rest Station. On Christmas Day, we were to meet in the marquee, and they had beer there, and a piano for a bit of a concert and all that sort of thing. We were all standing there like a lot of sheep and the Sergeant Major came in. He'd been well at it, enjoying himself. He said, "Before we start, lads, we'd better ask the officers to come and drink our health." In comes the Colonel and all the officers, and they'd had a couple too, and one of them, and this was unpardonable according to army rules, he was telling dirty stories, if you please. I can remember him singing a lewd song, "I've a hole in an elephant's bottom." This went on for about half an hour until the officers had had enough, so they shot off and the Sergeant Major said, "Well, that's it, lads, we'll call it a day now." None of our blokes had had even a drink and of course there was a riot. It ended up in a free fight. I had a little pal called Barney Bridgewood, and he'd had a couple at lunch time, and I hung onto him as he was wanting to have a go at the Sergeant Major. It was going to get to court martial stage, but it was all hushed up. We didn't get any beer. Christmas 1916 was a dead loss as far as we were concerned, a complete shambles.

CHAPTER FOUR

1917

CAMARADERIE AND COMPLAINTS

IT IS EASY TO FORGET that old soldiers are just mere mortals like everyone else, with all their gripes and grumbles. The tendency to eulogise them as a special generation, the like of which we have not seen and will not see again, is deceptive and misses the point. My fascination with these men has always been that they are flesh and blood, men no different from you or me. What makes them remarkable is that they endured the apparently unendurable; they suffered the extremes of violence and for an unparalleled length of time. They saw sights that no one should see, endured cruelties no one should suffer, and felt a comradeship few of us will ever experience. They were stripped down to the bare essentials, and had the opportunity, whether they survived or not, to see and understand what was important in life. Nevertheless, little of what they had gained during those years could be replicated in civilian life, and with the peace came the inevitable let-down that could hardly compensate them for their endeavours.

We may be tempted to portray them as superhuman, but veterans are prone to the usual petty dislikes and moods. It was important for some to have had longer service than others. There was a lasting irritation amongst those, for example, who missed out on the campaign medal, the 1914/15 Star, particularly those who had seen action from early 1916. They might have served in France for three years, but as far as medals – the public recognition of service – were concerned, they were no better off than those who arrived on a draft at

Calais on the morning of the Armistice.

Worse still, a veteran might have been a 1918 conscript, dragged reluctantly from his place of employment to fight, four years after another man, a volunteer through and through, had enlisted in the heady days of 1914. Indeed, later in the war some men had deliberately chosen to enlist just prior to being called up so as to be a volunteer rather than a conscript. To all intents and purposes, on the march past the cenotaph or at the British Legion, or latterly on a tour to France, they were indistinguishable from each other.

Such important distinctions were recognized during the conflict. In early 1918, blue chevrons were awarded for each year of service abroad, sewn onto the right sleeve; indeed, there was a much coveted red chevron for those who had seen action in 1914. There were wound stripes, too, introduced in 1916 and worn on the left cuff, again indicating not just that the wearer had seen plenty of action but also showing by default some length of service. "Wipe your nose on that," was a popular offering amongst soldiers who, feeling slighted by others, offered their sleeve, thereby highlighting the presence of one or more of the brass insignia. Once the uniform was taken away, those distinctions were gone. Medals were the only alternative, and the holder of the 1914/15 Star had a kudos denied millions of other men who received only the silver British War Medal and the bronze Victory Medal.

The 10th East Yorkshire Regiment arrived at Alexandria, Egypt, at the very end of 1915. The 11th East Lancashire Regiment and the 12th York and Lancaster Regiment landed on New Year's Day 1916. All three battalions belonged to the 31st Division. Yet the men of the East Yorkshire Regiment received the 1914/15 Star, whereas the rest did not qualify for the medal as they had not landed in a war zone by the end of 1915. In addition, these men had been in far greater danger of enemy U Boat attack out on the open sea. Nevertheless, no medal was awarded, and this embittered many in the two battalions. I know of at least one veteran who defiantly wore the 1914/15 Star until he died, even though he was technically not eligible to do so.

Awards for gallantry such as the Military Medal, the Military Cross, the Distinguished Conduct Medal, or the Distinguished Service Order, and the highest of all medals, the Victoria Cross, gave the holders various levels of distinction. The last Victoria Cross holder from the Great War, Charles Rutherford, died in Canada in June 1989; he also held the Military Medal and Military Cross. The last gallantry medal holder from the Great War was James Lovell, who died in Bristol in January 2004. He held the Military Medal. Many wore their medals with pride; others refused to wear them at all, and some chose to put them away except on special occasions.

During the course of an interview with Royal Engineer Percy Clarke, I was flagging, not quite knowing what else to ask, when he said, "I've got a medal here somewhere." I assumed he meant a campaign medal, to which all men were entitled. He picked up a shoebox and took off the lid, rummaging around amongst pencil sharpeners, paperclips, screwdrivers, and sellotape, until he found the medal, ribbon-less and tarnished. It was the Distinguished Conduct Medal, an award given to other ranks and NCOs and second only to the Victoria Cross. I was astonished. "What did you win that for?" I asked. "Oh, nothing really, it came up with the rations," a phrase used occasionally, and often unfairly, by men in respect of the Military Medal, a lesser distinction, but never true of the DCM. He had done something extraordinarily brave, but he would not let on and the medal went back into its shoebox.

Service, or lack of it, could be the charge made by one veteran against another, simply because they, the two old soldiers, did not get on. Stan Clayton did not take to Smiler Marshall, not that Smiler was ever aware of this or that he would have cared. In many ways, they were two peas from the same pod: tough men, one from the north, one from the south, and perhaps that explained the antipathy. "When did he go to France?" Stan asked me once. "End of the war, I bet." "Er, not really, Stan, he was out in 1915." (Stan hadn't gone out until January

1916.) "That's what he tells you." "Stan, he's wearing the 1914/15 Star." "Oh, that doesn't mean anything," he replied, regardless of the evidence. Stan did, however, take to Mike Lally, a former regular soldier from Manchester, an ex-Regimental Sergeant Major, and as tough as they came. Although they had never met before, they appeared to understand each other immediately. Both were sitting in front of the fire at a reunion of old soldiers in the Lake District, when Mike, then aged 104, raised his feet up and rested them on Stan's knees, a liberty I had never seen one veteran take with another. Whatever the message, Stan understood, and the pair of them became immediate friends, challenging each other to impossible races and other physical competition.

Those who had once enjoyed outdoor life, sports, horse riding, or simply health and fitness, often enjoyed revisiting their once considerable prowess for a willing audience. Former professional footballer Stan Clayton had a party piece: to stand, arms fully extended, before he bent forwards, legs straight, and touched his toes. There was always rapturous applause for 105-year-old Stan, admiration for his agility and enjoyment too at the theatrical way in which it was delivered. Others had less overt displays of prowess, but displays they were, nevertheless. Walter Humphrey, aged 104, enjoyed using his powerful hand-shake/grip, proving that his fingers really were still as strong as he had built them up to be. Smiler Marshall's gambit was slightly different. He enjoyed nothing better than opening his vocal cords and giving a willing audience a rendition of the old Great War songs or reciting the alphabet backwards faster than most people can say it forwards.

The delight for many of the veterans in later years was that they were the centre of attention and wonderment. Most, too often confined to bedrooms in their homes, enjoyed the fame. "You're a film star," said one very young boy to Reg Glenn, a centenarian who had appeared on television shortly before he went to France for the annual commemoration of the Somme Battle. Reg laughed, but he was also tickled by the compliment. However, when the veterans came together, that limelight had to be shared. All of a sudden, being a centenarian and a Great War serviceman was not so special after all.

The pecking order that insinuates itself into all areas of life existed amongst veterans too. Fred Taylor, then a 98-year-old ex-gunner in the Royal Field Artillery, was being filmed at his home for a documentary programme in 1997. To save relocation time for the camera and equipment, it was arranged to bring another interviewee, Jack Davis, over to Fred's house. Jack, then aged 102, had seen action from 1915; Fred had been in France from 1917. Jack, realizing Fred was just 98, quipped "Ah, a youngster" but the 'youngster' was not happy about the remark, and, while not unfriendly, was certainly cooler towards his guest.

Competition apart, the bond between veterans remained strong. Appeals for former comrades continued well into the 1990s, the height of optimism perhaps, but these men were keen to make contact with pals even so late in the day. Occasionally, a speculative letter met with success. In 1990, Andy Andrews, then aged ninety-three, placed an advertisement in the British Legion magazine for any former D Company men of the 7th Royal West Kent Regiment to get in contact. Within weeks, he met Donald Hodge, then aged ninety-five, in London, and they reminisced about life seventy-five years earlier. In 1989, Charlie Young was delighted to hear that Ernest Ford was still alive in Reading, as both men were former privates in the 10th Queen's (Royal West Surrey Regiment). Charlie and his wife Gertie were all for taking the train to Reading to visit, when Ernest, who was painfully shy, felt he couldn't cope; the meeting was postponed, and, much to Charlie's regret, never took place. Even when old soldiers did not share a battalion, the regimental association could draw them together and there is often great camaraderie. Harry Patch had enormous fondness for Jack Davis, both men having served with the same regiment, the Duke of Cornwall's Light Infantry. At one point, Harry, born and bred in Somerset, even contemplated joining Jack at his residential home in Berkshire. Jack, 108 at the time, died shortly afterwards, and Harry would have been left alone had he gone ahead with his idea.

The veterans were "Chums" or "Pals" during the war, and that shared experience created a bond that would last a lifetime, even if the men themselves did not always stay in contact.

1917

It was not evident to anyone, least of all the soldiers in the line, but the tide of war was beginning to turn against Germany and its associated powers. True, it would take almost two years to win the conflict, but German forces were not just on the defensive but more often also on the back foot. The Somme had been ruinously expensive for all sides in terms of lives lost, and Germany could afford the losses least of all. At the same time, the growth in war production in Britain afforded to the soldiers at the front artillery support undreamt of eighteen months earlier. Artillery could be used to pulverize and demoralise the enemy, breaking up counter-attacks, and softening them up prior to an advance. The tactics as well as the lessons learnt during the Somme and those further developed in 1917 would be used to break the line decisively the following year.

The winter of 1916-17 was as cold as anyone could remember for thirty years, with weeks of unbroken frost. Horses became bogged down in the mud and were unharnessed in favour of mules with their smaller, daintier feet, picking their way through the morass created by an army going nowhere. The Somme mud mixed with chalk created a glue that was worse, according to many veterans, than any met elsewhere, even at Ypres; clinging to the feet and legs, it ingratiated itself onto every bit of uniform, especially the greatcoat which hung heavy with filth. Out of the line, uniforms, if they were removed, froze solid; both friend and foe suffered, and fought the weather rather than each other.

The soldiers who were sent to France and Flanders in 1917 were overwhelmingly conscripts, lads who had been called up in designated age groups since the middle of 1916. They included Arthur Barraclough, an apprentice hairdresser from Bradford, called up at 18 for training. His flat feet might have precluded his service in the heady days of 1914, but not any more. He was sent to France in January 1917 with the 2/4th Duke of Wellington's Regiment, a territorial battalion. Another new arrival was Cecil Withers, aged eighteen, a lad from London. Cecil had enlisted in the days of the Derby Scheme, when the Government made a final attempt to revive voluntary enlistment. The Scheme invited men to enlist, but allowed them to return to civilian work until the army required their services. Cecil enlisted under age without his parents' consent, and left for France just prior to Christmas 1916, joining his battalion in the small French village of Grand Rullecourt. Harry Patch would also arrive at the front in 1917. An eighteen-year-old apprentice plumber turned conscript, from Somerset, he already had two brothers in khaki and was a reluctant soldier, having heard about the terrible nature of the fighting from his eldest sibling who had fought at Mons.

For the Germans, other issues were more pressing than fighting. Their desire to defend their position in the west necessitated a tactical manoeuvre: a limited retreat. Their army, worn down by the fighting in France, was too thinly spread to hold the whole line in depth. By retiring to newly-constructed positions forty miles back, they could shorten their lines and therefore proportionately increase the number of troops holding the front. In mid-March, in the face of the British forces, the Germans retreated to the Hindenburg Line, begun in September 1916 by the then new Chief of Staff, after whom it was named and Ludendorff, his Quartermaster General. This was just one of a series of positions held by the German army, that stretched from the coast to Metz, east of Verdun, but it was the most complex and believed to be the most difficult to break, characterized by vast belts of barbed wire and strong points that supported one another.

The German withdrawal came as a surprise to the Allies, who were preparing a renewed offensive in the spring. The French, under their new Commander in Chief, General Robert Nivelle, wanted a joint offensive, and British forces were temporarily placed under this charismatic officer, who promised a surprise attack and victory within forty-eight hours. For the forthcoming offensive, Nivelle would launch a massive attack in the south on the Aisne while the British would go forward with fourteen divisions in front of Arras.

On 4 April, a furious bombardment of the German lines began, utilizing over 2,800 guns of all calibres. On 9 April, the British attacked with fourteen divisions, including four of the Canadian Corps, ordered to storm the formidable height of Vimy Ridge. At the northern end of the British line, the attack was an overwhelming success, as infantry supported by tanks tore into the German lines covering almost three miles. Vimy Ridge was captured as well as ten thousand prisoners. At the southern end, the resistance was stronger, and for five days the fighting raged as the Germans threw in reinforcements to halt the British advance. On the 14 April, the British attack was halted to allow the French to advance on the Aisne but here the offensive turned to catastrophic failure. Mutiny began to spread through the French ranks; by mid-May, fifty-four divisions were affected, as men refused to undertake further offensive operations, while there was a general complaint of poor pay, poor conditions and cancelled leave. Nivelle was ignominiously sacked and Petain, the hero of Verdun, was made the new C-in-C. He immediately set about pacifying the army, and by June all resistance was at an end. Around Arras, Haig continued to make attacks well into May, but for little further gain and the campaign ground to a halt. Very little news of the French rebellion reached the ears of the other Allied powers, and, mercifully, the Germans too remained in the dark.

The end of operations at Arras had seen the British army make useful if costly advances, resulting in a higher daily rate of casualties than at any other period of the war. Once again, the Germans had also suffered greatly and there was another reason for pessimism among their ranks: just prior to the British assault in April, news had filtered through that the Americans had entered the war on the Allied side. It would be the best part of a year before their troops would enter the battle zone in any numbers, but dark clouds were looming on the German horizon.

The offensive spirit of the Allies knew little rest in 1917. No sooner had the Arras offensive petered out than the Germans were attacked again, this time on the Messines Ridge, southeast of Ypres. This attack, launched on 7 June, was one of the most audacious of the war: the Ridge, held since 1914 by the Germans, was captured in one morning when nineteen mines dug under German trenches were detonated at 3.10am, literally blowing the enemy off this important strategic position. The decision to burrow underground and construct over 8,000 metres of tunnels was originally taken in April 1915. It was a wonderful feat of engineering. Although a bombardment had ensured that the Germans knew an attack was imminent, nothing could prepare the defenders for the horror of watching, in the breaking light, one mine after another being blown along the Ridge. The mines were planned to explode simultaneously however the watches supplied to tunneling officers were not synchronsised correctly and so the mines blew over the course of thirty seconds. Such was the devastation caused, so demoralizing the effect, that the attacking British and Empire forces found that they were able to occupy the entire Ridge within hours and at minimal cost. The Germans launched several half-hearted counter attacks over the following days, which were all beaten off. For the first time in the war, the cost of defence exceeded the cost of attack. This was an important milestone, and a pointer to the evolving tactics that would eventually break the deadlock on the Western Front.

The decision to take the Messines Ridge also showed Haig's desire to move operations north after the failure of the Nivelle attack, in order to conduct his own independent offensive around Ypres.

Third Ypres was the last great battle of attrition on the Western Front. Haig's aim was to break out of the Salient, pushing British forces towards the German submarine bases along the Belgian coast, from where the German navy had been conducting a successful war against Allied shipping in the Atlantic. Haig also believed that the German army was in a parlous state and was likely to collapse if one last great offensive could be mounted. A conventional ten-day bombardment prior to the assault prepared the way for a successful attack on 31 July. Once again, there were significant gains as the enemy was thrown back. However, the weather was about to come to their rescue. In the afternoon, a downpour drenched the battlefield, churning up the ground into a quagmire made worse by the preliminary bombardment that further destroyed the drainage ditches. All attempts to renew the offensive came to grief as men, animals and tanks floundered in mud. Haig pressed on and made localized assaults whenever there was a break in the weather, but the gains grew smaller and smaller. Ultimately, the village of Passchendaele, on the last of the low ridges that surrounded the town of Ypres, was taken, ninety-nine days after the offensive began. The costs were terrible on both sides, but it was the Germans who could not afford such like-for-like attrition, and therein lay a marginal, if hollow, victory for the Allies.

In previous years, the approach of winter had been the cue to close down major military operations until spring, but Haig did not want to do so now. One last assault would be launched at Cambrai, involving over 300 tanks in an attack over better ground. It broke the German lines in a single stroke and forced the Germans into flight. Yet in the aftermath of Third Ypres the army simply had too few resources to capitalise on the breakthrough. As the Germans fell back on their reserves and supplies, so the British became overstretched. A German counter-attack on 30 November won back all of the land gained in the previous week and a half. The year finally drew to a close, with all sides in need of recuperation.

At home, public exhaustion with the war was evident, as food queues lengthened in the streets and industrial disruption grew. Exasperation at the lack of success was evident, too, between politicians and the army commanders. The rift between Lloyd George, the Prime Minister, and his Commander in Chief had grown to outright hostility. Lloyd George simply did not believe in Haig's capability. The Field Marshal required more men on the Western Front if he was to win the war, but more men were not forthcoming, Instead, Haig was required to release his reserves of five divisions to the Italian Front. Italy was in a state of civil despair and unrest, as fuel and food queues lengthened. In the autumn of 1917, a joint Austro-German offensive made spectacular gains at Caporetto, driving the Italian forces back. In total, eleven Allied divisons, six French and five British, were diverted to Italy to shore up the front and halt the enemy's advance. They were troops that Haig could ill afford to send.

[Ed.The beginning of 1917 saw limited engagements on the frozen Somme battlefield. Lieutenant Richard Hawkins took part in one, the Battle for Boom Ravine.]

Lieutenant Richard Hawkins, 11th Royal Fusiliers, 1895-1994
Our forming-up place was just in front of a depression known as the Gully and our target was Boom Ravine a short distance ahead, seizing the high ground in order to provide observation over the upper Ancre Valley.

I was commanding D Company and on the night of the 16 February we began to move up. There were two routes to the forming-up line; both were very congested and in the dark it was almost impossible to get the men up. The journey was made more difficult by the weather. For at least three weeks it had been freezing hard, indeed, that winter was one of the coldest periods I can ever remember, but this night a thaw had begun to set in. We waded through the mud and slime to be in our positions by 4.45am and were harassed all the way by artillery and machine gun fire, causing a lot of casualties just to get my company into position.

At 5.30am I went round the line with some rum and gave all the men a good tot, chatting to them as I did so. I finished about 6am. The only thing I could do then was to establish my headquarters at the top of a small ravine that ran at right angles to the main objective, Boom Ravine. At 6.20 I clambered to the top of the ravine which was 25 or 30 feet high. I just managed to see from my watch that it was 6.25am; it was still dark. The time went on, 6.26, 6.27, 6.28. It was 6.29 when the biggest bloody barrage I had ever been through suddenly descended on us. It was obvious that the Germans had wind of our attack. Captain Collis-Sandes, who was commanding B company, turned up at my side. "I think this is going to be a pretty awful show." "Yes," I replied, "I think I am going to get myself a rifle and a bayonet," and I collared one from a fellow who was dead.

At 6.30 our barrage opened with a blinding flash behind us. We were still bogged down with the German barrage when there was another flash and Collis-Sandes fell dead and I was hit in the shoulder. It was like being kicked by a mule. As the force spun me round, I lost my balance and fell right down the ravine, crashing into some barbed wire at the bottom. I lost consciousness for a while. I awoke as it was beginning to get light, to hear a cockney voice say, "Cor blimey, 'ere's Lieutenant Hawkins, the poor so-and-so is dead." "No, I'm not," I replied, "but I shall be if you don't get me out of this lot."

I'd lost a lot of blood but they helped me to my feet and took me back a couple of hundred yards and there I met dear old Doctor Sale, from Australia. He stripped my tunic and put some dressings on before he called over three German prisoners, "Here, come and get hold of the end of this stretcher." He needed a fourth man and, looking round, he saw a German officer. This German officer was a good looking young fellow with a ginger moustache and he explained in fairly good English that it was not the job of a officer to grab hold of a stretcher with three private soldiers. Dr Sale was a pretty busy man, and he hadn't time to argue, so he just repeated himself, "Get hold of the end of that stretcher!" The German said "Nein." Dr Sale was a very good rugby three-quarter and he stuck his boot into this fellow's behind and he took off. They started to go round in a very big circle, down in the shell holes, and up the other side, the doctor launching a kick at this officer every few yards and missing practically every time because of the impossible state of the ground. In the end, dear old Sale caught him and kicked his backside several more times, after which the officer decided he would take the end of the stretcher after all.

When you get up on the shoulders of four fellows, it's a long way down to the ground and we were walking on a very muddy slippery duckboard, with not really room for two people abreast. I looked down into the shell holes and didn't like what I saw. I said, "Oy, I'm getting off." I didn't want to get tipped down into one of those shell holes, so I walked out, weak though I was.

[Ed. With hindsight, the fighting proved of little consequence. Just weeks later, the Germans began their voluntary withdrawal to the Hindenburg Line, 30 miles to the east. The wasteland of the Somme was abandoned to the Allies and to nature, at least for the time being. Important lessons had been learnt during the Battle, but not all were positive. The Somme had finally dispelled any residual hope that the war could be brought to a speedy and successful conclusion. Guts, dogged determination and simple endurance would decide the outcome of the conflict. By 1917, war weariness was beginning to set in and not everyone was ready to continue this seemingly open-ended task.]

Lance Corporal Vic Cole, 1st Queen's Own (Royal West Kent Regiment), 1897-1995
By 1917, I was not particularly anxious to get back to France; my enthusiasm for the war had waned since being wounded on the

Somme. By volunteering for a number of different courses, I managed to stay on at Shoreham for several months. Thus I passed out as a bomber, a pioneer (latrine digger), a sniper and was about to take a course in army cooking when I once again got my marching orders, this time to join the 1st Battalion of the regiment.

Driver Alfred Benjamin Finnigan, No1631, A Battery, 15th Brigade, 5th Division Royal Field Artillery, 18 September 1896-11 May 2005

I had a friend called Milne who served in the Gordons. He'd been hit and wounded in the back and was sent home to recover, and for a long time he was convalescent. And the morning he was supposed to be going back to his regiment, he went outside, stood and stared at the sun, deliberately, to damage his eyes, not permanently, but it stopped him going away. He was an honest man, he was not the sort of man who would do a dirty trick, and yet he did that. He'd had enough.

Rifleman Robert Renwick, MM, 16th King's Royal Rifle Corps, 1896-1997

A mate of mine, Percy Milburn, was wounded in the shoulder, got home and was in a rest camp for a while. I had a sister who had taken my place in the grocery store in Hexham and he called in and told her how I was getting on. He said to my sister, "Never worry about your brother, he'll come back, but I won't." He came back to France and was in very bad heart when he joined us again. He was killed the first time up the line.

Private Henry 'Harry' John Patch, No29295, C Company, 7th Duke of Cornwall's Light Infantry, 17 June 1898-

I didn't want to join up but I was conscripted, so there you are. I came from a very sheltered family, the youngest of three brothers. The army didn't appeal to me at all, and when I found what a rough and tumble life it could be, I didn't like it one little bit. I had no inclination to fight anybody. I mean, why should I go out and kill somebody I never knew? We had a week's embarkation leave and then we were sent in an old paddle steamer from Folkestone to Boulogne. Then up the hill into camp. I wasn't carrying enough, so they gave me a fifteen-pound pack of bully beef. On arrival, we were separated and drafted to various regiments. I had a chum with me who came from the same village; I went into the Duke of Cornwall's Light Infantry, and he was drafted to a regiment in Egypt, and we never met again.

Private Arthur Barraclough, No238014, C Company, 2/4th Duke of Wellington's Regiment, 4 January 1898-26 August 2004
There were people who'd never done owt in public life, sometimes office jobs, and they've read all this stuff in the paper about what goes on in the war, and they come out and they are frightened to death, especially when they get to France. That's when the trouble starts. And they see fellows coming down wounded and others going up the line, and it puts the wind up them, of course, and they think, "Oh, I hope I'm not going to that place." Everybody was a bit nervous, and you couldn't help your knees knocking.

Private Cecil Withers, 7th East Surrey Regiment, 1898-2005
We'd not been long overseas when this sergeant conducted a roll call. As the sergeant called out the names he reached the letter "S". "Smith." No answer. "Smith." No answer, so he says to this man, "What's your name?" "Smythe, Sir." "Smythe be damned, Smythe's an officer's name, your name's Smith!"

And that reminds me of another occasion. This old sergeant major we had was bringing up a man in front of the Colonel for not shaving, dirty boots, dirty buttons, the want of a haircut. All those things that were wrong were put on a crime sheet, and the Colonel said, "Who's brought all these allegations against Private so-and-so?" The sergeant major stepped forward and said, "'Sir, I am the alligator."

Corporal Brian Shaw, MM No2395, 2/5th South Staffordshire Regiment, 10 February 1898-November 1999

The first time up the line, I was sent on a ration party to a road where we were to meet the horses to collect food and water. As we arrived, the Germans started shelling the road. So I stood there bravely, telling people to get up, but most of the people were older than I was and had more sense and had taken to ditches straightaway. I had a romantic notion of war, so I stood there braving shot and shell, but after I'd seen what they could do, I was the first into the ditches. I was brave, oh yes, very brave, trying to get them out of the ditches.

Private Harry Patch, 7th Duke of Cornwall's Light Infantry, 1898-

You were scared all the time. You couldn't deal with the fear. It was there and it always would be. I know the first time I went up the line, we were scared; we were all scared. I would get a butterfly in my stomach and my hands would shake, so for a moment or two I would have a job to coordinate my nerves to do anything. We lived hour by hour; we never knew the future. You saw the sun rise, hopefully you'd see it set. If you saw it set, you hoped you'd see it rise. Some men would, some wouldn't.

Private Cecil Withers, 7th East Surrey Regiment, 1898-2005

You see when you're in the trenches, your life's measured by the second. You never know one second to another whether you're going to be blown to bits. It's so imminent that you never trouble your head about it, it's too terrible to think about.

"Don't forget to tell mum I died instantly." That was something every chap would ask. It might be a damn lie, of course, but it was done for the mother's sake.

Private Ernest Ford, 10th Queen's (Royal West Surrey Regiment), 1896-1995

You had to accept the position you were in; there was no point dwelling on your fears or pondering on the thought that death could strike at any time. You shut off feeling, ignored reality. Whenever I was under a bombardment, I would sit and stare at the end of my boots, clear my mind of everything, communicate with no one. What would be the point in letting your imagination run away with you? It couldn't possibly save you, or do you any good. A man could light a cigarette and be dead before he smoked it. That was a fact.

Private William Golightly, No65065, 1st Northumberland Fusiliers, 29 October 1898-February 1992

We were taken into the support lines first, on a day when it was raining like hell, and we went up in the dark. That first 24 hours, I changed from a boy to a man. There had been an advance the day before; we were perspiring like mad, the trenches were half full of water and duckboards were floating about. Very lights were going into the air, and when we felt down, we found there were dead bodies under the water and more lying on the parapet. That was our first job in the morning, to find and bury these dead.

Private Andrew Bowie, 1st Cameron Highlanders, 1897-2002

You see pictures of men sat on their bottoms doing nothing and because the picture was taken during the day, you think that's what their life is. Far from it. Once it got dark you had to get a move on, you were on a working party and you'd to work like blazes to keep up, wiring, carrying sleepers, carrying duckboards, corrugated iron, all the things you needed to build and maintain a trench. You are working like a slave. And if there were dead to be buried or taken away, you did that too.

One job started with the "you, you, and you" business, about six of us. "There's a dead mule lying outside our parapet," we were told. "Go out and bury it." A dead thing like that always gave off a bit of a stench, and someone decided that it must be buried. That was the order but it was easier said than done. We went out, and I don't know if you have ever handled a dead mule, but we couldn't move the blasted thing, so we took our spades and put mud on it, thinking that would hide it. But the next morning we looked out, and there was the poor beast still visible with these pats of mud on it.

It was no joke being a private soldier in a line regiment at night, and if the weather was bad you had to work through it. You needed that tot of rum they gave you in the morning, no doubt about that, then you'd try and get a bit of sleep or tend to your own affairs, writing letters, looking for lice.

Private Arthur Barraclough, 2/4th Duke of Wellington's Regiment, 1898-2004

Working parties were sent out every night and the lousiest job in the world was the barbed-wire job. We went out in pitch dark on our bellies. White tape was handed to the one at the front, and this white tape was let out wherever you went. No Man's Land was full of shell holes, and in winter it got wet and anybody falling in, they'd had it. So the lance corporal took the tape and about four men would go round the shell holes so that when the wiring party started you wouldn't topple in. Handling that stuff, barbed wire, it were terrible. The wire had inch-long needles and you daren't get clipped to it because you couldn't pull yourself off, it was like somebody grabbing hold of you. You'd have to go out with special wire cutters trying to clip them off the barbed wire but there was more than one lad shot, fastened on. Before the wire came out in balls, we used to put it through the loops of wire pickets, and wrap the wire round. We wore gloves, of course, just ordinary thick gloves, but you got awful scratches. It was a terrible job at night, it was a job the men feared.

Driver Alfred Finnigan, 5th Division Royal Field Artillery, 1896-2005

I've seen several horrible sights, bodies of which only the trunk remained, head, hands, arms, legs gone. Heads with no faces, empty skulls. I hadn't been out in France long and we were at Achiet Le Grand station, in the railway yard. There was this man and he had been placed out front with his tunic thrown over his face and head. He was a member of a German medical team that had been caught by our artillery and they were just lying around, all dead, in various stages of decay.

I hate to think of it now, but out of curiosity I pulled his tunic aside, and his head was an empty shell, his face had gone.

UNDER BOMBARDMENT

Lieutenant Richard Hawkins, 11th Royal Fusiliers, 1895-1994
A group of us were behind the lines in a corrugated iron hut one morning. We were having a pow-wow with General Maxse when all of a sudden an 8inch howitzer went off from somewhere very close by. It frightened the lot of us, a ruddy great gun like that, we thought we were being bombed. Anyway Maxse, who appeared the only one unruffled, turned to his ADC. "Monty, go and tell the young officer in charge that General Maxse is here. If he fires that gun again I shall have him shot at dawn, in fact I shall not wait for dawn, I shall have him shot straightaway."

Lieutenant Norman Collins, 1/6th Seaforth Highlanders, 1897-1998
My teeth started to chatter because we were under bombardment. I was in a hole in the side of a trench and the sergeant was making me a cup of tea with a candle and a billy can. I apologized to him and said, "It's cold, isn't it?" Actually, I knew perfectly well that my teeth were chattering because I didn't like the shells dropping closer and closer. "Yes, it is cold, Sir," and he passed it off, you see. And then it stopped and I pulled myself together, but I don't mind admitting I was never the stuff that heroes were made of.

Lieutenant G B Jameson, C Battery 72nd Brigade, Royal Field Artillery, 1892-1999

Getting up to the front line, you were all zig-zagging about. When there wasn't a battle in progress, the back areas were always subjected to searching and sweeping by the enemy's 5.9 inch batteries, which would try and hit supplies. You studied where these shells were falling and listened to them for a while, and then you made off in a slightly different direction to get out of the way. You were always weighing up your chances.

When a battle was in progress, you just listen to the various salvos and watch them drop and then take a deep breath and run for the next bit of cover, and wait again. I had to make for the front line during the attack on Vimy Ridge. I was with three telephonists and all their gear, so I spread them out. "Right, you go first and make for that shell hole and dive in there, and when you've got there, stick your hand up and I'll come and get in a shell hole and I'll put my hand up and the next one will come," so we weren't all in the same place. Soon as I got there, I pointed out another place and he'd run there, so that we were leapfrogging each other all the time.

Lance Corporal Vic Cole, 1st Queen's Own (Royal West Kent Regiment), 1897-1995

We were up on a ridge near Arras, looking down on this field. We were moving up to what was known as the Brown Line in support, and the Royal Field Artillery had a battery of 18 pounders in this square field, each gun with a dugout next to it. We saw this battery, and they were shooting away, and Jerry must have spotted them because he retaliated. As shells started falling, four chaps came out of a dugout and started playing touch around this field, running around like kids. They must have been at the rum bottle or something, and now and again a shell would land and a fountain of earth went up in the air. It was the most amazing sight, and these lads carried on playing, and no one seemed to get wounded. After a time Jerry stopped shelling and the men went back to their dugout.

Private Cecil Withers, 7th East Surrey Regiment, 1898-2005
You could see the shells go over, like a misty dark patch going down, then as they hit the ground it was like a bottle of red ink spraying, but all in one direction, all red flames and shrapnel. It meant that if you were standing to one side of a shell-burst, you could remain practically untouched.

Corporal Brian Shaw, MM, 2/5th South Staffordshire Regiment, 1898-1999
A British battalion was advancing to take up a position, moving up in sections. I can remember watching them going forward when a shell burst apparently right on top of them, and I thought, "Oh Lord, that's finished them." When the smoke cleared, they were still going, but the man next to me gave a groan and collapsed. A piece of shrapnel must have travelled over, hit him in the chest and killed him. Extraordinary, the shell burst just yards from these people, none of them injured, yet one who was 600 yards away was killed.

Sapper Stan Clayton, 457th Field Company, 62nd Division Royal Engineers, 1894-2000
Whilst we were at Bapaume, our cook made a stew out in the open and blew a whistle for us to go and fetch it. I was with a friend, and together we walked out of our billets. Overhead there was a fight going on between two aeroplanes, and we looked up for a moment as we walked. Now, this man is at the side of me when all of a sudden I heard a scream, the like of which I'd never heard in all my life, and he dropped dead. I looked at him and couldn't see anything, so I called the officer and he came and stripped his coat and found a wound, a bullet had passed through his shoulder and into his heart. He had been killed by a spent bullet fired by one of the aircraft overhead.

THE BATTLE OF ARRAS

Alfred Henn, 3rd Battery, Warwickshire Royal Horse Artillery, 1897-2000

It was dark and there was a hell of a noise going on, guns firing, shouting, and the noise of wheels rumbling over cobbles. We were going through a very narrow street in the outskirts of Arras when we came to a sudden halt, causing the horses to swerve. The gunners behind started shouting and bawling for us to go forward but we couldn't move. The horses were scraping their feet and neighing, and then came a terrible smell. I couldn't make out what was happening. Then a Very light went up and I saw steam rising up all around me. To my horror I could see that the wall opposite was absolutely blasted by meat, flesh torn from horses and men blown to pieces. The steam I saw was ascending from the blood.

Private Tom Dewing, 34th Divisional Royal Engineers Signal Company, 1896-2001

The attack was timed for 6am on 9 April. The day before, a few of us were sent to the advanced signal dugout a few yards behind the front line. We had a very quiet night but promptly at six, a shell from a 16-inch naval gun roared across with the sound of an express train and every gun on the front opened fire. There was no prolonged bombardment but now every German battery was subjected to devastating shellfire. The troops left the trenches and moved towards the barrage, so that when it lifted they were able to jump down into the enemy trenches almost at once. Harry Bradfield had heard that tanks were going over and he wanted to see them. So when the gunfire started, he ran up the dugout steps and put his head up above the parapet. Presently we heard him shout, "Come here quick, come here quick!" We thought he was wounded, but when we got to the top of the steps we were amazed to see scores of German prisoners hurrying down the communication trench as fast as they could go.

Private James Hudson, 8th Queen's Own (Royal West Kent Regiment), 1898-2001

We were loaded down with bullets, a box respirator, tin hat, a bottle full of water, a haversack, and iron rations. Then just before we went over, they came round with an extra fifty rounds of ammunition to go round my neck and a Mills grenade in each pocket. When we went forward, the men managed to jump the German front line but I was only a small man and didn't. The trench had been badly affected by snow and rain, and I failed to clear it. Instead I hit the parapet, and slid down onto the floor. It was all clay and very slippery. I struggled and fought but I kept falling back. Eventually, on almost giving up any hope of extricating myself, I got out after I don't know how many attempts. By that time, the line wasn't very much ahead. The Germans were shelling our old front line trench, so we were comparatively safe for a time as their infantry were beating a retreat. I saw my platoon sergeant, a brave man, and he shouted, "Come on, I thought you weren't coming with us. Extra rations tonight!" and he waved a slice of German black bread.

Private Arthur Barraclough, 2/4th Duke of Wellington's Regiment, 1898-2004

Some lads used to get drunk when they knew they were going over, and they'd go over fresh, others used to grab onto someone else, they'd be frightened to death, but I wanted to act like a man. I could face up to what was coming. So I used to say a prayer before I went over. "Dear God, I'm going into great danger, would you please guard me and help me to act like a man. Please bring me back safe," and I used to go out without a fear. I went over with confidence.

We had been practising for weeks going behind these tanks, a platoon behind each, in two ranks. Now we could hear them coming a mile away, and four tanks got set up in front of our trenches. We set off behind one of them. The idea was that when it came across the German line, it was supposed to flatten the wire and our platoons would open out and attack. The problem was there had been a lot of rain at the time; it was terribly flooded. We had hardly gone twenty yards when the tanks got stuck in the mud, and others went nose down into old trenches. The tanks had bundles of wood tied to their tops and these were supposed to be dropped into the hole to give the tank tracks some grip to get out, but it didn't work that way, the tanks were too heavy and smashed up the wood. None got any further than the first line of trenches and not one of them reached the objective on our bit of front.

Lieutenant Norman Dillon, MC, 2nd Battalion, Heavy Section, Machine Gun Corps, 1896-1997
Inside the tank it was frightful. You couldn't hear a word, and so when the driver wanted the gear-changing man to change gear, it was no use shouting, so they had a code whereby they took a hammer or a spanner and rapped on the engine casing, which made a loud clang. One clang meant bottom gear, two clangs meant second gear, three clangs meant neutral. No matter what the temperature was like outside, it was like an oven in there, terribly hot, and of course a lot of chaps lost their lives by opening flaps and sticking their heads out of the top of the tank.

As we went forward, bullets hit the framework of the tank and had the unpleasant effect of knocking off, on the inside, a tiny piece of red hot steel, so if there was a lot of machine gun fire in one place on the side of the tank, you got quite a cloud of these fragments, smaller than a pin-head. That is why the tank crew wore masks.

Private Archie Richards, D Company, Heavy Section, Machine Gun Corps, 1897-1998
The Germans turned these guns on us, particularly on the trap doors, and the bullets smacked against the tanks, causing the metal to splinter. Tiny flakes would fly about and cut you all over. Our faces often bled, and we wore goggles to stop ourselves being blinded.

Inside the tank, the atmosphere was sickening. When you are in action and all the traps are down, the fumes are hardly bearable. There is a thick haze of petrol and gas and cordite fumes. With the engine running, it was incredibly stuffy. The engine was in the centre of the tank and there was a little passage to step around it, but we were very cramped, and you had to watch your head. It was impossible to speak to anybody, so we had to make pre-determined signals with our hands and fingers. I had a good stomach, but others were sick, spewing up all over the place and passing out. You can imagine what it was like, eight men cooped up in a tank with no air for five hours.

Your nerves get worn, the noise and everything, it gradually gets to you. We had two men in the tank and their nerves gave out and they went funny in the head. They had a kind of glazed look in their eyes; the smells were affecting their minds, they didn't know what they were doing and they were unsteady on their feet. But we were all on the verge of collapsing sometimes.

A/Lance Corporal Cecil Withers, 7th East Surrey Regiment, 1898–2005

The sergeant major came round with the rum jar, and we had a little tot of rum in our mess tins. Soon after, we fixed bayonets and climbed onto the firestep. Before I went, I'd say a little prayer, "Lord help me," you know, a plea for mercy, but sometimes I didn't say anything. We knew our duty but we never calculated what was happening, or worked things out; it was so swift, we lived from second to second not minute to minute.

It was freezing cold, and our arms felt like blocks of ice. We were waiting for the whistle, shells were whining over, bang, bang, crash, crash. Then over we went. As I climbed the parapet, the chap next to me collapsed. "Get up, get up!" someone shouted, but as far as I know he didn't get up, that poor boy, he showed all the signs of a stroke.

As soon as we got on top, we went as fast as we bloody well could, because the quicker we got to the German lines, the quicker we'd be out of the range of their guns which were fixed on our own trench. Even so, we tried to keep in line with each other, not stray all over the place. As we were going, a football appeared, and landed in front of my right foot. So I just kicked it to the officer on my left, Captain Maxwell, and the first thing he did was kick it straight into the German line, and as he did so everybody rushed forward into the enemy trench which we found was empty. They'd cleared off.

Private Arthur Barraclough, 2/4th Duke of Wellington's Regiment, 1898-2004

I came across a badly wounded Jerry and he was shouting out, "Water, water!" I just stopped for a second, and thought, "I'll give the poor so-and-so a drink", and a sergeant shouted, "Barraclough! Get on with your work, don't worry about him." I suppose he thought he might have had a gun or a bomb in his hand, perhaps the sergeant thought I was trying to dodge the attack, I don't know.

I felt really hurt, though, to leave that fellow there with half his face blown off and me walking past. I've thought many times, if he'd lived, what he'd have thought of a British soldier who knew he was wounded and wouldn't give him a drink. I've never forgotten that man. He haunted me a bit.

A/Lance Corporal Cecil Withers, 7th East Surrey Regiment, 1898-2005

Close to the German trenches, near a shell hole, there was a German lying on his back, blood all over the place, dying obviously, and he said one word, "Wasser". I got my water bottle out and poured some of it on his lips and down his mouth as best I could, and I've never forgotten the look of gratitude in that man's eyes, as much as to say thank you. I was just pausing for a few seconds but I was out of line with the wave of men going forward, and I remember the sergeant saying, "Come on, Withers. You ought to give the so and so a bullet, not water."

Rifleman Robert Renwick, MM, 16th King's Royal Rifle Corps, 1896-1997

I remember the corn was just coming through the ground as we moved to attack the Fontaine Line on 23 April. We went up on the Sunday night, and we were lying out at the side of a quarry, to go over the next morning. It was a surprise attack and the signal to go over was one big shell. Our platoon was held back in support. After some time, Jerry counter-attacked and we got orders to go forward which we did and took their line. I remember Nicholas Dodd, a Hexham lad, and another from Gateshead, Bob Thompson, they both got a bullet through their wrists, and I can hear this Nicholas Dodd yet. "Good luck, Bob, we're off for Blighty." I envied those two men that day, I'll admit that, I really envied them.

After things had quietened down, we were mopping up when a German sergeant appeared from a deep dugout. For a moment he seemed amazed at the sight of our troops and picking up a rifle and fixed bayonet, he had a go at a sergeant of the 2nd Queen's who had somehow got mixed up with us during the attack. He was wounded first in the shoulder, then he got the German in the same place but rather more severely, and the rifle dropped to the ground. Instead of having another go, the Queen's sergeant put his rifle aside, took out his water bottle and had a swig, handed it to the German, put it back, then took out his cigarette tin and produced two cigs, lit up, and gave one away. "Come on with me, Fritz, we are finished with this game." By this time, the German was losing a fair amount of blood and feeling weak, so he put his arm around our sergeant and off they went, out of the trench and on to the open ground towards the dressing station, looking like a couple of friends. There were two men prepared to fight to the death and, when both were wounded, they went down arm in arm to the dressing station. As I watched them I thought to myself, "What on earth are we fighting each other for?"

We were trained to hate the Germans; we called them either the Hun or the Boche but when we took prisoners we called them Fritz.

THE DEAD

Driver Alfred Henn, 3rd Battery, Warwickshire Royal Horse Artillery, 1897-2000

We stopped on a road once and there was a German sitting quite normally on the edge of a shell hole, not far away, and I could not understand what he was doing there. So I went over to have a look. He was sitting with his mess tin in his lap. He'd been eating when a shell had split his head open and his brain had fallen into the mess tin. If that isn't sudden death, I don't know what is.

Sapper Stan Clayton, 457th Field Company, 62nd Division Royal Engineers, 1894-2000

I came to the remains of a large church and saw a door and steps. I walked down and counted fifty-one steps and found myself in a German headquarters. At the bottom there was a corridor and a series of entrances on each side. I saw a door with a number five on it and I looked in and there was a German lieutenant, sitting at a table, and he had a photograph in his left hand. He was staring at a picture of a woman and a little curly headed girl, about two-years old, beautiful she was. I looked at him. He was white and quite dead. He must have taken poison because he was not wounded at all. I had to drag the picture out of his fingers tips and gave it to an officer. I heard no more about it, but I hoped it might be sent home to his wife, so she'd know for certain that he'd died.

Gunner Frederick William Taylor, No207742, 13th Battery, 17th Brigade, 29th Division, 12 May 1898-19 March 2000

It was my turn to go on duty, walking around the silent gun pits, the length of the battery, perhaps one hundred yards in all. We'd only just taken over this position after recent advances, and when I got to No.1 gun I noticed a shell hole half filled with muddy water. In the gloom, I made out a face looking towards me. It belonged to a German. Why his body was still there and hadn't been cleared away, I don't know. But suddenly, as I looked, his face appeared to laugh at me, it was so uncanny, supernatural, that I moved quickly away and kept away for the rest of the night. In the morning, his body was pulled out of the water and taken away for burial. I realized afterwards that a wisp of cloud had passed over the moon and made it look as though the man had laughed. Very scary when you are on your own, I can tell you.

Driver Alfred Henn, 3rd Battery, Warwickshire Royal Horse Artillery, 1897-2000

We were going along the Monchy Road, and we saw a big log of wood and three soldiers sitting there with their hands on the top of their upturned rifles. They'd got their eyes closed and I thought, "Fancy sleeping through all this lot, some men have got a nerve." The next day they were still there – the flash from a gun must have killed them outright, instantaneously, and nobody had bothered to move them.

A/Lance Corporal Cecil Withers, 7th East Surrey Regiment, 1898-2005

It was pitch dark and there was a chap out in No Man's Land, groaning, right in front of the trench we'd taken, and he was saying, "Mutter, mutter." It was enough to break your heart. A cockney man was going through the trench at the time, and said, "It's no good him calling out for mum, he won't see her no more," and I thought that was a callous thing to say, cruel words. When your mind goes back to these occasions, they come up like a record in your mind, you can't help it. It makes you very bitter. These things stand out so vividly that they make a deep impression on you as an eighteen-year-old, like a pencil making a dent on paper, it's the same on the brain.

There were so many wounded after the attack at Arras and no one left to attend to them, so the sergeant said to me, "Withers, we've no stretcher bearers and this chap's wounded. Would you carry him down to the 5th Southern General Aid Post?" So they hoisted this man over my right shoulder and I was obliged to carry my rifle in my left hand, I absolutely had to carry my rifle. It was dark and while I was going across with my rifle dangling on my left arm, two military police on horseback went by and asked where I was going and if I had my rifle, that was their concern. They saw it and let me go, satisfied I was not a deserter. I made my way to the Aid Post, about two kilometres, and as soon as they took the wounded man off my shoulder, I collapsed. They put me on a stretcher and gave me a dose of sal volatile, a stimulant, a few drops in water, to restore a fainting person. That brought me round. They gave me a half hour's rest on the stretcher and then I went back to rejoin my unit.

Private Arthur Burge, 1st East Surrey Regiment, 1895-1999
Another badly wounded man came in. He was shouting and swearing. I was annoyed, as they brought him in and placed him amongst some sacks where I was supposed to read signals. They dropped this man down and I said, "Don't leave him here," but they said, "Sorry, mate, but we're too busy." On my right, there was a pillbox, the top of which was being used by a surgeon. He wasn't ready for the casualty and he said to the sergeant, "For God's sake keep that man quiet!" The sergeant spoke to the man and said, "Stop that bloody noise, will you?" The man stopped for a moment and started again once the sergeant had gone. The sergeant came back again and repeated himself, and the same happened. The third time he came back, he had a syringe and he rolled up the man's sleeve and gave him an injection, and put him right out. The surgeon had said he couldn't work with the noise, and to my mind he asked the sergeant to finish him off; he was very badly wounded and couldn't have lived.

A/Lance Corporal Cecil Withers, 7th East Surrey Regiment, 1898-2005
After the battle men were fainting, we were so exhausted. It was terribly cold, so cold in fact that the water in our bottles froze. A group

of men would be standing still and one by one they would collapse and there they lay in a thin covering of snow. When the medical officer saw this, he turned to the sergeant major and said, "Don't disturb them, let them remain where they fall, they will get up when they are ready." After a while they started to come to and we were taken out, back to Arras.

We were tired beyond words, and many men put their hands on the shoulders of the man in front to stop themselves collapsing. I was standing by a concrete post, I was so exhausted, almost dead. Next to me was a Salvation Army hut and a lady opened a tin of Carnation condensed milk and poured it in my mess tin, mixed with hot water and Horlick's malted milk, and that brought life back to me. It restored my life.

Air Mechanic Henry William Allingham, No8289, No12 Squadron Royal Naval Air Service, 6 June 1896-

It was the men in the trenches who won the war. What they put up with, no one will ever know. I've seen them coming out of the line, poor devils, in a terrible state, plastered with mud. They were like hermit crabs with all their equipment on and they'd plonk down in the middle of the road before somebody helped them up. How did they manage? They were at the end of their tether. They were worn out, absolutely done up. They could hardly put one foot before the other, they were gone, depleted, finished, all they wanted to do was sleep, sleep, sleep. Salvation Army there, "Cup of tea?" Further down the road, Church Army. "Cup of tea? One penny."

Driver Alfred Finnigan, 5th Division, Royal Field Artillery, 1896-2005

I got into the Grand Place, the great square in front of the Ypres Cloth Hall, before moving up the line, and towards me came an squad of men, perhaps twenty in number. An officer was in front of them and they moved mechanically, lord knows how they'd suffered at the front.

I'd never seen men so absolutely done up, finished. They were healthy but they were beaten, physically beaten.

[Ed. Many of the infantrymen who passed through Ypres into rest, also marched through the town of Poperinge, 10 kilometres to the west. Although damaged by shellfire, much of the town was largely intact. One of the best-known havens there was Talbot House, run by a short bespectacled padre, Tubby Clayton, a man who was loved by all who met him. Talbot House, known to the men as Toc H, was opened in December 1915 and offered friendship and relaxation to all: a club for Everyman. Just as importantly, the house also had a chapel at the top, the Upper Room, in which many thousands of men took communion, before going back into the line.]

Air Mechanic Henry Allingham, No12 Squadron, Royal Naval Air Service, 1896-

One day a week, I had some time off and I was wandering about in the town of Poperinge with nothing much to do. As I walked up this road, I saw a chalk message on an old board, all smeared, and there was something about a meeting. "What's that all about?" I thought, and so I walked down the side to find an old stable that was knocked about a bit and there was old Tubby Clayton just making up a lovely bowl of roses. With all the trouble in the world, the sight of those flowers was a right tear-jerker if you were that way inclined. "Aren't they lovely?" he said. "They've just arrived from Blighty this morning." I admired them, and said, "What goes on here?" He was an army chaplain. "There are three or four other fellows in there and I'm going to have communion," and I said, "All right, I'm in." And I went in and took communion.

Tubby was a good man, he did a lot for those boys. They could spill the beans to him. If they'd trouble at home he'd listen and try and iron it out for them, if he could.

Private Harry Patch, 7th Duke of Cornwall's Light Infantry, 1898-
You couldn't relax unless you had the chance to go down to Poperinge into Toc H, that's the only time you could forget the strains of war for a couple of hours. Tubby Clayton ran the place and was the life and soul of the party. He had a deep, almost bass, voice, and he could sing a good song and tell a good tale. He would sing any old chorus including, I remember, the Ivor Novello song "Keep the Home Fires Burning". The only time I heard that song in Belgium was Tubby singing it in Toc H. There were games going on, and you could join in, or, if you wanted to borrow a book, you could, and the price of a book was your cap, which was returned to you when you brought it back. I believe Toc H at one time was used as a grain store, and all the grain had been stored in the upstairs room. I take it the wheat was in the centre, as the middle was a bit dodgy and everyone used to sit around the edge.

The room at the top was his chapel. Tubby upstairs became a different man to the Tubby downstairs. He tried to reassure people in that room, to the best of his ability, that everything was all right. He knew damn well it wasn't. The altar was an old carpenter's bench he'd found somewhere, and he knew, as I think most of the people who went in that room knew, that there were people there who were about to go up to the front line and would not come back.

STRESS AND COMRADESHIP

Rifleman Robert Renwick, MM, 16th King's Royal Rifle Corps, 1896-1997
We had a big, fit Welshman, a bit older than me. We were in action at Arras and facing a lot of machine gun fire, and he kept on turning to go back. In the end I said, "For goodness sake, Taffy, pull yourself together, you have a sporting chance going forward, you have a chance

to come through, but if you go back down the line unwounded you know what to expect." I talked to him until he pulled himself together and the incident was never mentioned again. He gave way that day, but he came out all right. You never know how any two men will react and he was the last you'd expect to go back.

Lieutenant G B Jameson, 72nd Brigade, Royal Field Artillery, 1892-1999

People crack, you can't blame them. We got as far as the old German line, roughly a hundred yards from the crest of Vimy Ridge. The Germans had been driven back and their heavy guns began pounding the land they'd lost. We were up there for a week after it was taken, and to avoid the enemy fire we were shifting our guns about, just to get out of the general pattern of salvos that were coming over.

The rain was lashing down as we tried to work in the old German front line trench, calculating our barrages. A gun sheet protected us from the filthy weather, but as shells crashed around us, the canvas sheet billowed and the light would go out. It was very trying. One of the subalterns was called Lancaster, known to us all as Husky Jake, a striking-looking fellow from South America. We'd love to listen to him on the telephone, saying such things as "You're no bloody good in this battery if you can't talk about pampas grass."

Well, we were in this trench and the light was going off and on, and eventually he grabbed a pair of gumboots. "My God, I can't stand this any longer," and he dashed off into the night. Of course it was muddy outside, you could hardly put a hand out without it going into a shell hole full of water. We looked at each other and thought, five minutes and he'll either be buried in a shell hole full of water or killed.

About half an hour later he turned up again, soaked to the skin, covered from head to foot in mud and filth. He'd obviously fallen into a shell hole, and he looked a sorry mess. The pressure was so great, his nerve just cracked, yet, he was still carrying these gumboots. "Jake, why the devil didn't you put your gumboots on?" we asked. "I took the wrong ones. I took Macdonald's." Jake was about six feet two and Macdonald was about five feet four.

Driver Alfred Henn, 3rd Battery, Warwickshire Royal Horse Artillery, 1897-2000
A good pal of mine was a damn good wheel driver on the limber, but he was very, very windy. If there was danger about and there was a railway arch, he wouldn't miss the chance to get down and under cover. One day, we were waiting to go up the line with ammunition when suddenly there was a lot of shellfire. Horace, he got the wind up, made a dive for an empty trench and left the mules. But this time, as he dived, one of the mules kicked him in the face. Anyway, a month or two afterwards he had a recommendation for a medal from one of the corporals who used to like him. He'd said that Horace had been wounded looking after his mules but he hadn't, he got wounded running away. He got the Military Medal. Horace was ever such a nice chap, he was too good to be in the army. We all liked him and I thought it was a damn good way to get a medal.

Private Archie Richards, 25th Battalion Tank Corps, 1897-1998
You are mates. You're so closely associated all the time, see, and when you're in action it's closer than ever. You're all so near to being annihilated and of course that draws you together. There was a brotherly feeling and that extended to the officer. Outside the tank, he would have to change his attitude, be a little more formal, but cooped up inside the tank with us, when we might all go up together, he was pally.

Private Dick Trafford, 1/9th King's Liverpool Regiment, 1898-1999
Being a machine gunner was a lot different than having a rifle because you'd more protection, and you'd all the men beside you, your party, five in all. So you'd always somebody with you if you were injured

and that was a great comfort, if anything happened you'd always got somebody with you.

Private Smiler Marshall, No195155, 8th Machine Gun Squadron, Machine Gun Corps (Cavalry), 1897-2005
The biggest thing is holding your fire. We'll say a German reconnoitering party, perhaps 100 or 120 men, and half are going round one side, half the other with the idea of caging you in, and the officer is telling you to hold your fire, well, that's the biggest shock of the lot, the biggest test, and you get the wind up a bit because they're coming on and you're not allowed to fire. Of course as soon as you fire they scatter, but perhaps you'll only kill a couple, wound a few more, and the rest might scarper back to their trench, well, the officer wants to bag as many as he can.

Then he gives the order and you press that button brrrrrr, and you can see them fall or jump for cover, and you don't feel the slightest thing, not the slightest. You are there just on a job. It's either you or them. What are you going to do? You're going to defend your mates, of course you are.

Private Dick Trafford, 1/9th King's Liverpool Regiment, 1898-1999
Your mind was on the job in hand because your life depended on your friends and theirs on you. Have I got the height right, am I too low or am I dead centre…dead right. Things like that pass your mind. Am I sweeping the gun too fast or too slow? If you're on the slow side you've a better chance of hitting the target than what you have if you're swivelling the gun too fast. The better the sweep, the better chance you have of hitting somebody, and one bullet could kill one fellow and wound another or it might pass through and kill two. You've always a chance, but a lot of it is guess work and experience; that's the art of being a machine gunner, when to fire and when not to fire, when to sweep or not sweep.

Private Harry Patch, 7th Duke of Cornwall's Light Infantry, 1898-
We were a little group on our own, five of us, although we were part of C Company, part of the Regiment, of course. Number 1, he was a lance corporal and he came from Henley on Thames. I was a plumber; he was an electrician. Number 3 came from Truro, numbers 4 and 5 came from Falmouth, one was a shoemaker; the other a grocer. That was our team.

We took our orders from the officers but when we were in the trenches we were just that little body alone, and we shared everything. I used to get a parcel from home about every fortnight, and in that parcel there would be an ounce of tobacco, two packets of twenty cigarettes, some sweets – if the grocer could scrounge them – and a few cakes. Number 4 on the Lewis gun and I were pipe smokers so that ounce of tobacco was cut in half, half was mine and half was his. The forty cigarettes were divided amongst the other three, thirteen each and they used to take it in turns who should have the odd one. Cakes, chocolates, anything else, were all divided. If you had a pair of clean socks and a fellow had socks with holes in, he'd have the clean socks and throw the others away.

Private Andrew Bowie, 1st Cameron Highlanders, 1897-2002
We tolerated and understood each other. Men would swear at one another, swear about each other, but the true fact was there was always that other bond of friendship; we were still friends. We accepted things, and our role in the army. We might call someone a bloody so-and-so one day, but if we heard that chap was badly wounded in the next bay, everyone would go at once to see what they could do for him. Your pals are almost family, a very rough family, mind. Everybody would have their own pals, the teetotallers got together, and those who liked a drink. Likewise, there was brotherly love within the signallers, and it was the same with the machine gunners. I was a bomber when I went out first time, and you shared everything with your group.

Comradeship was a necessity, and it was difficult thing to accept if you lost your pal. You had to get over it, but there was no way of sharing any feeling with anybody else; it was your personal loss. Mind, you often didn't know they were good until you were parted.

Air Mechanic Henry Allingham, No12 Squadron, Royal Naval Air Service, 1896-
The friendship in that war was something else, it really was. Everybody was your pal. The man you sat beside, you'd talk to him as if you'd known him for a thousand years, as it were, and he was a complete stranger.

Private Ted Francis, 16th Warwickshire Regiment, 1896-1996
I saw a friend, a pal I'd enlisted with. He was struck down during an attack with a terrible leg wound, his leg half blown off. We were under instructions not to go to him – his screams, sometimes, really, I can hear them now. He was in front of me, and a shell landed practically a yard from him. He fell into a shell hole while I had to push on and leave him in a very dangerous position. I knew no Red Cross men or stretcher bearers would go near him, they would merely get killed themselves. His screams, not for one hour but for several hours, you could hear them above everything else, even above shell fire. It was at least ten hours before anyone could get to him, and by that time his breath had failed and his wounded leg had sunk into mud and water, hastening death.

He was left there, he wasn't gathered in, because there are hundreds of dead lying about and stretcher bearers have no time to mess with dead people, they are left to the rats. Now is there anything more horrible than that? He was wounded in front of my very eyes; that was really when I felt that I'd lost something that could never be put back. I'd lost a friend, who for years had talked and laughed and joked and gone for walks with me, and the idea of losing such a friend was not in my thinking at all.

[Ed. The sense of comradeship and fraternity with other men could often be so strong that some soldiers removed from the fighting line felt an element of guilt at their relative good fortune. Equally, those whose lives were considered 'cushy' by other soldiers were often looked down upon and even scorned.]

Lieutenant Norman Edwards, Tank Corps, 1894-1999

I was posted to the Tank Corps School of Gunnery, where I became O.C. Battle Practice Wing. It was very hard work because we had six hundred men a week going through the school.

I used to feel rather ashamed of myself at being down at the base, training these chaps. They were going up to the firing line and I was able to sleep in a billet every night, and I couldn't help feeling a bit of a cad. I was posted to do this training job and I did it to the best of my ability. Nevertheless, I tried to get out of it, to go back up the line where I could look my brothers in the eye. A General was doing one of his tours and came round the gunnery school. I said, "Is there any chance, Sir, of my being transferred to a fighting unit? I've got two brothers up in the front line and I feel I should be up there with them and not at a base." "If you can find somebody who can do your job as well as you are doing it, then yes," he said. I thought, "If the General says that, I can't do any more." I'd been wounded in action, which was a solace in some ways. I went and got on with my job.

Trooper Ben Clouting, 4th (Royal Irish) Dragoon Guards, 1897-1990

I was a servant to an officer who had been made an instructor at the Cavalry School of Equitation at a town called Cayeux sur Mer, where the mouth of the river Somme met the sea.

At Cayeux, those billeted with me were glad to be out of the war, but I became restless. I considered myself a fighting soldier and I was bored with being everybody's servant. Being at Cayeux felt like being in the peacetime army again, and I increasingly became tired of the school and in the end I asked if I could be returned to my Regiment.

When I got back to the billet I told the others, and they all pronounced me mad for giving up such an easy job. They were all content to see out the war in luxury. The corporal in particular had had three days' leave to get married in England, and had no intention of going anywhere near the front again if he had any say in the matter.

My decision was prompted by an incident that hurt my pride. I had been exercising an officer's horses. Both were fine, thoroughbreds. I was riding one and leading the other, when I happened to pass a stationary battery of artillery, and as I went by, one of the drivers turned to his mate and shouted, "And what did you do in the war, Daddy?"

We were all miles behind the line, but he, at least, would be heading towards it, and that was enough for him to feel I was having a cushy number. I rode on because it was my business to ride on, but it stung me.

[Ed. Ben Clouting was born and raised in the countryside and grew up with horses. For this reason he, like so many others such as Smiler Marshall, had joined the cavalry in order to continue working with the animals and to ride. Before the advent of a fully mechanized army, animals played a vital part in military life, and during the war hundreds of thousands of horse and mules were transported overseas and subsequently maimed or killed close to the front line.]

Lieutenant G B Jameson, 72nd Brigade, Royal Field Artillery, 1892-1999

It wasn't always possible to send ammunition in wagons; you often had to pack it, six shells to a horse. As we were going up on one occasion, I saw this fellow, he was lying in the road cuddling his horse's head and weeping his heart out. The packhorse he'd been leading had been hit and killed. Men got so attached to horses, in some ways men could look after themselves, the horses couldn't, they were dumb animals.

Driver Alfred Henn, 3rd Battery, Warwickshire Royal Horse Artillery, 1897-2000

We had harnessed up the horses when Captain Dixon came down and told us that we had to take mules, as horses were in short supply. I'd never ridden a mule before and I got along pretty well as we approached Hellfire Corner, just beyond Ypres. We used to pause quite a distance from this important crossroads, because the Germans regularly sent a salvo of shells over, and then we used to make a rush for it. We saved a lot of lives doing that. Anyway, I rushed with the others right into the middle, and then the mules stood still. They would not move. All the others had gone and left me stranded. I got off and pulled them back, front, everywhere, and I thought it's just about time now, I'll get a salvo of shells. Sure enough, one shell dropped just behind us and it shot the mules forward. As I happened to be hanging on to the reins, they dragged me along and into safety.

Driver Alfred Finnigan, 5th Division Royal Field Artillery, 1896-2005

Near Hellfire Corner the ground was frightful, absolutely frightful. I was leading a horse loaded down with ammunition shells. I was very tired and like a fool, I mounted the animal across the pack and it walked into a shell hole and toppled over. I couldn't get it to move. It was lying on its side, and, I am ashamed to talk of this, the horse looked at me out of the corner of its eye as much as to say, "What did you do that for, boss?" I tried to get him out, I tried and tried, but he was stuck. I was distraught, then he made one last tremendous effort and got up. All his offside was thick mud.

Private Harry Patch, 7th Duke of Cornwall's Light Infantry, 1898-

You looked out into No Man's Land between the firing points, and all you could see was a couple of stray dogs looking for something to eat to keep alive. I thought, "Oh well, I don't know, there they are out there, two stray animals, and if they found a biscuit to eat they would start to fight over who should have a bite. Well, what are we doing that's really any different? We're fighting for our lives, just the same."

Private William Golightly, 1st Northumberland Fusiliers, 1898-1992
We had a forward post in front of our trench with the Lewis gun in it. We had managed to camouflage it pretty well and the Germans hadn't spotted it. I remember looking out one night through a little hole and I saw a pair of eyes looking back at me. God almighty! Do you know what it was? It was a bloody cat. It scared the living daylights out of me. There were domestic cats, lost or abandoned and left to run wild, and they survived by eating off the dead, fighting with the rats for food.
[Ed. There were not just domestic cats in the trenches. One senior officer adopted a lion cub he named 'Poilu', won in a Red Cross raffle. Reared on horse-meat, of which there was an abundance, Poilu happily padded along the trenches to the amusement of the men. However, in the end the cub grew too big and the officer was ordered to remove it from front line service. The Germans are also known to have had a lion cub in the trenches. Both animals, one assumes, must have come from a zoo or circus.]

Private Andrew Bowie, 1st Cameron Highlanders, 1897-2002
This man had been sent out from England because of an acute officer shortage. He was in the same dugout as I was, which was built into two sections, one for the officers, with wire beds, and one for the telephone section. There was about a twenty-yard passage between us. One day, he came screaming into my quarters, "Signaller, signaller, mice have pinched my emergency rations!" which consisted of a hard biscuit and a tin of bully beef. Evidently they'd eaten the biscuits. "Mice? You don't see mice round here, it's rats." And he jumped with the idea of rats being there.

Air Mechanic Henry Allingham, No 12 Squadron, Royal Naval Air Service, 1896-

The ground was all colours, it stank and it was offensive. As we moved forward, we passed over Hellfire Corner. There were rats round there as big as cats, and that's no exaggeration. We used to shoot them if we had nothing better to do. You'd shoot at them and if you could hit them end ways, they would be like a tunnel with four legs.

Private Joe Yarwood, 31st Division, Royal Army Medical Corps, 1896-1995

At night time, somewhere about 11 or 12 o'clock, a great big rat used to come right under our bed, snorting away, it used to sound more like a pig than a rat. One evening I thought, "I'll wait for you," and I got an old bayonet that was lying about the dugout and I waited for that stinking rat and sure enough he came snorting along. I crashed down but I only succeeded in breaking the bayonet; that rat got away.

At Festubert, our dugout looked like a glorified chicken coop, with galvanized iron and a pile of sandbags. We were under shell fire and as we made a dash for it, we saw a rat sitting on the doorstep to our dugout, and as we ran towards him, he dived into our dugout and under the blankets.

No sooner were we inside than we went mad, we ran around with our boots in our hands smashing all about us, or with whatever we could lay our hands on. We killed the beast and hung him outside, but the next morning his comrades had disposed of him all right, his body was gone, they'd eaten him.

Lieutenant Norman Dillon, MC, 20th Tank Battalion, Tank Corps, 1896-1997

In battle, pigeons were the only reliable means of sending back information. Each tank had two, and often they carried news of vital importance. During an attack in the Salient, one of my friends, Wagstaff, reached his objective, and, taking pity on his pigeons, fed them on seedy-cake and whiskey. Soon after, his tank got stuck on a tree stump and although the tracks went round, it was immobile. So he tried to send off a pigeon to report his predicament. Opening a port over a track, he pushed the pigeon out but it sat on the track and refused to move. So they started the track, thinking that it would carry the bird forward and it would then fall off and fly when the track doubled under. But the pigeon was having none of this, and, no doubt hoping for more whiskey, started keeping station by marching against the flow of the track.

Private Robert Renwick, MM, 16th King's Royal Rifle Corps, 1896-1997
I had a mate called Jim Morris from Macclesfield. About half a dozen of us were sent out on a reconnoitering patrol to try and get a prisoner, and we met a very heavy German patrol. Jim said, "I'll give out such a yell they'll think there's a battalion coming." He did, and the Germans scattered, but we collared one prisoner and a dog. I suppose the dog was meant to smell our scent and warn them of our approach. When we got back into the line, the bombing officer was on duty and he said, "Halt! Who goes there?" And Jimmy shouts, "King's Royal Rifle Patrol, a prisoner and one dog, Sir". We adopted the dog. Once Jerry's mascot, now it was ours.

Private Harry Patch, 7th Duke of Cornwall's Light Infantry, 1898-
Roaming around the destroyed villages were not just rats but cats, dogs, mice; you name it, we had it. Stray cats would come into the line, and a stray dog occasionally, and, as a rule, they'd be as vicious as hell.

After the war, I worked with a builder who had a terrier that had been born in the trenches. If you were in the same room as the dog, the only way you could get out was if you had a saw in your hand and you showed him the teeth. He was fierce. It was the way they had to live. They survived on what was dead or abandoned.

THIRD YPRES: THE BATTLE FOR PASSCHENDAELE

Lance Corporal Vic Cole, 1st Queen's Own (Royal West Kent Regiment), 1897-1995

The battalion went in by night over the duckboard tracks through Zonnebeke and Sanctuary Wood down to the Menin Road. We spread out, two companies on either side of the road occupying a rough line of craters. I had a Lucas signal lamp on a spike with which I was to flash messages back to Brigade headquarters established in a pillbox on a ridge half a mile away.

When dawn broke, it showed the true horror. As far as the eye could see spread a vast sea of mud and every inch of it lacerated and churned up. Shell craters touched and overlapped on all sides to the horizon, many of them full or half-full of green, slimy water. Beaten down into this mess and half-obliterated were pieces of equipment, fragments of shells, shattered guns and even tanks and the blackened bones and rotting corpses of thousands of men. The new dead lay here and there in khaki heaps. Over this terrible terrain it was our job to go forward and take the next line of pillboxes four hundred yards away.

Lieutenant Norman Dillon, MC, 20th Tank Battalion, Tank Corps, 1896-1997.

It is hard to describe adequately the appalling conditions that existed. The whole countryside was featureless; everything had been obliterated. It resembled a desert covered with shell holes full of water and dead men, and mules pointing rotting limbs to the sky. Many had gone below the surface forever, and the smell of decaying corpses, gas and cordite made it a place for strong stomachs.

So bad was the condition of the "soil" that it took up to 12 hours to extricate a wounded man from the front to a point where an ambulance could reach him. There were duckboard tracks, but to step off them was to invite being bogged down, and of course they were frequently breached by the continuous shellfire.

Corporal Brian Shaw, MM, 2/5th South Staffordshire Regiment, 1898-1999

Some of our forward posts had started to fall back on the orders of an officer, and the word had spread. I was with Lieutenant Butler, an inefficient officer known to us all as 'Blob'. On this occasion, however, he really came to the fore because we started to retire and he suddenly said, "This is wrong, we must stop." He went forward again while I stopped a group of about four men and said that we must go back up.

I suppose everybody in that war has seen a shell go. If you stand behind a six-inch howitzer, you will see the shell vanish to a spot in the distance. Conversely, if you are in the line of fire, you will see the shell arrive but you won't survive because it will burst where you are, but I did. I'd stopped these men, and a three or four inch shell landed at my feet and burst. It laid out these four chaps and knocked me down.

I got up and felt myself all over and found I wasn't wounded, although a small piece of shrapnel about the size of a walnut had hit my small box respirator. This shrapnel had gone through my gas mask and finished up denting a brass button on my tunic and that had stopped it. If I had not had my gas mask on my chest it would have gone straight into my lungs and I would have been dead.

There were lots of gas masks lying about and I could have picked another one up. But I was so pleased with this gas mask that I patched up the hole with a field postcard and a bit of jam, and kept it until we came out of the line.

Private Harry Patch, 7th Duke of Cornwall's Light Infantry, 1898-
I came across a lad from A Company and he was ripped open from his shoulder to his waist by shrapnel, and lying in a pool of blood. When we got to him, he said, "Shoot me." He was beyond all human help, but before we could draw a revolver, he was dead. And the only word he uttered was "Mother". I was with him in the last seconds of his life.

It wasn't a cry of despair, it was a cry of surprise and joy. I think, although I wasn't allowed to see her, I am sure his mother was in the next world to welcome him and he knew it. I was just allowed to see that much and no more, and from that day I've always remembered that cry and that death is not the end.

Two or three Germans had got up out of the trench, and one of them came towards us with a fixed bayonet. He couldn't have had any ammunition, otherwise he would have shot us. My right hand was free; I'd just changed a magazine. I drew my revolver and I shot him in the right shoulder. He dropped his rifle but he came stumbling on, no doubt to kick us to pieces if he could. He shouted something to me and I don't expect it was complimentary. I had four seconds to make my mind up. I had three rounds in that revolver. I could have killed him with my first; I was a crack shot. What shall I do? Four seconds to make my mind up. I gave him his life. I shot him above the ankle, and above the knee. I brought him down but I didn't kill him. For him, the war was over. He would be picked up, interrogated, passed back to a prisoner of war camp, and at the end of the war he would rejoin his family.

Lance Corporal Vic Cole, 1st Queen's Own (Royal West Kent Regiment), 1897-1995
At zero hour the regiment went over, slipping and sliding in the mud, bunching up, spreading out, going single file. Meanwhile, our artillery, large and small, with incessant scream and thunder, flung tons of shells towards the enemy. Then came a strange pause in the general uproar, with both sides trying to ascertain the new positions of their respective front lines.

For ten minutes the battlefield was deathly quiet; it was pouring with rain. Then again the sudden rattle of machine guns and rifle fire and the smack-smack of bullets as they passed overhead or sloshed into the mud, followed by the whine of projectiles coming over in counter-barrage. I sent some signals, but whether headquarters received them, I've no idea, because nothing came back. I stuck the lamp into the top of a pillbox that was being used as battalion headquarters and soon after, a lump of metal hit it and put me out of action. A number of stragglers from other units began to accumulate behind our pillbox and there we crouched together whilst the storm of missiles passed overhead.

A kid came over, spewing up blood. There was a concrete hut on the Menin Road, a dressing station about fifty yards from the pillbox, and I took him down. He'd been shot in the chest and I expect he died, but I pushed him down through the mud and shell holes and got him to this first aid post where chaps were lying outside waiting their turn for treatment. I squeezed in and there were men everywhere, and blood, and coughing and moaning, that was enough for me.

I returned to the pillbox where half a dozen men continued to take shelter, and they looked at me with amazement. "They were shooting at you all the way across and you didn't notice!" I didn't. By this time they'd got another man on a stretcher, badly wounded, and they were told to take him down. Everything was in such a mess that as I leant over him to say, "Good luck, old man," the water from my tin hat tipped onto his face. "Get out of it," and he swore at me.

A few Germans began coming across. We had a pot at them round the side of this pillbox before we realized they'd been taken prisoner, and were being left to make their own way back. We stopped shooting and the ragamuffin crew I was with, not West Kents I'd like to say, began nicking everything they could off these poor buggers, making them empty their pockets of watches and money and suchlike, while the rain slashed down in their faces.

From the interior of the pillbox our Colonel emerged. His name was Twistleton-Wyckeman-Fiennes, a wiry grey-faced figure. He was very agitated and was waving his Colt .45 revolver around. Spying me, and practically sticking his revolver in my face, he gave me an order. "Corporal, get hold of these men and take them up to the next line of pillboxes." Apparently our C Company on the south side of the Menin

Road had been captured, and there was a hole in the line that we were to help fill.

I got as far as the next row of pillboxes, when an officer came along with a group of jocks. They were shouting and pointing to a man stumbling across with his head in his hands as if he was blind. "Look after him," they shouted. I couldn't, of course, it would have taken half an hour to get over to him and, in any case, he was going in the right direction. Shortly afterwards I looked back and he was gone. Just then a shell burst in the air above me, casting shrapnel all about. Blood streamed down my face and my arm felt immediately numb. I was wondering what to do when another officer came by, wounded in the shoulder. "You going back to Headquarters? Tell them that Lieutenant Lithgow is wounded and he's gone back." That was all the excuse I needed, so I struggled back and into the dugout and reported to the Colonel, wiping blood out of my eyes as I did so.

Lieutenant Norman Dillon, MC, 20th Tank Battalion, Tank Corps, 1896-1997
I went up the Menin Road with Basil Groves, another Section Commander, to show him the area. There was another attack in preparation, which fortunately did not come off. We got pinned down by shellfire and took shelter in an old German dugout under the road, where we found a two-bunk bed with a dead German in each. There had been a small advance and these poor creatures had been left to die. As we were squatting on the ground, rigor mortis apparently ended and a wet arm flopped over the top bed and caught Basil a clip. We examined the bodies for signs of life, but there were none.

Corporal Brian Shaw, MM, 2/5th South Staffordshire Regiment, 1898-1999
The Germans had concreted all the houses in the area with five feet of concrete facing the British lines, but very little at the back, just enough to stop the splash of shrapnel. About twenty of us were sheltering in a

former barn of some sort. There was plenty of concrete over the top, plenty facing our lines, but only about nine inches to strengthen the back wall and of course the enemy knew exactly where everything was because they'd been there. I remember very well that each time a shell burst on the roof, the concussion put the candle out, so after a time we stopped bothering to light it. Nobody said anything, we knew the situation we were in. This went on for a long time, until two of the boys decided to make a dash for it but a shell caught them outside and they were killed. I made up my mind to wait, wondering when the next shell would be. It was very wearying on the nerves. I'd got a tin of 50 cigarettes and I was lighting them one after the other. One shell had already hit the back wall creating a hole through which we could see the stars. If another one came through, it would burst inside and we would all be killed. Eventually one shell did come, and buried itself in the floor. It was a dud and it was the last shell they fired.

Private Arthur Barraclough, 2/4th Duke of Wellington's Regiment, 1898-2004

The battalion was being held up in an attack, and we were told to take the Lewis gun and go to the flank and enfilade the enemy. So we found this old building, it was only a few bricks, and we got down and gave them a blast or two. I was lying beside the gun, firing it, and the other two lads were behind, filling the magazines. Within a minute, bullets started flying past us and then shells started to come over and one hit bang in the middle of the four, but all the blast seemed to go one way, taking the gun and the two lads with it. They completely disappeared but the gunner and I were untouched.

Lance Corporal Vic Cole, 1st Queen's Own (Royal West Kent Regiment), 1897-1995

We held our position all that night and all the next day, crouching in shell holes and enduring a vicious strafing by German aircraft. Night again. As each man was relieved at his post, he made his own way down to the rear. Personally I had just about had enough. My only food for the previous 24 hours had been a tin of apple jam (with a strawberry label on it), I was plastered with mud from head to foot and had the damaged Lucas lamp and battery to carry as well as my ordinary equipment.

It's so very vivid. Even now I can shut my eyes and see where I am, and then I open them and I'm back out of it.

I made my way with my broken lamp, my rifle slung over my shoulder, until I hit the Menin Road, which was identified by the stumps of poplar trees and cobblestones. There were various shadows moving here and there, dimly-lit figures, glimpsed now and again in the pale moonlight or the flickering Very lights, but I was on my own. They had markers on the way out and a bloke would shout, "West Kent?" "Yes." "Down there."

Crossing over the next ridge, it was possible to relax and give one's mind and muscles a rest. I arrived dead-beat at our assembly point at Dickebusch, followed by more chaps gradually coming down one by one, covered in mud. At the YMCA, I knocked back an enormous mug of tea laced with rum and then slept like a log for eighteen hours.

Private Harry Patch, 7th Duke of Cornwall's Light Infantry, 1898-
The battalion had been relieved at ten o'clock at night and we were going through to the support line over a piece of open ground, when a whiz-bang burst just behind me. The force of the explosion threw me to the floor, but I didn't know that I'd been hit for two or three minutes; burning metal knocks the pain out of you at first. I saw blood, so I took a field dressing out and put it on the wound. Then the pain came.

I don't know how long I lay there. It may have been ten minutes, it may have been half an hour, but a stretcher came along and I was picked up and taken to the dressing station. There were a lot of seriously wounded there, so I had to wait. I lay there that night and all the next day, and the next evening a doctor came and had a look at the wound. He could see shrapnel buried inside and said, "Would you like me to take it out?" I said, "Yes, it's very painful, Sir." He said, "Got no anaesthetic. All that was used in the battle and we haven't been able to replace it. I shall have to take it out as you are." I thought for a minute and said, "How long will you be?" He said, "Two minutes." So I thought, well, two minutes of agony and I shall get rid of all the pain, so I said, "Okay, go on, take it out." Two orderlies got hold, one on each arm, and two got hold of my legs, and the doctor got busy.

In those two minutes I could have damn well killed him, the pain was terrific. I take it he must have cut his way around the metal and got hold of the shrapnel with his tweezers, so that he could drag it out. Anyway, he got it and asked, "Do you want it as a souvenir?" The shrapnel was about two inches long, broad at one end, and about half-an-inch thick with a sharp edge. I said, "No, I've had the bloody stuff too long already."

I didn't know what had happened to the others at first. But I was told afterwards that I had lost three good mates. The three ammunition carriers were blown to pieces. My reaction was terrible, it was like losing a part of my life. When one day they sound the last post for me, I'm sure I'll be meeting my friends again.

Private Dick Trafford, 1/9th Kings Liverpool Regiment, 1898-1999
To go through Passchendaele is to go through hell. There's no other way of putting it. We succeeded at Passchendaele when the Germans left it and said, "Here you are, here's Passchendaele – it's all yours." That's the way I look at it.

Private Andrew Bowie, 1st Cameron Highlanders, 1897-2002
We were coming out of the trenches into rest. I was in charge of the signal section and I asked the captain beforehand if we could go out of the line on our own; we generally did that because we could read maps and I knew the rendezvous. He said, "Yes, signaller, take your men out." As we went, we came to this wire put up by the South Africans, and just as we were passing through, the Germans decided

to send a salvo over. I was carrying a Fuller phone on my back, and one of the party, a nervous type, shouted that he was stuck. I went back to help him and pulled him off the wire, but in doing so, I got stuck. Another salvo came and went over my head, and there I was stood upright, stuck. The next lot came over and exploded; the force of the percussion threw me out of the wire, dashing me on the ground. I didn't know what to do, but I got up, picked up the Fuller phone and made for the railway line. I knew there was a ditch, and flung myself in, being stung all over the backside by nettles, and lay there panting. Then I heard Jock's voice, "Andrew, where are you?" He had come back for me. I made a noise of some description and he picked me up and brought me out. I had a touch of shell-shock, I lost my voice for a week and could only make husky noises for "yes" and "no". The doctor wanted to send me to hospital but I wouldn't go, because if you got to hospital you would come back to another battalion, and you'd lose all your friends.

Private Arthur Barraclough, 2/4th Duke of Wellington's Regiment, 1898-2004

Within a couple of days of losing my mates I was wounded in the heel while out collecting the rations. I was picked up and sent down to a base hospital where, through a bit of luck, I was sent to England and a hospital in Wigan. While I was there a couple of people came round the wards with a list of missing soldiers. They asked if we knew anyone called so and so, and they called out one of these lads' names who'd been with me in the machine gun team, so I said, "Yes, I know that lad, he's dead." They asked, "Are you sure?" and I said, "As sure as I can be, he just got blown to bits." Then they asked me, "Would you like to go to Chesterfield? That lad you just named lived in Chesterfield and it would be a great pleasure to us if you could go and tell his mother, tell it to her nice, that he isn't a prisoner of war or anything like that, that he is dead and won't be coming home." The man had lived in a mining district. I found the house and told them they wouldn't have to expect him coming home. I said he was killed, but didn't tell them how it happened. They had been hoping he was a prisoner, and I had to say to them, "Sorry, no, I know for a fact he won't be coming home." It was a bit of a hard do for them. He was only a young man like myself, about twenty. They were heartbroken really, but they thanked me for going to tell them.

Private Samuel Allen Short, No36556, 2/10th London Regiment, 26 May 1899-3 January 2000
A family friend, Teddy Wells, was reported wounded, then wounded and missing, then missing believed killed; they never discovered his body. Teddy had been serving with the Royal West Kent Regiment, when he was killed on the Somme. His parents were relatives of our family doctor, Dr Paxton. He was a widower and they kept house for him and helped bring up his son, George. Mr and Mrs Wells had a daughter, Dorothy, and we were close friends with the whole family.

About a year later, his mother had a visit from a soldier who produced his wallet and the contents and said that he had found it on the body of a sergeant. All we could presume was that this sergeant had recovered the wallet from Teddy's body with the intention of sending it home and in turn he had been killed and it had got into the possession of this other soldier who brought it back.

Private Alfred Anderson, 1/5th Black Watch, 1896-

I was badly wounded in the neck by shrapnel and sent home, and a friend of mine, Lyon Jeffrey, took over my job as an officer's servant. Since our youth, Lyon and I had spent a lot of time together. We were both apprentice joiners and we used to get together in the shed at the back of the shop and do fretwork in the evenings. We were in the same class and there was just a few months difference in age between us. Like me, he'd gone out with the battalion in 1914.

Some time after I came home, I heard that Lyon had been killed. He had three sisters: one was postmistress and the other two worked in the house. So I said to my mother, "I'm going round to see the Jeffreys to give them my condolences." It was the youngest daughter, Rose, who came to the door. She was the postmistress, and someone I'd known from school, so I said, "I've come round here to offer my condolences for you losing Lyon," and I said, " I'm very sorry about it all. I hope the three of you can accept this, me calling round here like this." "Oh, it's not that," she said, "but you're here and he's not." You know, I felt terrible. I said, "I'm sorry you feel that way about it. I wasn't even in the country when he was killed." The other girls were in the back kitchen and came in when they heard my voice, and they kind of broke it up.

[Ed. When men returned to France after a period in hospital, they were rarely sent straight back into the line. Arthur Barraclough, Andrew Bowie, and Frank Sumpter all passed through the Bull Ring, the training camp at Etaples. The Bull Ring was infamous; it was used both to harden new men sent out to France and to act as a refresher for those who had been convalescent. Its rigid discipline, enforced by men called 'Canaries' because of the yellow band worn around their caps. They were universally hated by the men, and led in 1917 to a famous mutiny.]

Private Frank Sumpter, 1st Rifle Brigade, 1897-1999
The men had to fix bayonets and charge the sandbags. A sergeant ran alongside and as the man was about to stick the bayonet into the sandbag, he knocked the bayonet out of his hand, telling him what sort of a bloody fool he was, and what use was he with a bayonet. "If you're going to stab a man, stab a man, don't play at it." The man wasn't holding the rifle tight enough, of course he's holding it tight enough to stick it in a sack but not ready for a man knocking it out of his hand. Then, when he bent down to pick it up, they'd give him a kick or punch him. They'd call him everything under the sun for dropping the rifle, giving him a shove one way and another man would shove

him back. "This man needs waking up!" Men were being pushed around, some of them straight from convalescence or hospital and sent for re-training. I saw two Canaries, one each side of a man, and both of them were shouting in his ear and when he put his hand up to stop the noise they knocked him down. This brutality was going on all over the place, and people would apply to go back to their regiments, they'd had enough. This was a month before the mutiny.

Private Ted Francis, 16th Royal Warwickshire Regiment, 1896-1996
At Etaples, young fellows aged between eighteen and twenty-two were put to drill with sergeants who were as cruel as could be to these chaps, who, by this time, were mostly just conscripts. They would march them till they almost fell down, and if they fell, they would get a kick up the backside to get up.

I was watching this until a Military Police sergeant came over and says, "What are you looking at? Get off." I think from that day to this, I detested the army. I saw these poor chaps in their drill with these sergeants who had no idea of being easy with fellows who knew nothing about being soldiers.

Private Frank Sumpter, 1st Rifle Brigade, 1897-1999
We had a very unpleasant situation. All the men were disgruntled and grumbling but they were afraid of the Canaries. The men were threatening all sorts of things, that they'd get one canary on his own to do him up. Others said, "No, don't do that, you'll have to do the lot or we'll all get punished for it."

Everything had to be done at the double. They didn't have to give any punishment, the whole thing was a punishment. If the Canaries were taking a man to the captain to get him punished, they punished him on the way, pushing him around to each other, punching him under the chin and saying, "Hold your head up." We couldn't understand it, we'd never seen anything like it before, none of us had.

Private Andrew Bowie, 5th Cameron Highlanders, 1897-2002
We were in the main street at Etaples, and a party of about twelve men marched past me with one man in the middle without any hat on. I can see his face now, he was aged about 25 and was staring straight in front. As they went by, I said to a soldier, "What are they doing there?" And he said, "Oh, they are taking that fellow away to be shot." Just like that. I went over the words in my head, "Taking him away to be shot". It looked mighty like it, too, the set-up, I mean, they were all round him, twelve of them. The sight was a terrible blow to a young soldier like myself.
[Ed. In 1917, Andrew had contracted trench foot and was sent to hospital in England. He arrived back in France on 11 September 1917 and proceeded to Etaples, where a mutiny had broken out two days before. It seems certain that the prisoner he saw was one of the mutineers, and may possibly have been Corporal Jesse Short who appeared at a Field General Court Martial on 12 September and was sentenced to death. Short was not executed until 4 October and was the only mutineer to be shot.]

Private Eustace Rushby, 1/4th Royal Berkshire Regiment, 1896-1996
The first execution I saw was at Kandis, not far from Doullens, in September 1916, near a Flying Corps aerodrome, and the other occasion was behind Poperinge, and this was September 1917. The firing squad consisted of eighteen men and the witnesses would be anything up to fifty, including ten men from four regiments. I was in the firing party at Poperinge. We found out afterwards that he was from a Worcester Regiment. There were six men lying, six kneeling, and six standing, and we were rehearsed before the victim arrived. We would receive instructions beforehand, but during the actual event there was not a word, not a sound, it was all done by signal. As soon as we fired, we dropped our rifles down where they were, and stepped back clear in our three ranks, and they would come along and check to see that we'd fired. Anyone who refused to fire or fired wide would

be severely dealt with. The shooting took place in an orchard. The man was led out by two red caps with a gas helmet round the wrong way. They would warn you it was an order, but they knew it was no good choosing someone who would point blank refuse to fire or whose nerve wouldn't allow them to do it. We were excused fatigues or guard duty for a week.

[Ed. It seems likely that the first man Eustace saw shot for desertion was Private Charles Deeper of 1/4th Royal Berkshire Regiment. Forty men from the battalion were paraded as witnesses to the execution. The second man shot was probably Sergeant John Wall of the 3rd Worcester Regiment, also for desertion.]

Rifleman Robert Renwick, MM, 16th King's Royal Rifle Corps, 1896-1997

A mate of mine was on a firing squad, and it was a long time before I dared ask him how the chap had died. I still remember his name, Thomas Donovan, a London lad, and he was no coward. He was just fed up with the life. I knew him personally. He was more of a daredevil than anything else. The first time he deserted, he dressed himself up as a Frenchman; his intention to make it to the coast. But he couldn't resist his cigarettes and he kept coming back to our canteen in Amien, and the chaplain recognized him and gave him away. He was a prisoner for a while.

We had a Sergeant Myttion, who was going on guard duty one night, and, knowing Donovan, I said to him, "Don't let him escape, mind. If he wants to go to the toilet, send two men." He made a mistake, he just sent one man. Myttion thought Donovan was a long time coming back, and when he went he found the guard with his hands tied with a rifle cord and a dressing pad wedged in his mouth and Donovan gone. He nearly got to the coast this time before he was picked up. Of course he had to face the penalty. My mate was one of the firing squad and I asked him how Donovan had taken it and he said he'd never wavered.

Private Walter Green, No3275, 20th Durham Light Infantry, 26 November 1897-5 March 1998

There was a windmill at Reninghurst, near Ypres, and the guard who was on duty that day noticed that the sail started to go around, stopped, then started to go round again. And he said, "That's funny, there's no wind, but it keeps stopping and starting." He couldn't understand it, so he got it into his head to call out the guard. The duty officer took some men and observed what was going on and then went and arrested a Belgian who was using the position of the sails to signal to the enemy. I'd seen this farmer on several occasions going about his normal work. Anyway, they took him away and about half an hour afterwards somebody came along and said, "They've shot that bloke," and we said, "Really?" He said they must have tried him straightaway and brought up a firing squad and shot him.

[Ed. A number of civilians came under suspicion for similar actions. The men of the 1st Cheshire Regiment were very doubtful about one Belgian farmer who ploughed with a white horse. Whenever this horse appeared in the field, a German battery opened up on the troops. Whether this was pure coincidence or actual collaboration is not known.]

Lieutenant Norman Collins, 1/4th Seaforth Highlanders, 1897-1998

There was to be a court martial of two men: one had a family of about six children and the other was an officer in a Highland Regiment. My job was as an 'officer's friend' – and officers had to have a personal guard. I had to look after him for twenty-four hours and we got to know each other quite well and had a chat. He told me quite a few things about himself. He had taken too much rum when he had gone over the top and he was incapable of carrying out his duty properly. He was a charming man and I felt very sorry for him. I knew the least punishment he would get would be to be reduced to the ranks and sent back to the regiment. But the next day he shot himself, and of course they wanted to know where he'd got the revolver. He didn't get it from me and I was able to prove that, but I was almost court-martialled because I was the last one with him.

Lance Corporal Vic Cole, 1st Queen's Own (Royal West Kent Regiment), 1897-1995

After the fighting at Ypres, my brigade was withdrawn and sent to the comparatively quiet Italian front. While there, I was sent with a little party to Padua for a course on the gentle art of pigeon flying. It was the day before Christmas Eve and that evening a few of us went out into the town, but while walking about I got toothache that only got worse as the evening wore on. In the end I went into a café to sit down and the owner started plying me with grappa, which he thought would help. Later, when I stepped out into the cold, my head went round and I started to stagger about. I saw the bridge I had to cross, but in getting there I managed to walk into a wall, which cut my nose and bruised my face, and before I knew it, a couple of scruffy Italian Red Caps, military police, arrested me and threw me in clink. I was put in a cell, and they took away my shoelaces and belt.

I looked around the stone-built room. It had a hole in one corner in which to urinate, the smell from which almost made me vomit, and a straw mattress to sleep on. It was indescribably filthy. About two hours later, someone brought a dixie of soup which I didn't like the look of, but, fiddling around, I found a pack of playing cards on a beam that ran across the cell, and from then on I played Patience all day to pass the time. The next morning I was taken to see an Italian Captain who told me I was arrested for causing a disturbance of the peace, but that he'd sent for an escort from the regiment to take me back. No one was in any hurry to retrieve me. For ten days I remained in prison, eating soup brought three times a day, and I was allowed out for half an hour's exercise every morning. I was unable to wash or shave throughout my incarceration.

My escort arrived, and after a good clean up I was taken back to my unit to see Colonel Twisleton-Wykeman-Fiennes. I don't suppose he liked a Kitchener man upsetting the discipline of the regiment, so he put me down for a Field General Court Martial. I carried on normal duties for several weeks until the day of the trial, which took place five miles away in a village. I was charged with drunkenness whilst on active service – I had not realized the magnitude of this charge – which, some kind person informed me, could be punishable by death. When I was marched in for my trial, I found that I had also been accused of assaulting the police of a friendly country. My sergeant major made an able defence of my character in front of the court (hardly recognizable to myself, let it be said!) but it worked. "Forty-nine days No1 Field Punishment, reduced to the ranks, with pay stopped under Royal Warrant," which meant that I was to lose twice that number of days' pay. I was marched out.

I'd got off with a comparatively light sentence. They brought the Regiment out on three sides. I was in the centre and the Regimental Sergeant Major read out the sentence. The stripes on my arm had already been loosened so he could pull them off. After the ritual humiliation was all over, the regiment marched away and I walked back to the billets to be told "Right, you are orderly man, fetch the soup", because NCOs don't do that job. Three days later, the battalion went into the firing line on the Piave River and, according to army regulations, all my crimes were automatically erased, except my loss of pay.

CHAPTER FIVE

1918

WAR WOUNDS AND OTHER SOUVENIRS

ON RETURNING HOME, veterans hoped to pick up their ordinary lives and forget about the war. Inevitably, they could not help but be reminded, especially in big cities, where unemployment meant that the street had a scattering of destitute former soldiers, sometimes missing an arm or a leg, sleeping rough or peddling matches to scrape a living. Yet the trauma of the war was such that reminders were not solely visual. A car back-firing or similar sudden noise, and a man might be seen to dive for cover, hit the pavement, or simply start to shake. Doug Roberts served in France in 1918. In early 1919 he was coming down by train from Waterloo Station to Guildford, when the shock of another train passing brought an instant reaction. "I went under the seat. That's the sort of state you get in. It wasn't so much nerves, it was self-preservation, to get out of the way of a shell." Doug Roberts' reactions were instinctively those of a soldier, ready to take cover at a split second's notice, or to repel a sudden attack. "On another occasion I went by bus to see my uncle in Fulham. I dropped off at Wandsworth Bridge Road, and when somebody tapped me on the shoulder, I put him on the floor. I right hooked him. You get like that. And he was one of my mates from the army."

Such reactions were common amongst those who had served, and many tried to resist them. Ben Clouting's reminders of war included sudden and profuse nose bleeds, the result of a chlorine gas attack in 1915. He also learnt to restrain his physical reaction to loud noises, so that his head just nodded slightly, a reaction hardly discernible to the outside world.

Night-time for many former soldiers was when the war was relived. Stan Clayton married his sweetheart not long after the end of the war, when he had yet to recover from memories impinging on his sleep. He described vividly how his nightmares disturbed his wife, although she was never alarmed by his reactions. "When we got married and went to bed, she said I used to disturb her in the night, saying, "They're coming, they're here, they're here!" I was reacting to dreams, events. "Come on, get down, get down, they're firing, they're shelling, get down," talking to my mates. His comrades were always in his thoughts, and he recited their names as he slept. Eventually he got over the trauma, but it took time. Richard Hawkins had similar problems. "I married and had two sons, and was very happy, but I didn't sleep until three or four o'clock in the morning. I used to go up through the ceiling and down again, dreadful business, the after-effect of being shelled for nineteen months."

Even seventy years later, the memories could resurface without warning. Don Price took part in an attack at High Wood in July 1916, and was one of only 150 men to march into rest from the 600 who had gone over the top. "Do you know," he told me in 1988, "three months ago I woke up in a terrible state. I was bathed in perspiration and, for a moment, I couldn't understand why. I have never suffered after the war: dreams sometimes, but no nightmares, or uncontrollable nerves, nothing like that. Then I realized. During the attack on the Wood, I had taken shelter in a dugout and fallen asleep. Now at any time, any passing soldier, British or German - and there were thousands fighting in that wood – could have thrown a grenade straight into that dugout, no questions asked, and I would have been blown to smithereens. It had taken all these years for that fact to dawn on me, in a dream."

In interviewing veterans, I was aware that stirring up such memories might cause an old man to sleep badly. Several wanted a period of time away from remembering the war, so that they could relax and clear their minds again before they went to bed. Walter Green was well aware of the downside to talking about his experiences, although in his case the months as a prisoner of war were the memories that flooded back. He often woke in a sweat, he told me, having returned to the German mines where he had worked, swinging a 7lb hammer for all he was worth.

The effects of war and the physical trauma suffered remained quite literally embedded in some veterans. Artillery in the Great War was responsible for around half of all battlefield casualties and its immediate legacy was shrapnel buried deep in soldiers' bodies. Under surgery, most metal was removed and was commonly given to the patient as a souvenir. Harry Patch was offered, but refused, the lump of shrapnel removed from his stomach, whereas Walter Popple decided to keep the bullet he received on the morning of 1 July 1916, which was subsequently removed from his shoulder – 'the second intercostal space' as he told me. Richard Hawkins, coming round after an operation, found his piece of shrapnel wrapped in cotton wool and pinned to his pyjamas. Like Walter, he chose to keep the souvenir.

Other veterans were given no choice. When the metal proved too difficult or dangerous to extract, it was left alone. For the rest of his life, Vic Cole had a piece of shrapnel in his back, received in 1918. Its most notable annoyances, as far as Vic was concerned, were a stiff back and its habit of setting off alarms at airport security. Ernest Ford's souvenir was the smudge on his left hand, a piece of shrapnel still trapped under his skin which, in his case, was missed or ignored during surgery. Walter Burdon kept two fragments of metal embedded in his skull from his time on Gallipoli.

Such souvenirs, whether they were kept voluntarily or not, gave veterans a physical as well as psychological link to the past. Some would rather not have kept them; others morbidly clung on to momentos that their wives did not always like. Fred Francis, a veteran of 1 July, was so critically wounded that day that he was given the last rites. After many operations, Fred was "patched up" and sent home with a glass jar full of shrapnel and several pieces of bone taken from his foot and leg. For whatever reason, he wanted to keep them, and he was most upset when, many years later, his wife threw them away.

As Fred lay critically wounded on the battlefield that July day, he was robbed of his personal possessions by a stretcher bearer who believed his casualty would not live. Taking from the dead, never mind the living, was disapproved of by many soldiers. They saw the removal of property as blatant theft, robbing the dead man's family of precious keepsakes that, in the ordinary course of events, would be returned home.

Going through the pockets of the dead, either in pursuit of souvenirs or during the course of identification before burial, could often throw up disturbing images. Pictures of family members, particularly children, upset even hardened soldiers; Smiler Marshall wrote to the family of one man he buried because of letters he found strewn about the body. However, Jack Irving had perhaps the most unusual shock of all. In examining a badly disfigured body close to Delville Wood, he came across some family photos. As he looked through them, he instantly recognized a girl whom he knew well, for she lived just a few doors down from his house on the same road in Newcastle upon Tyne. Jack had found her father.

Souvenir collecting did not always have to be morbid. In the first rush of enthusiasm, soldiers newly-arrived at the front were liable to collect bits and pieces without any thought as to how they would carry them around, and with little discretion as to what they acquired. Tom Dewing ran to pick up the first piece of shrapnel he saw, like a schoolboy chasing shrapnel after an air raid. As with all collectors, discrimination between what was worth picking up and what might be left was learnt, particularly as anything found had to be carried. One soldier estimated that his collection of shell fuse tops, rusty bayonets and funny-shaped bits of shrapnel weighed 20lbs before he eventually saw how ludicrous this was, and jettisoned the lot. Picking the right souvenir was not only sensible but could be financially rewarding too. The 'top' finds were invariably near the front line in German dugouts, or stripped from prisoners as they marched into captivity. The veterans I have met with the best souvenirs have typically been the infantrymen rather than former gunners, airmen, or members of the Army Service Corps. However, it was the men working far behind the line, at Base Camps and Depots, who were most bereft and as a consequence bought their souvenirs from front line men, happy to sell at a good price to 'Base Wallahs' as they were called.

When it came to the collecting instinct, rank was irrelevant when there were souvenirs to be picked up. After all, Richard Hawkins and other officers of the 11th Royal Fusiliers were watched through field binoculars by Major General Maxse, commanding 18th Division, as they wandered around on the skyline, searching for momentos. Their enthusiasm was commented on by Maxse, who pointed out that as the officers walked on the skyline they made themselves nice targets for any sniper who might have remained nearby. For the most part, collecting souvenirs was a harmless pastime. However, the enemy well knew that men were keen to pick up prized possessions and set about booby-trapping many of them. Richard Hawkins, who picked up a pickelhaube on 1 July, had one of the most sought-after finds, and therefore one that was more commonly rigged to explode. On one occasion, as Norman Dillon recalled, the "mania for collecting" resulted in a senior casualty in his tunelling company. "Our Major Wellesley (a relation, I believe, of the Duke of Wellington), was dismantling a grenade of the type fired from a rifle when it exploded. He was a fine chap, well-liked, and his departure caused unusual grief." Major Edward Wellesley, MC, was in fact on leave from France when he 'accidently killed himself by a bomb which he had brought home illegally,' a report noted at the time.

Bringing dangerous souvenirs home was forbidden and any man

caught could expect the immediate cancellation of his leave. Vic Cole tried to break the rules and had a tricky moment when he boarded the boat. Powerful lights trained on the men threw into relief any irregularity of dress or any bulge concealing forbidden material. "I must confess to some apprehension," he told me, "for tied to my rifle inside its dust cover was a German saw bayonet, and in my pocket a Hun forage cap." Vic's souvenirs went undetected and all was well.

As I talked to veterans, I was fascinated to hear about the range of items they brought back to Britain. Alfred Finnigan had on his sitting room wall a barometer retrieved from the rubble of a chemist's shop in Ypres. Ben Clouting had a Very pistol, from which he had had to remove a severed hand. He surrendered this and a Belgian pistol during a weapons amnesty in the late 1960s. Bullets, buttons and coins were more common as souvenirs. Perhaps one of the most interesting finds belonged to Robbie Burns, a veteran who lived in Whitley Bay. In 1917, he had been sheltering in a house when the building took a direct hit. As the roof timbers fell and glass flew about, Robbie was struck in the mouth by a small piece of shrapnel that removed his two front teeth and sliced open his top lip, a very evident scar remaining all his long life. When the dust settled and Robbie collected himself, he saw that a cabinet in the corner of the room had been damaged. Inside was a set of medals dating from the Franco-Prussian War of 1870. He reckoned that they deserved a better home, such as his, where they were to receive pride of place, hanging in a glass cabinet in his sitting room.

Inevitably, most souvenirs were lost, jettisoned, given away, sold, or packed away in the bottom of a drawer. Doug Robert's only souvenir from the trenches was a Mauser pistol with thirteen rounds of ammunition. Yet in the end Doug turned against his souvenir, and it ended up, with the ammunition, at the bottom of a fishpond. Eustace Rushby had a German forage cap tucked away in a chest and brought it out only when someone expressed an interest in his war; likewise his German Zeiss binoculars taken from a pillbox on Pilkem Ridge. His wish was that these would eventually make their way to a regimental museum; I hope that in the end they did.

Just occasionally a souvenir brought life-long reassurance. Smiler Marshall picked up a crucifix in the rubble of Albert Basilica. Even then he cherished the memento, secreting it in one of the regiment's limbers with the collaboration of the driver. "Keep it for as long as you can. Don't lose it unless you can't possibly help it," he told him. The driver kept it for Smiler, and after the war it found a permanent spot on his bedside table, remaining with him until the day of his death earlier this year.

1918

The war entered its fifth year with both sides recuperating from the exertions of Third Ypres and the fighting at Cambrai. On 8 January, President Wilson of the United States put forward Fourteen Points, a programme for a negotiated peace, based upon a declaration of war aims by all combatant countries. Wilson's Points were popularly reported across the globe, but none of the combatants was yet willing to give these proposals proper consideration while the outcome of the war remained in doubt. In any case, the Germans still had one major advantage: after the October Revolution and the overthrow of the Tsar, Russia's participation in the war had been rapidly brought to a close in December, first with a ceasefire, then with the negotiated peace treaty of Brevst-Litovsk twelve weeks later. The Germans now had the scope and the opportunity to turn their attention to the west. After the Armistice in December, the Germans began to transport huge numbers of men and materials westwards in order to launch a final, decisive offensive that would win the war before the American Expeditionary Force could arrive in enough strength to tip the balance against Germany.

The realization that Germany was planning such a huge offensive hardly came as a shock to the Allies, and immediately Haig began to stockpile ammunition in readiness for the onslaught. The real issue was manpower, or rather the lack of it. The Germans would be in the tactical ascendancy for the first time in years, fielding 191 Divisions against the Allies' 164. Reinforcements were needed. However, deep mistrust between the British Prime Minister, Lloyd George, and his Commander in Chief in France, had created such a rift that the Prime Minister had taken it upon himself to restrict the numbers of men available to the C. in C. There could be no British spring offensive, as Haig had at one time intended. Defence was the only viable option and even this appeared to have been seriously compromised.

The German offensive began on 21 March, and was directed against the British Fifth Army, recuperating around St Quentin. A short but devastating artillery bombardment preceded a massive infantry assault that was aided by a heavy spring morning fog. This afforded the attackers an element of surprise far more effectively than any conventional smokescreen. In a matter of minutes, the forward position of the British line was over-run, as the Germans deployed the tactic of rapid infiltration, used successfully for the first time the previous autumn.

German units, rather than attacking strong positions head on, swept around the sides, overwhelming weaker points in the front line before moving on to the second and third lines of defence. They attacked artillery positions, helping to eliminate, or at least throw into confusion, the guns that had been used so frequently to break up and even shatter enemy assaults. Faced with such tactics, huge numbers of British soldiers, unsure what to do, held their ground only to find their retreat was cut off and they were taken prisoner.

The German drive appeared relentless, forcing the release of freshly trained units to France, men and boys with little or no experience of battle. Amongst the eighteen-year-old boys drafted to France in March 1918 was Harold Lawton, a lad from Rhyl, in Wales. A keen member of the army cadet force at school, he registered with the authorities at just seventeen, and was called up for military training a year later. As a conscript, he found himself shunted from regiment to regiment before he was finally sent to the East Yorkshires in France.

Fred Hodges was another *Men of 18 in 1918*, the title of his autobiography. Born and raised in Northampton, the grammar school boy was highly patriotic and eager to serve at a time when enthusiasm for the war was waning and few recruits saw service in France as anything other than a inevitable evil. As the Germans crashed through Northern France that early spring, he and his friends were sent overseas.

British and Empire soldiers fought a desperate and courageous rearguard action but were thrown back across the old Somme battlefields, only bringing the Germans to a standstill close to the strategically important town of Amiens. The Germans, in the first major tactical error of the campaign, switched the main thrust of the offensive north. They attacked again on 9 April near Armentières throwing the heaviest weight militarily against two divisions of Portuguese troops. Portugal had joined the Allies in August 1914 owing to colonial rivalries with Germany. However, internal dissension ensured that there was no Portuguese military involvement until mid-1917 when 40,000 troops reached the Western Front. The new German offensive had put these troops under intense pressure and they had immediately given way.

Desperate fighting by the British and Empire forces thwarted the enemy's ambitions once again, and the Germans switched the direction of attack to the south, to the area of the Chemin des Dames, east of Paris. The effect of each new offensive, while initially stunning, could only dissipate the strength of the German army, leaving it in control of great swathes of land bulging into Allied lines, salients that were difficult to hold and vulnerable to counter-attack.

The Germans had methodically lengthened their lines a year after they had sensibly sought to shorten them. When their offensive spluttered and then stalled in June and early July, it was only a matter of time before the Allies, America included, were able to regroup and attack a weakened and an increasingly demoralized enemy.

The Germans had expended their last major source of reserves and used up vast quantities of ammunition. Although it was not articulated widely at the time, this had been their last significant throw of the dice.

On 8 August, British and Empire troops forced a breakthrough on the Somme, driving the enemy back eight miles and capturing huge numbers of prisoners and equipment. Coordinated and honed battle tactics that incorporated air superiority and improved artillery fire, in conjunction with better tactical use of tanks and infantry, proved decisive.

The German Chief of Staff wrote that this was the black day for the Germany army, a tacit admission that the war could not be won. The last hundred days commenced with the Germans being slowly and inexorably being pushed back across the Somme to defend the Hindenburg Line once more. The Allies' storming of the Line on 29 September was hugely significant. The shattering 24-hour bombardment before the assault only underlined the pre-eminence of Allied fire-power.

Once the Hindenburg Line was breached, the Germans had no expectation that they could hold the Allied advance anywhere except in their own homeland where the River Rhine's natural barrier might hinder the enemy. It would never come to that. In October and November 1918, open warfare was resumed and the world of static trench lines left behind. The Germans were now incapable of making a concerted and prolonged stand.

President Wilson's Fourteen Points suddenly become acceptable to the Germans as the basis of a peace treaty, but it was too late, and the Allies were in no mood to negotiate. German capitulation could only be a matter of time. Even so, on the morning of 11 November, when news of the Armistice spread, most people, especially those fighting on the ground, were taken aback at the sudden cessation of hostilities.

Lance Corporal Vic Cole, 1st Queen's Own (Royal West Kent Regiment), 1897-1995

I can distinctly remember sitting in some bloody trench somewhere in Italy and saying to a chap, "Do you know what? I'm 21 today." And do you know what he said? "Oh, are you?" He couldn't have cared less. My coming of age, 2 January 1918.

Private Harold Walter Lawton, No41648, 1/4th East Yorkshire Regiment, 27 July 1899-

Father was a tile-fixer. Someone would want a mosaic on the ground, he would do it, but his business tottered and fell during the war. Officer training had been as good as promised me but father had no money to help out with the kit. Instead I joined the rank and file at Wrexham where I met a terrific mixture of boys, lads from Lancashire, a real mish-mash of rough and tumble lads.

We were all aware of the awful lengthening of casualty lists, the news of retreats or bloody battles, sometimes successful, sometimes not, but always with terrible casualties. Shortly after Christmas 1917, we moved from Kinmel training camp in Wales to Great Yarmouth. Here we underwent our baptism of fire when a German cruiser bombarded the town as we trained on the assault courses. The war was getting very close.

Private Percy Wilson, No77033, 21st Manchester Regiment, 14 August 1899-15 October 2004

When they took us out on square drill and called us to attention, our sergeant would say "Right turn" and half of them would turn left, deliberately, because they weren't interested in the army and wanted to make life difficult. The sergeant had been wounded and wasn't fit for further active service, and he would stop and look at us with scepticism, cane under his arm, "When I was a boy, my father bought me a box of toy soldiers. Some got broken and some got lost," then he hesitated for effect, "and now I've found the bloody lot again." He was having a swipe at the conscripts, as he'd found them a lot of rotters, and he was right. They had all been called up and they weren't relishing it. Only a few of us were volunteers. We all knew what the war was about by then. I went to a little village school and six of the lads I went to school with never returned.

Rifleman Arnold Vincent Miller, No560, 2nd Rifle Brigade, 10 January 1899-19 March 1991

We were conscripts, aged about eighteen, and we really were a mixed crowd. We had one fellow who had a private tutor, he'd never been to a school; his parents were very well off. He just did not understand the army in the least, the idea of standing to attention, the constant cleaning, and in the end he rebelled. One Tuesday we went to the swimming baths in Northampton. He could swim but, because he stood out, the other fellows kept pushing him under the water, so he went up to the corporal and said, "Corporal, I shan't be coming on the next swimming parade," just like that, and the corporal of course said, "Well, we'll see about that".

The next Tuesday they couldn't find this fellow at all, until the Military Police found him in the public library reading a book, and he was most annoyed. Apparently they wouldn't even let him finish the chapter! It finished up with a Court Martial and the Colonel said, "Before I pass sentence, Rifleman Cox, have you anything to say?" So he stepped forward and said, "Well, to tell you the truth, Sir, I'm a square peg in a round hole."

He got fifty-six days in a military prison, and he was still sent out to France before me!

Private Frederick James Hodges, No57043, 2 Platoon, A Company, 10th Lancashire Fusiliers, 18 July 1899-10 February 2002

War, to my mind, was a kind of super sport. We were used to hard knocks in football and rugby, and healthy competition in cricket and running, getting into the first three and all that, and war was just an extension of this manliness. If I'd been put down as Class B as a soldier, I would have been ashamed of myself. War was something noble, and we were anxious that it shouldn't stop before we got there. When we took the train down to Dover, we passed a train of German prisoners and they laughed at us. They were safe, going into captivity, and we were youngsters who didn't know what we were going into.

Sapper Arthur Halestrap, 46th Division Royal Engineers, 1898-2004
As we marched into the camp, an order came. "Halt that squad! That man improperly dressed in a woollen cap, double up to me." That was me, and I had to double up to this Regimental Sergeant Major. "Why do you come into my camp improperly dressed?" I told him about my accidental loss, that my hat had blown off as I looked out of the train window, but that cut no ice with him. "Put this man on a charge for not looking after Government property." Then he turned to me. "You'll know me before you've been here very long. About turn! Double back." Marching at twice the normal speed was the order for everyone who was moving outside a tent or hut.

The discipline was very strict indeed because we understood there had been trouble in an adjoining camp. As a result, we had three parades every morning while we were there, 6 am, 7 am, and 8 am, to reinforce discipline and prevent us causing the same problems. When an additional parade was posted for 5 am the next morning, I said to my pals, "I'm not going on that parade!" They told me I'd get into trouble, but I said, "If I do, it will be my own fault." So I stayed away from the first parade and when I went to the next one, the Instructor Sergeant, who was in his mid forties, with a long moustache, came up to me shaking nervously and said, "I'm sorry, my son, I...I...I had to report you, I don't know what they'll do." So I said, "Don't worry, Sergeant, I did it on my own initiative. Now I'll have to take the consequences."

I didn't appreciate that I was on active service and under different discipline to that at home. I went before the Colonel and, in my youthful naivety, I thought he would respect my courage in giving him the chance to make an example of a silly order that made us parade four times in as many hours. Perhaps he would even promote me! Instead, I was given three weeks' Number Two Field Punishment. Every moment from Reveille to sunset that I was off duty or not under instruction, I had to empty the latrine buckets, pour away the liquid and then take the solids to the furnace to be burned.

Private Douglas Henry Roberts, No11470, B Company, 7th Buffs (East Kent Regiment), 14 January 1900–2nd December 2002
First time we went into the line, it took hours to get forward through the communication trenches. They load you up like bloody camels. I had a two-gallon can of water, three Lewis gun panniers, some toc emma [Stokes Mortar] ammunition and before I got to the end of the line, a sergeant said, "Give that big bastard some more" and they gave me a sack of bread.

[Ed. At 4.40am on a dark and misty Thursday morning, the Germans launched their long awaited offensive. This would be Germany's all-out gamble to win the war. In December 1917 the Germans had fielded 171 Divisions in France and Flanders. However, after the Armistice with Russia, they were able to deploy 192 Divisions, a full 23 more than the combined effort of the Allies. This numerical advantage on the Western Front had to be used to advantage. Three German armies would launch a ferocious assault on three weakened British armies, the Third and Fifth, to knock Britain out of the war.]

Private Andrew Bowie, 5th Cameron Highlanders, 1897-2002
We were at Gouzeaucourt on the night of 20/21st March 1918, when a message arrived. I wrote it down and it said: "Prisoners taken report troops massing on your front. Stand-To such and such a time, earlier than usual in any case. All ranks and ratings must be in the front line,

a big attack expected." I took the message to the Captain, Captain St Clair Grant. He read it. He was a big tall fellow, and he started to shake. Nerves. He said, "Signaller, what about a wee tot?" He took one himself and he gave me some rum, because I would be nervous too. In the morning everybody stood to, everybody, including signallers, we had to stand in the line just the same. We were in the most precarious position we could be in, we were right out at a point, and it would taken nothing for them to get into our back line.

A/Lance Corporal Cecil Withers, 17th Royal Fusiliers, 1898-2005
It was a very misty morning, and we were just getting ready to be relieved by the King's Royal Rifle Corps when the whole world shook, all the German guns opened up at once, it was like an earthquake, whoosh, just imagine. We could see very little, and you couldn't hear orders, nobody could hear a word. After a while we pulled back. The sergeant caught hold of the officer's mackintosh and followed him down the communication trench and we tagged on, that's how we retreated in the mist, in as orderly way as possible.

Private Ernest Ford, 10th Queen's (Royal West Surrey Regiment), 1896-1995
We had been back from Italy a fortnight when the order arrived to move up nearer the line, as the German offensive had now begun. On the afternoon of the 21st, we marched seven miles to a station and there, in the evening, we entrained, our destination being billets in a village five or six miles west of Albert. About 3.30am we arrived at our destination. The night was black and foggy and we had no idea where we were. We had only pulled up a few minutes when there was a blaze of light and a crash about 100 yards away; this we thought to be a bomb dropped by an aircraft. Five minutes later there was another, followed by a third. We then had the order to detrain and the battalion lined up alongside the trucks. There was a tell-tale swish and another missile arrived with a crash, and I realized that the station was

being shelled by one of the enemy's long-range high-velocity guns. We were very puzzled about this as we thought we were 15 miles from the line. Then we discovered that we were at Achiet le Grand, which explained matters to some extent. The German Push had proved much more successful than anticipated. Result: our Division was wanted very much earlier than expected, and instead of halting west of Albert, we were rushed right up to the railhead, seven miles from the line.

The battalion continued to stand along the siding, lined up in fours, while the train was unloaded; meanwhile the shells were arriving with a sudden rush every four or five minutes, and uncomfortably close. We were not at all sorry when the order came to move as it was a rather nervy process to stand still on parade and be shelled and in the middle of an inky night. Although loaded with full packs and blankets, the battalion left that station at quite a remarkable pace!

A/Lance Corporal Cecil Withers, 17th Royal Fusiliers, 1898-2005
The retreat took us back further and further. At one point we went past a canteen. It was what they called the Expeditionary Force Canteen, full of sandwiches, cigarettes, bottles of beer, cigars and tins of fruit, and somebody had burned it all down, a terrible waste, but they had to stop the whole lot falling into enemy hands. I remember there were French people coming down the other side of the road pushing prams and old carts with kettles, saucepans, bedding and mattresses – refugees getting away from the Germans.

We retreated until we got to a small incline and, looking down, we could see a road leading down to the enemy lines and crowds of blooming Germans coming along, rows and rows. There was a little hillock about five feet high and on top was an officer, Brigadier-General Carey, who took charge and ordered us to lie down on the grass on the edge of a copse.

There were officers, even a cook, all sorts of men, mixed up, and he ordered us to fire at the oncoming Germans as fast as we damn well could. I was on the Lewis Gun but a bullet lodged in the barrel, a number one stoppage it was called, and so the sergeant said, "Throw it over your shoulder, Withers," and so I took the bolt out and flung it as far as I could out of the way, making the Lewis Gun inoperable should the Germans capture it.

I picked up a rifle. I don't know about the other chaps, but my left hand, where it held the rifle, was all blistered because the rifle got so hot. You didn't fire at a man, you fired at the line, blindly, one clip after another. After twenty minutes, perhaps half an hour, I have no idea how long, the General said, "All right, that's stopped the buggers." The line broke and retreated but some had got within thirty yards.

Sapper Arthur Halestrap, 46th Division Royal Engineers, 1898-2004
I joined a convoy going up at night from Division to Brigade Headquarters. We had reached a crossroads when a Very light lit up the place, an eerie sort of light, and, as it fell, the darkness came again; then another Very light, and another one, and inevitably the shelling started. The fire was very accurate and in no time there was carnage and carcasses all over the place. The wagon to which I was attached was halted because the leading horse of the team got its left legs in the mud on the side of the road and it couldn't move, and the lead horse on the other side was pawing the air.

All the horses were screaming, and there's nothing worse than screaming horses, they are terrifying. The situation was immediately seen by an NCO in charge, and he ordered some of the men to get on the back of the wagon to push and others to get on the wheels to wind them. I was sent to get underneath the horse stuck in the mud. When the order came to move, I heaved and everyone pushed on the wheels and we got the wagon going.

That was my baptism of fire. It wasn't a nice one but strangely enough I wasn't frightened. I had a job to do. I look back upon this with amazement, but that's the truth. It was the result of the discipline instilled in us, to do the job that we were told to do, regardless of anything else.

Private Ernest Ford, 10th Queen's (Royal West Surrey Regiment), 1896-1995

The amount of traffic on the road was astonishing and gave some slight idea of the size of modern armies and the enormous amount of transport required. I was waiting with the transport at the side of a main road. We were there about twenty hours and during all that time, day and night, there was an unbroken line of traffic moving backwards – limbers, guns and lorries in one continuous stream. There were no troops at all amongst these.

During the morning we heard an anti-aircraft shell burst very low and close to us, and looking up saw a Boche plane at a few hundred feet. It had suddenly dived out of the clouds and evidently intended to attack the traffic on the road. Fortunately the anti-aircraft guns landed another shell right on top of the plane and put the engine out of action (it was very rare for an anti-aircraft gun to score a hit.) The German plane immediately made a hasty landing about eighty yards away from us. We grabbed our rifles, loaded them and made for it (thinking that they might turn on their machine guns) but the occupants, when they saw a horde of armed Britishers bearing down on them, apparently considered discretion to be better than valour, clambered out and did the 'Kamerad' act.

Private Fred Hodges, 10th Lancashire Fusiliers, 1899-2002

I, along with some others, was sent to the village of Mesnil for water. We went to one of those wells where there was a windlass and I fetched a bucket of water up and then tried to pour it into a two-gallon petrol can. I was busily filling the can on top of a steep ridge above the trenches when a German plane came up very close, over the brow, firing at me. What did I do? I ran towards him to shorten the period that I was in his sights rather than stand still or run away. I could see the bullets spraying the ground, passing me. The plane went right over the top and as I looked up I saw the black crosses on the underside of his wings. He swirled round and came back to have another go, by which time I was hiding in the rubble. We watched as he circled a couple of times before returning to enemy lines, whereupon we recovered our water cans and went back to the trenches.

Lance Corporal Vic Cole, 1st Queen's Own (Royal West Kent Regiment), 1897-1995
There were all kinds of dogfights we would watch, going round and round, weaving between each other. The ack ack guns would be popping away, and now and again you would see something flash and fall into pieces, and then sometimes you'd see a dot in the sky, and that was the pilot falling to earth. After a dogfight, one of ours would come down "falling leaf" we called it, seemingly out of control, then suddenly flatten out and scoot away home to fight another day.

Sapper Arthur Halestrap, 46th Division Royal Engineers, 1898-2004
At regular times in the morning and evening, an observation plane would come over and of course we would take pot shots at it with our rifles. This airman was so low that we could see him using his revolver. As the plane went over, I suddenly felt a bang on the table beside me, and there was a bullet hole in the wood; the bullet had missed me by an inch. No one was hurt in these exchanges and in fact we took it all as a joke and enjoyed it, really.

Private Allen Short, 2/10th London Regiment, 1899-2000
One side of the quarry was in darkness but the other was swathed in moonlight. We piled arms and I used my valise as a pillow. A German plane came over and spotted our movement, dropped some bombs and then signalled to the German artillery, which started shelling. A chap close to me, whom I knew casually, was killed just a few yards away as we left our rifles and packs and dived into the shelter of a bank.

In the morning we went back. I found that a large piece of shrapnel had diagonally cut my valise from one corner to another. It broke my toothbrush into three pieces, split open a tin of bully beef, and my face towel was nothing else but a hole with a border around it. My head had been resting on that valise just a second before we decided to flee. Our stacked rifles had collapsed and, above the upper band, a piece of shrapnel had cut a groove that I could get my finger in.

Rifleman Arnold Miller, 2nd Rifle Brigade, 1899-1991
Jerry busted right through. So instead of our draft being broken in gently, in a quiet part of the line, our battalion was rushed up to the front. We were taken up on lorries and we were in no way dispirited because we knew nothing about war. We were full of glory and self-belief: we were going to stop them. The old hands, who had been at Arras and Passchendaele, didn't try and frighten us, but we could see they weren't enthusiastic. That doesn't mean they wouldn't do their job but they knew what kind of a job it would be, and we didn't.

We were near a village called Pargny. There was a canal running across which Jerry was trying to cross. Another fellow and myself had to dig two holes and shoot at anything we saw, which we were quite prepared to do. It was cold and it was foggy and we didn't see anything except the bloke who brought up our rations in the early hours of the morning. We nearly shot him.

Later that morning, we heard a heck of a noise going on a couple of hundred yards up on the right. Nothing happened, so King, the lad who was with me, had a slice of bread and plum and apple jam while I kept a look out. I then cut myself a slice, when he suddenly said, "Run, there's Jerry behind us." He bolted and I never saw him again. The Germans had crossed over the canal and were streaming through about sixty yards behind us. I didn't stand a dog's chance because my rifle was lying on the ground by the side of the hole and I had to climb out of my hole, by which time the Germans were already pointing at me. There was no chance of resistance.

With other prisoners, I was told to pick up a wounded German who was lying on an improvised stretcher, just canvas with a pole through it, and we carried him back under fire from our own guns. We went slipping and sliding through a wood, deep in mud, until we eventually got out into the open where there was a row of field guns firing away like mad. The Germans were very friendly because they were advancing at such a speed, and offered us ersatz coffee while all the time they shouted, "Nach Paris. Nach Paris!"

Private Ernest Ford, 10th Queen's (Royal West Surrey Regiment), 1896-1995
The village of Gommecourt, was situated on the top of a bare ridge and was originally surrounded with trees. In 1916 it had been the scene of much fighting, now all that remained were a few heaps of bricks with here and there a fragment of standing wall and the blackened and slashed skeletons of such trees as had survived the storm of high explosives. We arrived there and it was all peaceful and quiet and made for quite a strange scene.

The following morning, a red-cap came dashing up on a horse and shouted, "Turn out every available man at once; the Boche cavalry has broken through!" There was immediately a bit of a rush; the transport hitched up and went off, and the cooks, shoemakers, tailors and the band and all the other oddments, including me, fixed their bayonets and loaded rifles and were lined along the top of a neighbouring ridge; meanwhile a battery of 18 pounders dashed about over ditches and through fences and took up positions. I strongly suspected at the time that it was largely a case of severe 'wind up' and such it proved to be, as nothing happened.

Private Doug Roberts, 7th Buffs (East Kent Regiment), 1900–2002
As we retreated through Albert, Jerry started shelling us and one of our officers, a young chap, got a bit panicky. We were using foul words and cursing but all he could think to do was to tell Corporal Allen to stop us swearing. A couple of shells landed on a house about fifty yards away. Bricks and tiles and dust flew everywhere, and out of it all strode our CO, Captain Morrison, with his Sam Browne belt

round his neck. He'd been having a crap. You know what he said? "What's all the bother?" He was so unconcerned that everyone stopped panicking and in no time at all we quickly returned to normal again.

Private Ernest Ford, 10th Queen's (Royal West Surrey Regiment), 1896-1995

After the scare we returned to Gommecourt. I was lodged with my section in the shafts of some old German dugouts on the edge of Gommecourt Wood. The dugouts themselves had collapsed and it was highly uncomfortable, packed in what had been the staircase, but preferable to being outside where it had begun to rain heavily. Shortly after, the Germans began pounding Gommecourt unmercifully. I remember a notice board fixed up at the entrance to the village to this effect:

> THE FRENCH AUTHORITIES INTEND TO PRESERVE THIS
> VILLAGE UNTOUCHED AS A RELIC OF THE WAR.
> IT IS STRICTLY FORBIDDEN TO REMOVE ANYTHING OR
> OTHERWISE ALTER ITS APPEARANCE.

I wondered at the time what steps the French were intending to take against the Germans for the infringement of the last paragraph.

[Ed. So grave was the situation in France that political sanction was immediately given to releasing large numbers of reserves and partially trained soldiers serving in Britain. The majority were young and lacked any experience of front line action. They were sent to France to help stem the German onslaught, arriving in late March and the first days of April.]

Private Harold Lawton, 1/4th East Yorkshire Regiment, 1899-

Suddenly all training stopped and we were given draft leave; home, with kitbags and rifles. However, on the second day urgent orders came to return to Great Yarmouth for some frantic kitting out before we made our way to Sheerness and across the Channel to France.

This would have been in the last week of March 1918. Up to this point, I had been in the Manchester Regiment – I had been in the Royal Welch Fusiliers and the Cheshires before then – and now I found myself part of a draft sent to another regiment, the East Yorkshires. This we found near Armentières, resting behind the lines after having a very nasty time. We were the new boys, and the old soldiers took no notice of us whatsoever; they had to get themselves better again. So instead of getting any sort of paternalism shown towards us, that one might have expected from our elders, it wasn't there at all. They told us nothing.

Private Allen Short, 2/10th London Regiment, 1899-2000
I was on the last lap of a signalling course when our brigade school was closed down, and we returned to our unit to be given home leave for six days. However, we'd only been home two days when a telegram arrived recalling us to our unit. We got back, were given our overseas equipment, and off we went. I'm sure we all had a mixture of excitement, anticipation and fear. I had decided that I would rather be killed than maimed for life, but I also wondered whether I was going to be afraid. Was I going to be shown up against the other fellows? All sorts of things passed through your mind, but we never spoke to one another about it.

My company went out to France 213 strong: 100 went to the 2/10th Londons, 100 went to the 2/12th Londons and 13 went to the Rifle Brigade, including my own particular chum, Charlie Sheen. There was no choice in the matter at all, you were posted and that was that. I said goodbye to Charlie on a Tuesday and heard much later that he was a prisoner by the Friday.

Private Percy Wilson, 21st Manchester Regiment, 1899-2004
After just 11 weeks' training we went out on a tremendous draft, shiploads of us. We landed at Boulogne and we marched up the hill to

Etaples, and lined up in ranks of four. I was second in on a line and there was a Welshman on my left. He'd been out before, been wounded, and was going out a second time. "Do you want to be on the outside? You'll see a lot more there," he asked me. He guessed I'd never been to France, so I changed places with him and then I cottoned on to his trick.

France was the dirtiest place imaginable. Every morning the women used to empty the chamber pots and anything else straight out into the gutter and so by swapping with me, this Welshman ensured that I and not he would be walking in all the filth and urine.

Private Fred Hodges, 10th Lancashire Fusiliers, 1899-2002
I got into the front line and it was all chalk. I sat there on the fire step, and the man I relieved gave me a two-inch square mirror to clip onto my bayonet in order to look over into No Man's Land. I sat there and thought, "Oh, I've got this mirror, I'm not much of a sentry if I don't use it," so I pushed it up over the parapet and all I could actually see was coarse grass and barbed wire. But the mirror must have glinted in the sun because in no time at all a salvo of shells began to burst near the trench, stones rattling off my helmet.

As I sat there, a great lump of jagged shrapnel, as big as my hand, thumped beside me and like a fool I touched it and burnt my fingers, I didn't realise such things would be hot. I looked around and felt like the only man in the trench. I went round the next traverse and people were sat writing letters or playing cards. The sergeant just looked at me and grinned. "That's reet, lad, ta'ake no'a'tice, Jerry'll geet fed oop sooner or la'ter". The boys were quite fatalistic, and during a shelling most people kept quiet and put on a bold front: "That'll do, Jerry. You keep on, you'll hurt somebody."

Private Doug Roberts, 7th Buffs (East Kent Regiment), 1900-2002
We got buried a couple of times in the trench, and had to dig ourselves out again. We laughed, though it wasn't a laughing matter really. But

if you didn't laugh, you would have been dead, you couldn't have stood it. It helps a lot. We had a shell drop in and half bury us, and a lad called Pierce, he was at the back of the trench in a hole, and his face was completely red. In fact I couldn't see his features at all, and I thought, Christ, he's lost his face. But do you know what it was? A tin of jam and it had exploded all over him.

Private Harold Lawton, 1/4th East Yorkshire Regiment, 1899-
The Portuguese had retreated under heavy artillery fire. We could see them coming back and we wondered what had happened. We were rushed to hold the line of trenches that was little more than a scrape in the ground, and so we had to get digging straight away. We hadn't been there long when one chap, who'd come out with us, looked over our new parapet and he was immediately shot through the head by a sniper.

We were cold and hungry. It was absolute chaos. Not a single British officer came to see us; nobody knew what was happening. The next morning we retreated, but the Germans had already infiltrated our lines and swept around the flanks.

We could hear firing but we hadn't a clue what was going on, not an officer was to be seen, it was shocking. We were stuck. For a while, we lived on our iron rations eating hard biscuits and sipping from our water bottles, hoping all the time that we would be found or someone would tell us what to do.

Eventually, the Germans returned and mopped us up. There were only half a dozen of us, there was nothing to do but put up our hands. What could you do?
[Ed. Harold Lawton, aged 106 and a former Professor of French at Sheffield University, is the last survivor amongst the near 190,000 British and Empire servicemen taken prisoner during the Great War. Around two-thirds of all these prisoners were captured during the chaos caused by the 1918 German offensive, including 21,000 captured on 21 March.]

Rifleman Robert Renwick, MM, 16th King's Royal Rifle Brigade, 1896-1997

We were near Armentières, the Portuguese had fled, and we were attacked from the front and both sides. We kept firing until our rifles were hot, even our Colonel was at it. Orders were given to withdraw one platoon at a time. I was in No2 platoon and being batman to the Sergeant Major, I automatically stayed with him but he had to see the rest of the company out and told me to go. We withdrew about half a mile to a pond where some men went to the left and some to the right. Those that went to the right, about thirty of us, were taken prisoner. The Germans had swarmed ahead, and placed machine guns on the bank side, and so they just lined us up.

At first I couldn't realize what was happening. I couldn't take it in. One Sergeant, Jack Wheatley, shouted to me, "Throw your rifle down, Renwick, or you'll be shot." He had laid his rifle down and that was a sign for the rest of us to do the same. I still had my rifle on my shoulder and on the spur of the moment I made a bid to get away. As I ran, an officer fired his revolver and a machine gun opened up. I'll give them credit, they must have fired overhead as they could have mowed me down. When I got back, the German officer butted me in the ribs with his revolver, "Silly English boy."

Sergeant Henson followed me in flight but they got him in the arm with the revolver. It was a foolish thing to do and I felt partly to blame. Sergeant Henson, always a brave fellow, was standing there crying like a baby. I think the idea of being taken prisoner hurt his pride badly. "When the machine gun started up I shut my eyes," he said. "I never thought I'd see you alive again." I was posted missing, believed killed. It was six weeks before my parents knew whether I was alive or dead.

Lance Corporal Vic Cole, 1st Queen's Own (Royal West Kent Regiment), 1897-1995

We got out of the train, and advanced into the sprawling Nieppe Forest in extended order when word came down that we were now the front line. There was no sign of war, the sun shone, birds sang in the trees and startled deer ran leaping off into the brush.

Beyond the forest we came into the open, and there was a field with a chalk road running across and we started along this road. Ahead of me the column veered right, and I thought, "What's up?" In our path there was a complete section of blokes lying in fours, dead. You couldn't help but look, but a voice said, "Come on, come on," and hurried us past. About ten yards away was a little bit of ground with the earth scooped out. It had been a shrapnel shell that had burst, and wiped the lot out.

We moved on up to a hedge and one of the lads said, "There they are, over there in that village," so we dug ourselves a hole and stuck our rifles through the hedge. Then, with a shattering crash, the fun commenced and in a moment the air was full of bursting shells, flying shrapnel and the smoke and noise of battle.

Pulling myself together, I noticed that most of the stuff was going over our heads and dropping into C Company lines. The world seemed full of the whine and crash of shell splinters. To our front across a ploughed field, the ground rose a little so that we had hardly any real field of fire, then suddenly, quite close, I saw the Germans – at least I saw the tops of their helmets bobbing up and down as they ducked and dodged in our fire. Aiming at these moving blobs, I fired again and again until there was no longer anything to shoot at and the 'cease-fire' whistle brought respite. A battery of our field guns now joined in the game. Concealed in the forest behind us, they fired over our heads. As poor Fritz came on, our guns shortened their range until their shells were falling just in front of our own position. One fell right among our men, then another, and several were wounded.

Private Joe Yarwood, 34th Division Royal Army Medical Corps, 1896-1995
The Advanced Dressing Station was an old brewery, but it was due to be withdrawn because the German advance was so rapid. We didn't

have the facilities to move everyone, so the Colonel came down and asked for volunteers to stay behind to be taken prisoner with the wounded. As he talked, I heard this stinking shell coming and I dived into the lee of a house as it burst. I was uninjured, but as I came round the corner, I was shocked by the scene. Colonel Stewart was lying dead, the adjutant, Major McEwen had his leg blown off and was hanging on to the femoral artery to try and prevent himself bleeding to death, Lieutenant Quartermaster Addey-Jibb was killed, and I lost two comrades, real comrades I was very fond of, Arthur Hartland and Wilf Uren. The scene was indescribable and as if it were possible to make things worse, the wounded, who were lying there on stretchers, had had a second dose from this shell too.

Arthur Hartland was a varsity student from Widnes and Wilf Uren was a church organist. Dear old Wilf, he was a sensitive sort of man. He was going bald and he had what was called a cap comforter, folded up and used like a head cap. At night time, or if he went into a billet, he'd quickly slip his peak cap off so that nobody would see his balding scalp, and put this cap comforter on. And there he was, lying on the decks, dead, showing his bald head and I thought it was rather pathetic.

Lance Corporal Vic Cole, 1st Queen's Own (Royal West Kent Regiment), 1897-1995

I tried my best to get through to the battery on our phone but the line had been cut. The Company Commander, Captain Scott, was furious with the artillery and ordered me to take a message back to the guns myself, so I shook hands with my friend Ralph Newman and set off. All kinds and calibres of missiles were crashing all about, shrapnel, whiz-bangs, high explosive, all in a frenzied mix-up and at the back of it the steady tap-tap-tap of machine guns.

I reached a little stream, crossed on the plank bridge and turned into the wood where C Company was dug in. Here I found a signaller complete with telephone in a hole behind a tree, and in a minute or so my message had been passed to the guns and the range had been lifted nicely.

As I turned to leave, something hit the tree behind which we were crouching, there was a blinding flash, a whirling sound of splinters, and there I was lying flat on my back looking up at a startled signaller. I had been hit in the lumber region and was already feeling numb from the waist down. Stretcher bearers arrived and dragged me over to a hole for temporary cover and turned me on my face. One of them let rip a stream of swear-words as he cut away my leather jacket and saw the wound.

Private Walter Green, 1/7th Durham Light Infantry, 1897-1998
The Captain came along and said, "I'm sorry, but we're surrounded. There's three alternatives as far as I can see: we can fight it out, a lot of us being killed, or we can lay down our arms, which will mean we will all be captured. The only other way is every man for himself. See that church over there? If you get through, we'll meet there at 12 midnight, as many as are still alive." I asked if I could go. "Yes, you can go, Green," and I picked up my rifle and set off on my own.

I went to the bottom of the trench where I knew there was an old communication trench that had not been used since 1915. It was overgrown and I began to fight my way through. I hadn't been going very long when I came across what we called barbed wire gooseberries thrown into a trench to block it; there must have been eight foot of them. The first one thrown in hadn't fallen to the bottom of the trench so I got down on my stomach and started to creep underneath when I heard a laugh. I looked up and on top of the trench was an unterofficer, what we'd call a senior sergeant, and two Germans with rifles. As soon as I saw them, I feared the worst, but they gestured to me to come on through, so I crept on and, as I was coming out, one fellow jumped into the trench and put his foot on my rifle and the unterofficer and the other lad came down, got hold of me and lifted me up. As I stood, they unfastened my epaulettes and stripped my battledress off. I stooped to try and pick up my haversack because I'd 250 woodbines inside, but they shoved my hand out of the way.

We came to an opening in the trench and climbed out, and the officer spoke to one of the guards who told me in English to return to where I had started. When I got back, there were seventeen of the twenty-five there, and I asked what had happened. "Two have been killed and five wounded. We were the other seventeen, you're now eighteen, that makes twenty-five."

A German stretcher bearer came along and two of us were told us to follow him. We went back to a field covered in wounded and killed. There, stretcher bearers worked in twos, putting field dressings on the wounded, while dozens of prisoners picked casualties up on duckboards and carried them to a sunken road, three or four hundred yards away to a field hospital. This continued all day until dusk.

Rifleman Robert Renwick, MM, 16th King's Royal Rifle Brigade, 1896-1997

Sentries escorted us to the main road where we were handed over to Uhlan cavalrymen who rode up and bumped us with their ponies as we walked. We were marched through Armentières where a few of the enemy were looting and one, the worse for drink, came up and pointed at my cap badge. I was in no position to argue, so I let him have it. It snowed that night and we spent the coldest night of my life in an open cart shed without overcoats.

In the morning we were taken to an intelligence officer. We were questioned; one lad went in first, and when he came out he gave me a wink that I took to mean he hadn't given away anything of importance. I was the second to go in. I must say this German officer was very polite. "Tommy, you are a prisoner of war now, and we would just like a little bit of information about what is behind you in the way of troops." We hadn't eaten for forty hours and I was offered a meal for my cooperation. "Look, Sir," I said, "I'm sorry to be taken prisoner, that's grieving me, but I'm not giving any information. I'm still playing cricket." I said, "You speak English very well. Have you ever heard that remark?" and he said, "Yes, Tommy, I have." He finished up by saying, "We'll be over that ground in a day or two, it doesn't matter much." He then asked if I had been home on leave recently, and when I lied saying I had, he suggested that London was very much knocked about by the Zeppelin raids and people were very short of food, which I denied.

Private Harold Lawton, 1/4th East Yorkshire Regiment, 1899-
The funny thing is, I can't remember them taking us prisoner. All I can remember is sitting on the bank of a ditch without any webbing, and not a soul about. What happened to the men taken prisoner with me, I can't say. From what I could see, I was somewhere near a transport park. I was sitting there, blank, watching these vehicles of one sort or another, and along came a tall, fine-looking man with a very remarkable air about him, and he generously gave me a packet of biscuits.

More and more prisoners started to come in, and we were held in a field for several days before we were taken through Lille to a fortress known as 'the black hole of Lille'. As we marched, the townspeople came out and tried to offer us bread, even though they were hungry themselves.

The fortress was a truly awful place; I hesitate to describe it. Hundreds of men were crowded into cells, men lying on wooden shelves for day after day, six to one bunk, jam-packed, men covered in scabies. You couldn't move in the filthy conditions. Sometimes the Germans came along and we were given half an hour's fresh air. Food was a mug of soup but what was in it, I can't tell you.

Men were dying every day from wounds and dysentery. I was kept for twelve days, and it was a relief to be taken to Germany. Like so many others, I was reported missing, believed killed, and it was some time before I was able to write home.

Private Tom Dewing, 34th Division, Royal Engineers Signal Company, 1896-2001

It is impossible to give a coherent account of that spring retreat. I remember crossing a river via floating duckboards, moored on the far bank of the Lys and pulled across by ropes. I remember the explosion when a bridge, mined to stop the German advance, was blown up. I remember intense artillery fire on our left; I remember an old man pottering about the road saying "Mon dieu, mon dieu!" There was a farmer leading a horse as his wife sat on top of a wagon loaded with their possessions. I remember a sergeant stopping him and insisting that he gave the old man a lift. I remember sitting down to sleep on the floor of an empty house with my loaded rifle beside me. I could see through the open back door and it wouldn't have surprised me if that evening I'd seen Germans approaching. I remember a bombing officer collecting a group of runners and officers' servants to go and plug a gap in the line and I remember, when the Very lights went up that night, they formed three quarters of a circle round us.

Private Fred Hodges, 10th Lancashire Fusiliers, 1899-2002

The battalion would be withdrawn to a village or town behind the lines, often still under shellfire, and a corporal comes along and he stands up on a galvanized water tank in a farmyard and shouts. A crowd quickly gathers round him. The corporal's got the mail and he calls out the names, and as they are read out, voices call back, "He was killed at so and so"…"I reckon he was taken prisoner"…"The last I saw of him…" And they would give their verdict as to where a comrade might be and I shouldn't think a third of the letters were claimed by anybody.

Lance Corporal Vic Cole, 1st Queen's Own (Royal West Kent Regiment), 1897-1995

My wound bandaged, I lay until the attack slackened off. They lifted me into an empty ration limber drawn by a couple of mules and we rattled off back through the forest. I hardly recognized the place as the same one we had come through such a short time before. Then it had been a lovely peaceful bird sanctuary and now it was a shambles, fallen trees and great holes everywhere.

When I came out of the wood, I looked right and left. There were red caps about fifty yards apart and I said to the driver, "What are they doing here?" and he said, "They're to stop anybody going back."

Private Fred Hodges, 10th Lancashire Fusiliers, 1899-2002
At night you're all alone, you might be the only man in the world. Your battalion's fairly near you, but you and your mate are the only two sentries awake and you look around and there's nothing going on. You look up and notice the stars, and I'd try and remember the names of the constellations. Similarly, in the day you'd see white clouds lazily drifting over the battle front, hear larks singing overhead, and nature just getting on with life, a bank of poppies sheer red, yet all around men were dying, and you couldn't help but be struck by the contrast between the horror that man had created for over four years and nature which proceeded in its quiet, beautiful way, stars, birds, flowers, the humming of bees. I had never lived so close to nature and was acutely aware of life, the abundance of colour and scent.

[Ed. Prisoners who were transported to Germany were, on the whole, formally registered as POWs. Messages could then be sent via the Red Cross to loved ones back home who, until then, knew little more than that a son or husband was "missing". Once registered, prisoners became eligible for food parcels sent from Britain, though not all men received them. Prisoners who were kept in France were far less fortunate. These men worked close to the battlefront and were rarely registered and so were "lost" to any help from home. They lived on watery soup and anything else they could steal or scrounge. Frequently, the first news that these men were still alive was when they walked through the door back home, perhaps a year later.]

Private Walter Green, 1/7th Durham Light Infantry, 1897-1998

We were taken to work in an ironstone mine. I worked with another English lad, two Russians and a chap from Luxembourg with a peg leg, who was trained to do the drilling and blasting. We had to break the stone up and load it into wagons all day long, then, during the night, Italians came along and pushed what we'd loaded onto a gantry and it was taken outside. We were awakened at three in the morning, given a bowl of soup and a wash, and then got ready to be taken down the mine to start work at four, for twelve hours, when you came back up for another bowl of soup and bed. The work was very physical, using a seven-pound hammer, a diamond chisel, and a shovel. The hammer had a rosewood shaft which would bend, so as you swung the head to hit the chisel, the effect was to turn a seven-pound hammer into one with the power of a ten, perhaps fifteen pounds, smashing stone three foot square into little pieces. For the first three weeks your hands blistered, and then the blisters got hard, and then your hands got hard.

You weren't conscious of how much weight you lost. You weaken as time progresses, so that towards the end of the day you are told to get on with it or else you're not going to get your quota, in which case you might face a punishment commando. They'd threaten you with all sorts, but the most effective was that if you didn't do what you were told, you'd go down the salt mines.

Mostly, we had soup. It was so thin we used to say that it was 'been soup', not made with beans, but that it was once soup. Lots of men, particularly the Russians, were dying through a disease called octin, which was caused by having too much liquid in the blood with no substance in it. The signs were pain and swelling in your feet, then right up your legs until it got into your body, and then it started to swell your head, and then you'd suddenly die. I was in hospital a week with octin. A cart used to come round, and bodies of those that had died during the night were thrown onto it. I had some advice, to try and strain the soup, if I could, and sacrifice the water and eat only what was left over. It's hard to do when you are so hungry.

The only way to supplement the meals was by scrounging, if you could, but this was difficult for us, being in the mines. If you could get out on a fatigue into a field when food was growing, you could eat raw potatoes to fill up. What won't fatten will at least fill. Those who were working near houses, repairing railway lines or working on goods trains were best off, as they could scrounge around in dustbins for peelings and cabbage leaves which they would bring back to the camp and boil up.

Rifleman Robert Renwick, MM, 16th King's Royal Rifle Corps, 1896-1997

They had us handling ammunition, and of course we let them know that we shouldn't, that it was against international law. We were loading shells, then handgrenades the shape of an egg, from a light railway truck to the full gauge railway, and a box dropped in between and exploded. Whether it was done on purpose, I don't know, but the whole thing went up in flames. I was in a big truck with a mate and a German, helping. The sentry jumped out first, then my friend, both being wounded. I was unhurt and I dragged my friend to safety, then, spotting a garden, I went into it and had a feed of anything I could find.

The Germans took it that it was sabotage. We were sent to solitary confinement in Fort Macdonald. We had six weeks of confinement in there, during which we lost most weight. It was a terrible, weary time. You were just called out for your coffee and your black rye bread, 1/3 of a loaf for dinner and breakfast, but we were all so hungry that we ate it there and then and had nothing else until the watery soup next day at lunchtime. We had no exercise, we just lay on wooden beds with no bedding, nothing to do, nothing to read. Two dozen to a cell.

I came home weighing seven stone, and my mother and sister cried at the sight of us. We were never in a registered camp and as a result we never got a Red Cross parcel. We were shunted from one farm building to another. I won't say we were ill-treated, but we were badly neglected.

Private Harold Lawton, 1/4th East Yorkshire Regiment, 1899-

Horse-wagons took us to Germany and as the train trundled along we took turns to reach up to the small barred window to get fresh air. Our first camp was in Westphalia, where we were cleaned up, our uniforms fumigated, and our bodies washed. Our boots were taken away and we were given wooden clogs that nobody liked.

Before I went to France, we heard that a local man, well-known in Rhyl, had been taken prisoner, and that he was not having a bad time at all. When I arrived at the POW camp, this man was there and he seemed to be in charge of the place as far as the POWs were concerned. Everybody knew who he was. When I went up to him, I asked if he could get me any tea and sugar, which he did. Then one day we saw a German, a real Prussian, bullying a young man, pushing him around, and this chap from Rhyl went straight over and knocked the guard out with one punch. Of course he was arrested straight away and put into the cells. Everybody knew about it, but when his trial came he was sentenced to one year in Cologne Prison and he was taken away.

A group of us were then taken on to Minden Camp, sifted, and a few of us put on one side to be examined by a friendly German Colonel. He talked English to us one at a time, asking what we were going to do after the war, while a man took notes. He asked me if I was going to university and which one I would like to go to. I told him I wanted to specialize in French and Latin and he asked some very intelligent questions to check whether it was true or not. At the end, he said to the man behind him, "A1 intelligent". What he was going to do with this information, I've no idea, but I've the impression we were given lighter work than the others.

Each morning the guards brought a cylinder of clear liquid, tea it was supposed to be, but everybody used it for shaving instead. I was able to speak to a guard and got a job peeling potatoes, and a group of five of us peeled them in a glasshouse. I still had underwear on under baggy blue trousers, and I used to tie a piece of string round the bottom of my pants, and while peeling, I took some slices and put them down my trousers to cook that night, just enough for myself and one or two others. I had to be careful, walking away, to stop them falling out, as the German in charge, a nice chap really, used to watch us go and I had to walk very steadily. It was awfully difficult to build a fire without raising suspicion, but we managed to boil the potato in a mug.

In time we got Red Cross parcels once a month, cardboard boxes which were administered by the Swiss. Occasionally they were damaged on purpose. Some of the Germans examining them stuck chisels through the contents to check nothing untoward was hidden inside. In some respects we were eating better than they were. They were very short of food and used to look with longing eyes when the parcels came in.

Flight Sergeant William George Hall, No216264, 216 Squadron Royal Naval Air Service, 23 May 1898-January 1999

I was posted to a place called Ochey, near Nancy, at the end of October 1917 where the Squadron took over a French aerodrome. The weather was all against us, raining and snowing, and we were up to our necks in mud. It was a miserable place and we didn't actually undertake operations in our twin-engine Handley Page bombers until March, just as the Germans launched their big offensive.

At that age, nineteen, I was anxious to do anything that pleased me, if you can understand that. As a boy, I was always climbing trees. I used to climb out of my bedroom window and shuffle along the rooftops. I had no fear of heights. I never stopped to wonder what would happen if I fell or a branch broke beneath me. Likewise, if I'd worried about flying, I wouldn't have been able to do my job properly. If anything happened, too bad, there was nobody else to blame.

At the Squadron, we used to go into the officers' mess and have a really nice dinner, and start flying as it came dark. At first, we only did short trips to places like Metz which we could bomb two or three times a night. Metz was a strategically important rail junction and it took a real pasting because it was an easy journey, two hours. If we were supposed to go on a longer, six-hour journey, say to Mannheim or Coblenz, and the weather was against us, right, we banked round and bombed Metz on our way home.

Very often we would set off and turn back, either because there was something wrong with the plane, such as an oil or petrol gauge leak, or with the weather. On one occasion, the petrol connection went and fuel poured out all over the plane. I got a bit of paper and stuffed it in the hole and we immediately flew home. Any little fault, you went home, you did not take the chance, and some were very minor indeed.

We never bombed the trenches. If you were only twenty yards out, the bombing would be pointless. At best, you might kill or injure a handful of men and that wasn't worth the effort of flying there and the cost of the bombs. You left that to the artillery. Our targets were anything that helped the German war effort. We bombed Cologne, Mannheim, all along the Rhine, different works, ammunition factories, aerodromes, an important bridge, railway junctions or yards, and, if we spotted anything quite interesting, we bombed that as well. On one occasion, I bombed a train.

There was one thing that worried me. If we were going on a raid on a Sunday night when people would be in church, I knew it was possible that I might kill them. So on one of my leaves I had a word with a clergyman and he told me, "No, you can reassure yourself there, you're doing your duty. If it happens, it is most unfortunate." After that, I never thought about the people below.

When you flew, you watched the pilot all the time, watched his switches, his clocks, you watched how he made manoeuvres, so that in an emergency you could take over. I did feel that I could get a plane down, even if I crashed on landing. We had no parachutes. We weren't used to them so it didn't enter our minds. If people wanted to know what we would do, we told them we'd slide down a searchlight's beam.

We didn't dwell on death. Rather, we were enjoying the adventure, no matter what it was, good or bad. We felt we were much luckier than the fellows in the trenches in every way, comfort, hot food every night and a bed. Frankly, that's why I joined the air service, because I didn't want to go in the trenches.

The only thing we were issued with, should we be shot down, was a tiny compass about the size of a farthing; we received no other help than that. Your life was in the hands of the pilot. One of our fellows, Staniland, missed the aerodrome coming back from a raid, and looking for a place to land thought he saw a field. Well, actually he landed in the middle of a wood, so he was killed, but he was the only one we lost from our Squadron.

If everything was in our favour, we could achieve 70mph, but that was with the wind behind us. I would plot the course before we went. I was navigator and bomber, and the pilot flew the plane and did as you asked him to do. When we took off from the aerodrome, we started off with five planes, half an hour between them, but by the time you got to the objective, the difference could be much longer or shorter.

Bombing Cologne, we'd follow the river to find the city, and as we got toward it, all the city lights would suddenly go out as if there was a switch, so by the time we got there it was all black, and we had to rely on the bridge behind the cathedral to give us a sense of where we were. We knew the city was getting ready. Anti-aircraft guns would start up and searchlights scoured the sky. Once they found us, a dozen beams would concentrate on us, a brilliant light; it was like looking at an oncoming car with undipped headlights, but twelve times worse. We couldn't see a thing below and we used hand signals to tell the pilot how to get out of them, waving to dip or bank. The pilot would immediately dive or fly higher to get out of the beam.

We fired at the searchlights as much as anything to relieve the pressure but the machine guns were really for defence against other planes. In the dark you couldn't see a plane, only a black mask. On one occasion we'd finished a raid and were coming back, and nearing the aerodrome we could see searchlights, so we knew something was happening. Eventually the searchlights went out, but as we prepared to land I saw a black object below me. I prepared the machine gun, not knowing if it was ours or theirs, before I suddenly realized it was just my own shadow from the moon onto the ground.

As a crew we all sat in the middle of the fuselage. The pilot and the navigator sat forward of the bombs, and the gunners stood further back. They had two guns, one to shoot behind and upwards and one to fire underneath the plane, through an opening. As the navigator, I sat alongside the pilot.

Only as we approached the target would I crawl forward through a hole about two feet by three feet, under the instruments, to the actual bomb-dropping position, right at the nose of the plane. There I'd prepare the bomb sight, adjusting for wind, speed and height. I would approach the town but not go straight for it. Instead I'd go right round and then get the pilot to close down the engines and sail quietly over the objective. That had two advantages: the plane wasn't shuddering or moving so your sighting was steady, and at the same time the searchlights couldn't find you because they couldn't hear you.

Underneath where the pilot and the navigator sat, there was an eight-foot square grid like a box of eggs into which these bombs would fit on hooks. Our plane took sixteen one-hundredweight bombs and to drop each one you pulled a lever that released a hook. The bombs had four wings and, if they had not been properly aligned, the tips could catch in the corner of the fitting and wouldn't drop. When this happened, you had to lean over from your end and the gunner would do the same and free them by hand by trying to square them in the fitting.

When we were bombing, we flew at five or six thousand feet, no more or we couldn't see the target. We could see the explosion of anti-aircraft fire in the air and the shrapnel would fly about, making dozens of holes in the fabric, but these were easily repaired. If I heard an explosion, I knew it was very close because our engines, one on each side, created a deuce of a noise, and to hear anything above them meant it had to be near.

It was very cold and so we had feet and hand warmers. We wore our uniforms under a suit like dungarees, woollen-lined, so we were warm. The soles of your boots were electrically heated, but they sometimes got so hot that they burned your feet and you switched them off, and it was the same with your gloves. At the front the wind buffeted you, and I wore glasses to protect my eyes, but I lost more than one pair and a hat to the wind.

Standing up at the front of the plane, you were covered only to your knees while the rest of your body was exposed. The machine gun was mounted on an iron ring and you used to hold on to that pretty tightly, especially when you were dropping a bomb, because at that moment you only had one hand holding on.

Because we approached the target from the rear, we were already on a straight course for home. That's when I would look back. Of course, as it was dark I couldn't see a bomb drop, but I could see it burst. If there was just a flash, you'd think, "Well, that was wasted," but if it caused a fire, oh, you were on top of the world. Then, as we flew away, you looked back and you'd see some of the city lights gradually coming back on.

Once back at the aerodrome, we would check we had no bombs. It was impossible to land with any that were stuck as they were already primed and might explode on landing, so we would fly a little way off and try again to release them, blowing a nice hole in a field.

Air Mechanic Henry Allingham, No12 Squadron, Royal Naval Air Service, 1896-

I was a mechanic so I wasn't meant to fly, but in the RNAS you were mechanic, gunner and head bottle washer, and so you did anything that was asked of you. You never knew when you might go up; if you'd done a job on a plane, the pilot would point at you and say 'patrol' or 'first flight.' This ensured you did the best job you could on it.

You'd take off just before light in the morning. As we went up, I always had to listen to the engine; the least change of note and you would come back, if you could. There were so many accidents. I've seen aircraft and they'd be going along and suddenly they'd come down, it wasn't very pleasant - I've seen fellows fighting for their lives to keep control as little things went wrong. Very often the lock nuts failed, as lots of them were poorly-designed, and the plane stood no chance, bucket and a spade that's all you'd need for the pilot.

Even when you landed safely, you had to bail out as fast as you could and leave the plane for 20 minutes. It would seem all right, then woosh, it would be all in flames. If pilots didn't get out quickly enough you'd see them burnt alive and you had nothing to put the fire out with, nothing at all. You had to stand and watch and their arms would slowly rise into the air. There were no fire extinguishers whatsoever.

When you were flying in the Ypres Salient, you could see our line all the way round and Jerry's line too, but you had your job to think of, you weren't there to daydream or sightsee. Jerry's anti-aircraft guns would pop at you but you generally knew the height you'd need, to keep out of harm's way. In the air the German pilots rarely engaged unless they had the advantage. In action you had to hold your fire, and that took some nerve; then you gave them a squirt with the Lewis Gun.

The pressure was terrible and the pilots had to be rested sometimes. You couldn't take too much, most people had a breaking point. They'd get what we called the 'jumps', nervous. Some could take a lot and some could hardly take any, it depended on the make-up of the individual.

The pilots would make a report when they got back and then they tried to forget the strain, didn't think on it. You'd never mention a man once you'd lost him, you dare not, you'd never stand it otherwise. You had to forget, become hardened, become callous to it.

[Ed. By midsummer, the German offensive was exhausted. Time and again they had sought to force a break-through and time and again they had been thwarted. Up and down the line, the Germans held

*salients penetrating deep into Allied lines that inevitably proved
impossible to hold when Allied forces returned to the offensive.]*

*A/Captain Norman Dillon, MC, 20th Tank Battalion, Tank Corps,
1896-1997*
On 8 August, we made a big attack on each side of the Amiens-
Peronne road. B Battalion was to lead the way, and my C.O. and I had
a few hours' rest in a shelter, after seeing that all the tanks had arrived
at their starting point.

Before dawn we set off and fell in with the tanks just before zero.
The silence was broken by the roar of the artillery barrage, the
Germans making no noticeable response. I accompanied the Colonel
down the road so that I could show him the route the tanks would take.
The attack was underway and we walked until we met a tank coming
towards us, looking very menacing. It appeared that the officer in
charge had not adjusted his compass properly and it was 180 degrees
out. With some difficulty, we persuaded him that he was wrong and
turned him about.

The leading tanks advanced so successfully that they quickly
reached the German field-gun positions. One gun was still in place
and was loosing off at point-blank range and a shell burst right
between my legs. I got a piece of aluminium nose-cap in the left ankle,
which lodged between the Achilles tendon and the bone. I also
received sundry small wounds in the back. I was placed on a stretcher
and carried by some German prisoners down the road to a Field
Dressing Station. I was in hospital for three months, so it proved the
end of the war for me.

Private Archie Richards, 25th Battalion Tank Corps, 1897-1998
A few days after the big attack on 8 August, the officer in charge that
day came to me and said, "Richards – are you Private Archibald
Richards?" I said yes. "Well, you'd better get a letter off to your
mother to say you're all right because we've made a mistake. We've

sent a letter to your family saying that you've been killed, but it's a man named Private Sidney Richards who's been killed, two different names, understand?" I didn't know the man because we never mixed, the crews never mixed. We were more or less kept isolated in our tanks. I don't even know if he was in my company. So I got a letter off to my mother right away to say that I was all right. When I came home, she told me she'd never believed it, that it couldn't be true. There were so many getting killed that odd things happened, and she was sure they'd made a mistake.

[Ed. Private Sydney Richards was serving with the 15th Battalion Tank Corps when he was killed on 8 August 1918. By coincidence both men were Cornishmen: Sydney came from St Austell, and Archie from a little village the other side of Liskeard, twenty miles away.

The most extraordinary example of this sort of error that I met was the case recounted to me by a 100-year-old veteran, John Steele (1898-1998), a former private in the 3/5th Lancashire Fusiliers. In an attack at Passchendaele in 1917, another soldier in the same battalion, Private John Steel (without an 'e') was killed. "I was officially reported killed," recalled John Steele. "I got my name in the paper and the Boy Scouts wrote an obituary. After I'd been reported dead, my sister received a field card and wrote to the War Office to tell them I was still alive."

Not only did the two men share the same name, if with a slightly different spelling, incredibly they shared almost the same number. John Steele who survived had the number 39332; John Steel who died was numbered 39331]

Private Andrew Bowie, 5th Cameron Highlanders, 1897-2002
I was gassed in 1918 but the War Office sent word to my mother saying that they regretted to inform her that I had been shot in both eyes and was blind, which was a terrible shock for her. My family wrote to the hospital and a Sister wrote back to say that while the gas had temporarily blinded me, there was every reason to hope that my

sight would return to normal. I was receiving hot fomentations on both eyes on a regular basis.

Nevertheless, the shock of the letter had more than contributed to my mother going from a lady with quite dark hair, with the odd streak of grey, to a lady with hair that was quite white. The wording of the War Office letter was to blame, she said, and the fact that the words they wrote were so very brief and harsh.

Private Allen Short, 2/10th London Regiment, 1899-2000
On two occasions, my mother received a letter announcing that I was wounded. On both occasions, she told me that she knew I was in trouble before any notification arrived. Mrs Wells, the mother of Teddy Wells, who'd been killed on the Somme, had a similar sort of experience.

She had a brother in the New Zealand forces and she woke up in bed one night to see the door open and her brother appear. He said, "Daisy, I'm quite OK, I'm quite happy." She could hear the music of the Londonderry Air, *Danny Boy*.

The door closed and she went to sleep. In the morning, she went downstairs and Doctor Paxton who lived in the same house, was there. She said, "I had a funny dream last night. I dreamt of my brother. He was in my room and I heard the sound of the Londonderry Air." The doctor, who had been called out that night, said, "When I came home about 1am, you came downstairs and went straight to the pianola, which used rolls of music, and you took some music, put it on, played it and walked back upstairs. All the time you were fast asleep. Go and look at the roll." It was the Londonderry Air. They found out later that about this time her brother was killed.

[Ed. Apparent sixth sense was not so uncommon during the war. In May 1915, when Ben Clouting was wounded by shrapnel, his mother collapsed at home two hours later in severe shock. When she later visited Ben in hospital, she said told him, "I just knew you were in trouble."]

Private Doug Roberts, 7th Buffs (East Kent Regiment), 1900-2002
Towards the end of the war, we were all youngsters of 18 or 19. We were carefree buggers, fit and strong. We didn't give a damn for nobody, because we didn't know if we were going to die next, day, next month, or next hour.

Sergeant Eastmond was our sergeant, one of the few old sweats still with us. He'd been out since 1915 and had risen from a private to a sergeant because he was trusted as well as being a nice man too. We were in the line under intense and prolonged bombardment for the best part of two days. Then on 22 August, Eastmond came round to give us all a spoonful of rum as we were to go over. We went over, but in doing so our company, B Company, got separated from C Company and so they sent Sergeant Eastmond and me forward to find them.

We had to run and jump over a high railway bank, and roll down the other side before Jerry swept it with a machine gun. We found C Company about a mile in front of us. As we came back, we charged over the top of the railway bank again and rolled down, as Jerry fired again. At the bottom I stood up, turned and saw Eastmond's legs shaking like a shot rabbit. I couldn't do anything for him. When I got back to the company, I found the CO and told him Sergeant Eastmond was dead but he wouldn't believe me, it was such a shock to lose someone as experienced as him.

Private George Rice, 1/5th Duke of Wellington's Regiment, 1897-
We had taken an important ridge and were digging in, waiting for the inevitable German counter-attack. We were roaming about and all at once the enemy came at us from nowhere. We didn't know what was happening. They had fixed bayonets – they wanted to bayonet me. I tried to compose myself as a group stormed forward, screaming loudly and firing wildly to intimidate us. In the confusion, the lieutenant in charge of the section was shot dead. I dropped down on the ground with the Lewis gun, kept it steady, then pressed the trigger. The Germans ran onto my bullets. They were so near. They ran on and I

kept firing and I shot them all. I counted eight dead on the ground, just in front of me, riddled with machine-gun fire.

Private Ted Francis, 16th Royal Warwickshire Regiment, 1896-1996
There was a call for men with experience of car engines for a special job with the tanks. Like a fool, I stepped forward and volunteered. They wanted eight men in all, and as a group we were told to report to a tank battalion the following morning to meet the officer in charge, who would tell us our role in an attack. I was shocked. Our job, we were informed, was to walk behind four tanks with a special attachment fixed to our rifles firing smoke bombs over the top to create a smokescreen. Two men would be allocated to each tank. I said to the fellow next to me, another man from my battalion, "We've had it this time." He said, "What do you mean?" I replied, "It's a thousand to one on that we shall be killed, because the moment we go over the top of that ridge, every shell, bomb, rifle and machine gun will be at us and we shall be outside."

The first hundred yards were quiet but, sure enough, when we got to the top of the ridge the shells began absolutely flying over, as we tried to hide behind the tank. When all the smoke bombs had gone, the officer in charge of our tank, God bless him, saved our lives. "Have you used all the bombs?" he shouted. "Yes". "Well, don't just stand there, get inside." He was the only officer of the four tanks who asked the fellows to get in. The other six were left to themselves.

By this time the fellow with me was shell-shocked, his face was so contorted he could hardly speak, and we had to practically carry him to the nearest cover when the tank ditched in a trench. Most of the crew inside were injured and bleeding from the bumps, and they struggled to get out, because they feared the tank would be set alight.

There was a brand new machine gun in the tank, but no one in the crew was in any state to carry it, so I volunteered to take it back.

Of the six other poor fellows who had followed the tanks, three were killed and three badly wounded. Of the eight, I was the only one to come out unscathed, and from that moment I got the habit of saying each morning, "Thank you, Lord, for this day."

Private Doug Roberts, 7th Buffs (East Kent Regiment), 1900-2002
I'd been out in France for several months when there was a campaign, I believe in *The Mirror* newspaper, about eighteen-year-olds going into the line, and the Government was worried because so many had been killed or injured. The tide had clearly turned against the Germans and it was felt that boys of my age should not be sent to fight now that the enemy were falling back. In response to the pressure, someone in the Regiment decided to remove me from the firing line. Being born in 1900 made me one of the younger ones in the battalion, and so I was given a job with the regimental police, but, to be honest, that was the worst job of the lot. Behind the lines, when the men were out on rest, they were often difficult to control. These buggers in cafés or estaminets might be killed the next day, and they didn't care a damn for the likes of me or anybody else.

If we had to turf them out of a place, the first thing the men used to do was shoot the light out, making the place inky black inside. There was a corporal with me from the Durham Light Infantry, or Devil's Last Issue as we called them, and he was a good chap. He said, "All right, Doug, you stop there, you count them as they come out." He went into this café. Next moment a chap comes flying out the door into the night air, landing with a thump. "Don't start counting yet, it's me," and it was this corporal. They'd physically picked him up and thrown him out.

We had a chap, Corporal Pope, who had been in prison and had had all sorts of disciplinary problems. He had been wounded at one point too, but returned to the battalion. He was marching with us, in my company, and he'd been out of prison for a long time, and he walked out of the line and he wrapped his rifle round a tree. Corporal Pope, I can see his face now, he said, "I'm not fucking well going any more." He was arrested and placed back in nick again, wasn't he? That's what he did it for. He'd made up his mind that he wasn't going back into the line again.

Private George Rice, 1/5th Duke of Wellington's Regiment, 1897-
It was night. We had pushed forward near a small village, virtually face to face with the enemy. We spread out along a lane that was bounded by a railway embankment, only just high enough to give us some cover but with a good field of view. There was a lull in the noise of battle. Obviously, we kept extremely quiet, deathly silent. In the moonlight, a lone German sentry patrolled the railway line above us. Although under orders to hold our fire, someone in our section could not resist a shot at this man, triggering a massive discharge of arms along the line. The German sentry, in the face of certain death, went into total panic, zigzagging, and ducking to avoid the hail of bullets. Suddenly, one of the more sensitive amongst us called out in a very loud voice, "Give him a chance, chaps!" The firing ceased. The sentry ran off. I felt very emotional and, strangely, hopeful.

Private Allen Short, 1/8th London Regiment, 1899-2000
It was 7am, Sunday morning. We were lying out under a ridge, hidden from the Germans, who were the best part of a mile away, ready for the order to go over. Lying there, we could hear a church bell, calling villagers to early morning mass, and there wasn't a gun being fired. The tension built up as we waited, but once on the move, as far as I was concerned, it went well. An officer, dressed as a private, urged us forward. As we were attacking, the Germans retired, and we went a mile before we met any trouble. Then the bullets came past like angry bees, and you were lucky if they missed you. I felt a tremendous whack on the foot and I looked down and there was a piece of shrapnel about four inches long. I picked it up. I thought, "Oh good, I've got a blighty," but I hadn't, it hadn't even broken the stitching on the boot, but when I took my boot off next morning, I'd a bruise as black as the ace of spades.

By this time a lot of men wanted out of the war and were desperate for a light wound or even worse. A friend of mine, Len West, was in an attack with the 10th Londons and was hit by one of our own shells. He lost his left leg, was paralysed down the right side and finished up in a wheelchair. He was in hospital for a year at least. When I was on leave after being wounded, I visited him and he laughed at me. "You've got to go back, I'm out of it." He thought he was luckier than me.

Private Ted Francis, 16th Warwickshire Regiment, 1896-1996
We were in a fairly quiet part of the line and taking turns on duty, looking over the top now and again, and a sergeant came to me and said, "There's a nice little dugout round the corner, enough for one; you're not on for two hours. I'll send somebody to call you." I got into this tiny dugout, just big enough for one man to lie down full length. On top were lumps of iron, railway sleepers, and wood that they put over the trenches to try and keep them bullet and splinter-proof.

I must have been sound asleep when a whizz bang hit it and the roof came down. I had one leg curled up but the other was outstretched and it was crushed. I screamed in pain. I knew immediately that my ankle was smashed, but of course I was in a fortunate position as only yards away were plenty of people, but it took them quite a considerable time to get me out, trying to pull me and jarring my ankle.

When I got to hospital, an American doctor came to me and whispered to the nurse, and this fellow in the next bed told me, "You lucky so-and-so, you're for England in the morning." I could have kissed that doctor. Those were the words that I'd longed to hear for four years. I looked at my foot, and thought, surely even if I get well, I won't be sent to France again, and that gave me such a great relief. As far as I was concerned, I couldn't get out of the army quick enough, and here was a splendid wound, painful but splendid. I was overwhelmed with delight.

I was put in an ambulance train. Of course, if you live in Solihull or

Birmingham, they put you as near Scotland as possible, to stop too many visitors, but when I thought about it, no one that I knew would be coming to visit anyway. I had no girl, I had no mother or father, and my older brother hardly knew me. There was only Harry and he was still in the army.

[Ed. During September, the Germans fell back on the Hindenburg Line. The outposts of this great defensive position were attacked one by one until the line itself, long deemed impregnable, was attacked on 27 September. In twenty-four hours, and after a million-shell bombardment, the line was fatally breached. The Germans had no expectation that they could make any sort of concerted stand. The war was in its last throws, although there remained much hard fighting until Germany finally capitulated.]

Private Allen Short, 1/8th London Regiment, 1899-2000
About 3 o'clock in the afternoon, Jerry started sending over gas shells and we got our gas masks on. He stopped shelling round about midnight; it was a bit breezy and the gas soon cleared. After eight hours of wearing these masks, we couldn't wait to get them off. All the time one's nose is pinched, making it difficult to breathe, while our temples were numb with the stretching of the elastic band round our heads.

I'd been without cigarettes for four days and was desperate for a smoke, especially as we'd had an issue of fifty cigarettes each that morning. We'd had a couple when a high explosive shell hit the parapet in front of my section, partially burying four of us. I remember a great clod of mud as hard as iron hitting my elbow and a piece of shrapnel grazed my forehead. A volley of gas shells followed and as we struggled to extricate ourselves we breathed in the gas. It was mustard gas, and it began to burn under the arms and between the legs, anywhere you were likely to perspire. I was anxious to get my gas mask back on, which wasn't easy as I wore glasses.

Our spell of duty ended and we climbed down from the firestep and dozed off, marvellous what you can do when you are tired. When I woke up, I was startled to see that I was bringing up green vomit; my sight was there but my eyes were all gummed as if by glue. I forced my eyes open to check that my sight was all right, while I discovered my voice had gone, all I could do was whisper. It was weeks before it came back.

A Welshman called Davies was swearing like anything, while another boy was crying for his mother. We were collected and taken down in a crocodile, each hanging on to the man in front. As we walked, everyone vomited over everyone else; I was lucky to be the last man in the line. My company, which had been sixty strong when we'd gone into the trenches, came out numbering thirty, that in normal times was meant to have a nominal strength of 250!

A/Lance Corporal Cecil Withers, 17th Royal Fusiliers, 1898-2005
It was dark and we were sheltering from the shellfire behind a concrete pillbox when we were ordered to leave. To do so, we turned sharp left and down a little passageway and then made a dash for it. We were taking turns to go when the man ahead of me stepped out just as a time fuse shell burst over the entrance. He got the full blast and his head and body were flattened like a concertina. The force of the explosion flung me back bodily against the chaps behind who fell like dominos onto each other until the officer, at the end of the line, was dashed against the back wall with such force that it killed him stone dead.

I picked myself up. My turn. I went out to the edge of the St Quentin Canal close to the river Escaut where the engineers had constructed a narrow improvised bridge, on top of which they'd laid straw. While I was going across, the Germans were firing machine guns blindly. If I'd got shot there, I'd have been down in the water and never come up. Talk about getting the wind up – I'll tell you straight, I got the wind up then!

Air Mechanic Henry Allingham, No12 Squadron, Royal Naval Air Service, 1896-

We were going forward over the battlefield as the Germans withdrew. It was getting dark and really the only safe thing to do was to stay where you were, so I got my groundsheet and got myself ready to go to sleep. Before settling down, I went to look at something and fell in a shell hole. I couldn't get out and it was all crumbling at the sides. I got frightened, all sorts of dead things were in there. The more I tried to get out, the more the ground crumbled and I got deeper in the shell hole. The smell was awful for as I struggled, I disturbed the water. I moved a little to the left and the ground shallowed and I dug my feet in and got my belly on the ground and wriggled out. I sat there in the dark and waited for daylight. I didn't even dare to find my groundsheet again, I was so frightened. Well, that night I was stinking. Heaven knows what was in there. I wore that tunic until I got into Germany.

Sapper Arthur Halestrap, 46th Division Royal Engineers, 1898-2004
For the attack on the Hindenburg Line, we had a transmitter receiver, a trench set as it was called, in a wooden case with a carrying strap. Then there were batteries, which were very heavy cells, also carried in a wooden box with a strap. We had two tubular fifteen-foot steel masts in three-foot sections to sling over our shoulders with ropes and guys all together in a sack with a mallet and aerial wire. On top of this we had our own rifles, ammunition and field equipment, a knapsack, groundsheet, and gas mask, amongst other things, as well as six days' rations of bully beef, canned fruit, biscuits and bread, which had been placed in a sandbag. We had been told a carrying party was coming to help us through the trenches, but we received a note from a runner to say that the infantry had no men to spare. The three of us struggled on but the job was impossible. We had to dump something and the only thing we could afford to lose was the sack containing our rations. When we finally got to the front line we found the infantry waiting to go over.

Because we'd had to dump our rations, we ate anything we could find. We dug biscuits out of the mud of the trench, washing them with water from petrol cans, and that's the way we managed until the corporal found a packet of oatmeal on a railway track, and we lived on that for some considerable length of time. When you are hungry and you find something discarded, you'll use any means to make it edible.

When we had the orders to go over and erect our aerials, the shelling was still very heavy. Then the corporal said, "Oh dear, he's no good," and the third man with us was lying at the bottom of the trench gibbering; he was absolutely shell-shocked, his teeth were chattering and he was moaning, because the barrage was so fierce.

The noise of the guns and the shells bursting, it's impossible to describe a barrage of that nature, the different tones of the shells, the high whine of the machine gun bullets, and small arms and the heavy shells going over: it was a medley of sound, all mixed together. The corporal looked at me, shrugged his shoulders and said, "Come on, we'd better get on with it." We went on without this man and came back for him afterwards. He'd recovered and didn't remember a thing about it. The corporal said nothing to him and neither did I.

Private Percy Wilson, 21st Manchester Regiment, 1899-2004
The Germans set booby traps on windows, doors, anything that could be moved. They knew men were looking for things, souvenirs and so on, and they rigged these things to blow. The officers used to lecture us. "Whatever you do, don't touch doors or windows." But the Germans were clever. We were clearing some old German trenches, making sure there was no one hanging back, hiding. There was a bottle standing on an old wooden box, with a glass beside it. Two men went over, and one got hold of the cork and pulled it, and bang, both men went up, we heard the crash.

Similarly, we came across a gun team of mules that had been shot. A group of us were ordered to dig a hole and bury them, to keep us occupied, I fancy. A Canadian, a Second Lieutenant, took us to a soft place where we could dig deep. He got down and was looking at the mules when all at once he came running back. "Get the hell out of there as fast as you can, those mules are booby trapped!"

Private Dick Trafford, No229158, 1/2nd Monmouthshire Regiment, 1898-1999

We seemed to be getting the Germans into a tight corner, and the officers were telling us "Keep on, lads, keep on." They urged us to give everything we'd got because there were a couple of times when our fellows nearly gave up.

They were tired with marching, and they'd nothing to eat or drink for a couple of days, and there was no sign of rations because the Germans had blown up the crossroads and that had made it difficult to get supplies up.

The men had all eaten their iron rations, which they weren't supposed to, except in emergencies, well, the men put down that it had been an emergency and they'd eaten the biscuits and cheese a while back. Anyway, we were all of one mind: unless we had something to eat, we wouldn't go on.

Driver Alfred Henn, 3rd Battery, Warwickshire Royal Horse Artillery, 1897-2000

Towards the end of the war, we were coming through French village after French village, and our officer halted us and said we'd got to take our canvas buckets and fill them with water to give to the horses. So we all trooped down this long street of working class houses until we came to a gap in the terrace, where there was a pump. As we approached, we were stopped by a crowd of people, who would not allow us any water.

After a moment, a woman shook her fist at us and said, to our total surprise, "Allemands bien, vous cochons", Germans good, you're pigs. It shook me and I can only think that some of our troops had gone in there before we arrived and misbehaved themselves.

Trooper Ben Clouting, 4th (Royal Irish) Dragoon Guards, 1897-1990
Increasing numbers of German prisoners could be seen, trudging back
to our makeshift prison cages. Many were ridiculously young and
looked as if their world had fallen to pieces. They looked dishevelled,
their equipment dilapidated, for their lines of supply were breaking
down, and many had been left to scrounge their own food. At one
farmhouse where I stopped right at the end of the war, I found the
owners in tears: the Germans had passed through, the previous night,
and had eaten their old guard dog, cooking it at the farm.

I passed a cage with sixty or seventy prisoners. Most appeared very
tired and hungry, and only seemed interested in swapping what bits
and pieces they still owned for food. One German caught my eye. He
looked exhausted and was offering his watch for a tin of corned beef.
I agreed. As his watch was flipped over the fence a three-quarter
pound tin of bully was lobbed in the opposite direction. However, the
German was so worn out that he completely failed to catch the tin and
it thudded into his eye, adding to his general misery.

*Private Dick Trafford, No229158, 1/2nd Monmouthshire Regiment,
1898-1999*
We were capturing the enemy all the time. I wouldn't say young boys,
I'd say young men. They were glad that it was ending because from
their point of view they would be right for meals, that's what they tried
to explain to us, they'd not seen a decent meal in a long time. The only
thing they could do had been to kill their horses and use the meat for
food. You saw dead horses on the side of the road and you could see
where lumps had been cut out, from the stomach or off its side.

**Private Smiler Marshall, 8th Machine Gun Squadron, Machine
Gun Corps (Cavalry), 1897-2005**
I thought this was smashing, we'd got them beat. I can't tell you any
dates, but we noticed the last lot that held us up were young boys and
they hadn't got the fight in them that the old ones had. If they saw the

cavalry coming with their swords drawn, they'd scamper. They kept putting their hands up, "Kaput, kaput!" The Germans would stand their ground if they'd got to, but if there was a chance to get away, they would.

Just before the Armistice, the Germans started throwing their rifles away. They weren't going to fight any more, they told us that. One or two spoke English, one had been a pork butcher from York before the war, another had been a hairdresser in London, and they'd had enough. They were ambling along, without their rifles, walking towards Germany, accepting defeat. We believed we could go all the way to Berlin.

CHAPTER SIX

1919

REFLECTIONS

IN TALKING TO VETERANS OVER THE YEARS, I found that many of them felt they could not talk about their memories, because, to a greater or lesser extent, everybody else had been through similar experiences. Why, they asked, should they be seen as special? They were men, and men were supposed to have the British stiff upper lip; to suggest that they were affected by the horrors of the past years would seem, to some, to be personal failure.

Veterans reacted to this in different ways. The immediate response of some, such as Norman Collins, was muted. "Whilst I was glad the war was over, I was not excited about it; I did not feel like going out and rejoicing with champagne. I felt sad. The war should have been stopped earlier: it went on far too long. I don't think anybody won, everybody lost." Nevertheless, Norman was able to use the maturity and understanding of leadership that he had gained in the trenches as a springboard to success in business: he became Deputy Managing Director of F. Perkins Limited, manufacturers of diesel engines.

Richard Hawkins also achieved responsibility and status in his work: he became a director of Bellings, the electrical goods company. He had his own battle, however: the nervous tensions of the war left him with a stutter that he found hard to control.

"It was awfully difficult in business. You would go to a meeting and have to say something, and it was a tremendous stress on the nervous system, which had been pretty well shattered. Nineteen months is too long. It ruined my digestive system, really, and my nervous system, for a good many years afterwards." As he became more senior in his work, coping with his stutter put even more pressure on Richard: "Nobody knew, but it was a strain to hide it. It took me a long time to get over it, a long, long time."

Other veterans, deprived for so long of a normal family life, wanted to marry, have children, and see in the comfort of their lives the rationale for all that they themselves had suffered. Unfortunately, the national economy at the end of the war was depressed, and some found that they had to fight for their families almost as fiercely as they had previously fought for their country. Cecil Withers arrived home, married, and faced unemployment and a desperate search for work. A chance meeting with an officer from his battalion led to a job in the Civil Service, but it was poorly paid, and, to feed his family, Cecil had to undertake supplementary employment in the Post Office, working there in the evenings until he took the last tram home. At Cecil's funeral in April 2005, his son summed up his father's life: "The long struggle to live a family life on minimum income built in his mind a wintry view of human nature and the strenuous cost of survival."

The reaction of the authorities to the suffering and courage of those who survived was sometimes merciless; former soldiers were quickly disabused of any idea that the state would support them beyond a bare minimum. In particular, the lack of any outward physical disability was to prove costly for many a veteran.

Walter Burdon was discharged and received a pension. After a while, he was hauled before two doctors at the Pensions Office, who asked him what he was complaining about. "I told them that my memory had gone, I stuttered with nerves and I had headaches with the wounds." They asked him about his profession, and Walter explained that he made the moulds for machinery, which would then be cast in the foundry. The doctor dismissed his work: "Well, all you need is a hammer, scissors and saw, there's no skill in that." "I beg your pardon, Sir," I said, "but if I told you that in your job all you need is a box of pills and a bottle of coloured water you wouldn't like it, would you?" And he said, "Impertinence. Out, dismiss, out." I lost my pension. My nerves were shattered. I was riding to town on my bike one time and a tyre on a car blew and I fell off my bike with fright.' Many years later, even at 96 years old, Walter still suffered with his nerves. "I'm getting more used to it now as I'm not so keen in hearing, so a loud noise doesn't affect me so much." In interviewing him as late as 1991, I noticed that he still had a slight stutter.

Many veterans either had, or soon acquired, a profound mistrust of officialdom.

Ted Francis already had a deep hatred of the army, which he ruefully contrasted with his youthful dreams of military glory. He wanted above all to put the conflict behind him and to concentrate all his thinking into his job. "That is the reason that I worked for forty years with not one word to anyone about the war."

Robert Renwick also never spoke about his experience. "Neighbours used to ask me, but my mother used to shake her head and say he'll not talk about it and I didn't, all through my working life." In his sleep, however, the war would not go away. "I was sharing a bed with my younger brother and evidently a plane flew over our house. I must have thought I was back at the front. I jumped out of bed half asleep and my brother said, "What are you doing out there?" and I said, "Oh, I'll tell you some time." I was running for shelter, you see."

For years, John Laister never thought about the war, but late in life, he found himself remembering.

"Things crop up, and I'll see myself in the trenches, which I don't want to do. It's been that bad sometimes that I've got up at four o'clock, made myself a cup of tea and tried to go to bed again. I get a mental picture, fantastic pictures, and I see every detail exactly as if I'm there."

At the end of an interview, inevitably, the war is at the forefront of a veteran's mind. However happy he has been to talk about his memories, he is aware that the horrors that he has called to mind might disturb his sleep. Midway between waking and sleeping, he could be instantly transported back to the battlefield. In the home where he lives, Harry Patch can see the light through the glass panel over his door. If a member of staff switches it on at night, the sudden illumination takes Harry back to the moment when a shell burst directly overhead, injuring him and killing his friends.

I asked G B Jameson, as I often asked veterans, if he had ever been disturbed by memories of the war. He thought for a moment, and then said no. Except, he added, on holiday. He would suddenly find himself studying the ground with a soldier's eye: "Gosh, that would make a damn good battery position, wouldn't this do fine?" He had been involved for so long in making such judgements that he couldn't switch off, and in the immediate post-war period it was at the back of his mind, although in time it faded. "I was aware," he said, "of my ability to walk about the place and not have to put my head down, and every now and again it would come back into my mind, "Goodness, I don't have to duck here.""

Some of the veterans I interviewed felt very differently about the war. They hated the suffering, but felt that the experience had offered them something that they would not have missed. "Taking it in the round," Frank Sumpter told me, "except for the tragedy, and the death and all the rest of it, the war was much more interesting than peacetime soldiering, different entirely. It was an experience."

Norman Edwards picked up the same idea, and felt pride in what he had achieved. "The war made a man of me, I think. I hadn't shown any funk. You felt you'd done your duty, that was the main thing and you had the satisfaction of knowing you'd not only done your duty, you'd been wounded doing it too. You had a wound stripe on your arm, which proved you had been in the front line and not just at the base. Fifteen months in and out of the front line."

For many veterans, the abiding memory was of the comrades they had lost, as James Hudson told me most graphically. "I lost a very dear friend towards the end of the war. He was an east end boy. I knew him well and he was a delightful fellow. He always seemed to want to be friendly with me when we came out of the line. We were waiting in a sunken road ready for an attack on a strong point when a shell hit the top of the bank and he was buried. The men dug frantically and they did get down to his hand, and he squeezed back, but unfortunately another lot of earth came down and poor Dickie Bell was buried alive. I don't forget that boy.

Any tribute should not be to us survivors, we were lucky, damn lucky, but to the thousands of young boys lying out there who never saw a life after the age of nineteen or twenty."

Cecil Withers stressed what many veterans felt, that the war was the responsibility of politicians, and that ordinary soldiers were simply doing what they had to do to stay alive.

"It was life – you or them – there was no animosity, no anger, I never thought about killing people, I simply defended myself. You shot them to stop them shooting you, and they no doubt did the same thing. When you look back, politicians are to blame; they organized it and gave the orders."

No matter how many interviews a historian conducts, the actual experience escapes. To the frustration, sometimes, of the veterans themselves, they cannot fully describe the indescribable. As Harry Patch says, with a certain resignation,

"You can't describe it, a smell of death, and you never will. And you can never get it over to the youngsters of today, what it was like. There's no smell on television."

ARMISTICE AND AFTERMATH

The Armistice might have signalled an end to hostilities, but the Germans were under no illusions: the ceasefire was dependent on certain conditions that, if broken, would result in a resumption of war. A peace treaty would be needed and there was no guarantee that the Germans would be willing to accept all that would, in time, be coming their way. The provisions of the November Armistice ensured that they left French and Belgian soil, handing over as they did so the disputed lands of Alsace and Lorraine, which they had taken from the French in the war of 1870. Huge quantities of equipment were to be surrendered to the Allies: 5,000 artillery pieces, 3,000 minenwerfer, 30,000 machine guns, 2,000 aircraft, and 5,000 lorries, although much of it was abandoned or destroyed as the German forces began their retreat to the Rhine and beyond. The German High Seas Fleet, which had not left port since the Battle of Jutland, was to sail into captivity in Scapa Flow, and all submarines were to be surrendered, along with the merchant fleet. Allied prisoners were to be released, with immediate effect. To ensure co-operation, the victorious Allies would follow the enemy closely all the way back to Germany, seizing one of the economic and industrial jewels in the nation's crown, the Rhineland, as surety against any backsliding. The Allied economic blockade, which had done so much to undermine Germany's manufacturing during the war, was kept in place as powerful leverage. Of the five British Armies serving on the Western Front, the Second Army was given the privilege of occupying one of the proposed allied bridgeheads: for the British, the city of Cologne.

The advance into Germany left hundreds of thousands of British troops in France to await demobilization. Soldiers who had signed up for the duration of the war hankered after a return to civilian life, a quick exit from the rigours of the army back to the comfort of homes and jobs, but the Armistice was only the cessation of hostilities, and it would be many months before peace was signed at Versailles on 28 June 1919.

When demobilization came, the land fit for heroes was predictably absent; there were too many soldiers, sailors and airmen coming home to enable a nation to be grateful to them all, too many other pressing national and international problems to deal with for the government to care greatly for those who had fought.

For too many officers and men, the welcome home amounted to little more than an introduction to a hard life, with unemployment soaring and an economy driven into recession after years of free spending during the war. For the likes of Joe Yarwood, Ted Francis and Frank Sumpter, the disappointment was tangible. Those who had been granted demobilization quickly, realised that others who had extended their service in the army to peacetime soldiering were often far better off.

THE ARMISTICE: HEARING THE NEWS

[Ed. News of the Armistice spread quickly across the battlefield, and was met by the troops with a mixture of anger, bewilderment and loss, but rarely jubilation. The war had lasted more than 1500 days, and a small but significant number of men, like Ben Clouting, Smiler Marshall, Dick Trafford, and John Laister had seen the majority of them. Others had nearly made it through the war, men like Ted Francis and Norman Dillon, and they were now back in Britain recovering from wounds. Ted Francis was glad to be out of it, and back home; others, such as Allen Short, were sad that they had not seen the war through to the very end.

Some men were angry, like Smiler Marshall, who wanted to push the Germans back to Berlin and was frustrated that the war had so suddenly and abruptly come to a halt. Yet for the prisoners in Germany, news of the Armistice could not come a day too soon. Many were starving and ill, and no small number were at death's door; another week or two and they would not have survived.

Private Harold Judd, 2/14th London Regiment, 1898-1998
On the night of the 10/11 November we were on the River Scheldt. The Engineers were putting a pontoon across and we were helping them to construct it. All of a sudden, we saw a blue Very light in the sky, a signal to pack up and return to our camp. At 10 am the next morning, we saw a cavalcade coming towards us, and there on his horse was Second Army's CO, General Sir Herbert Plumer, and behind him was quite a crowd of officers. The pipes played "On parade" and we ventured out. He said, "Now gather round, boys, gather round. You'll be pleased to know that an Armistice has been signed but this does not mean that the war is over, you still have to keep alert and you still have to carry on with the training. But immediately we get the peace treaty, we'll see about demobbing you." We were open-mouthed. He then turned to our commanding officer, Ogilvy. "Ogilvy, you still got rum?" He said "Yes" so Plumer said, "Well, you'd better serve it." So the cooks put it in big dixies, warmed it up and put sugar in it and I'll tell you, on that cold November morning it was lovely. We were lying about like rotten sheep, half drunk, for the rest of the day.

Trooper Ben Clouting, 4th (Royal Irish) Dragoon Guards, 1897-1990
We had received information that some Germans were making a stand near a village called Ath, and that at 2pm the infantry was to make a frontal assault, supported by two regiments of cavalry. Our orders were not to worry about the village itself, but to sweep past and harass any Germans we happened to come across.

That morning, our Troop Officer came round with a map to show us the direction we were to take. There would be further instructions before the attack went in, but meantime we checked our saddlery and all our equipment before the Regiment moved on again. It was full light when we halted along a tree-lined road. I had just begun to recheck my saddlery when I saw an old Douglas motorbike speeding towards us with a dispatch rider frantically waving his helmet. As he came closer, I could hear him shouting, "It's all over, boys, there's an Armistice. It's all over." At first I didn't know what he meant. What was all over? What was an Armistice? I'd never heard the word.

Sapper Tom Dewing, 34th Division, Royal Engineers Signal Company, 1896-2001
I was in an upstairs room when one of our men came in and said that the Germans had asked for an Armistice and that the war would end tomorrow. We didn't believe him, but he was most emphatic, and said we were to go round to the signal office and find out for ourselves. So I said, "All right, I'll be the fool." The news was true. One of the operators was taking down the conditions of the Armistice that was to come into effect at 11 o'clock the next morning. On my way back, I called at a café and told the girl there, in French, that the war would end tomorrow, and she said, "After four years. Four years!" The news soon spread and that night the battalions fired off every Very light they had left and an aeroplane flew over and dropped flares. It was a time of great excitement.

Private Harry Patch, 7th Duke of Cornwall's Light Infantry, 1898-
I was on the Isle of Wight, at a place called Golden Hill Fort that was our regimental depot at the time. I was A1 and on the next draft to go back and rejoin the regiment in Belgium. We were on the firing range and they told us that if the Armistice was signed, they'd send up a rocket. We watched for the rocket and about 11 o'clock we saw it go up. There was a lot of spare ammunition which we were using and the officer said, "Get rid of it, fire it out to sea, we don't want to carry it back." The fellow next to me started blazing away when I noticed that his rifle was across mine and I said, "What the hell are you firing at?" He said, "That bloody hut up there." I said, "That's where the markers

are!" All the markers on the targets were inside taking refuge on the floor as this lad fired ammunition through their hut.

A/Captain G B Jameson, C Battery 72nd Brigade, Royal Field Artillery, 1892-1999

At 4 o'clock in the afternoon, after the Armistice had been settled upon in the morning, one of the drivers saw a notice on the side of a drive into a big house announcing that as of 11am, today, the 11th November, an Armistice had been signed. It was so unbelievable that we didn't believe it. It was read back two or three times before anybody would believe it was possible, and even then you couldn't sort of contemplate that it should be possible. Then you began to think, "I don't have to keep my head down any longer." It was difficult to appreciate. The war had gone on so long, and was so beaten into your very character in every way, the daily routine, that you couldn't contemplate any other life. And then we began to backtrack a little bit. That morning I and a friend called Drew had been near the town of Le Quesnoy, which had been heavily fortified, almost Roman style, with twelve foot thick walls and drawbridges, and I said to Drew, "My God, to think that this morning, we were walking forward looking for another position, passing that town."

We had been casually walking on the road by the side of the entrance to this place and a New Zealand officer from just ahead of us, said,

"For God's sake get into the ditch, there's a blasted Prussian officer up there with two or three machine guns and he's wiping out everything he can see. We've decided not to bother about trying to take the town. We've circled it and left it to be dealt with, and the advance has gone on beyond it. We will take it in our own good time."

Naturally, later in the day, we thought back to what might have happened in the morning, "Heavens, to go through all this lot and be wiped out on the morning of the Armistice!" I said to Drew.

Even when we were getting along, and keeping in contact with the battalion we were supporting, by galloper from the battery, we still didn't think that the war was near the end. We were advancing to another battery position and if we'd not seen that notice we'd have dropped our tails and contacted the nearest battalion to find out what they wanted us to shoot up next.

Private Percy Johnson, 21st London Regiment, 1899-2002

To this day I could cry. We were marching through a town, and you've have never seen such a dilapidated place in all your life. Jerry had stripped it of every bit of brass for ammunition for their guns, and left the population starving. Anyway, the local people rushed out and we gave them what food we had, and the Colonel said, "Come on, we must get on", so we pushed them away. On the far side of the town, we could see Jerry getting away in railway trucks. We started to run and we could see them leaning out, sticking their two fingers up at us, and this dark staff car came up and a chap said, "War's over, boys, war's over now, an Armistice has been signed." It had just passed 11 o'clock. And the language! "Get out of it!" We wanted those blokes for what they'd done to the town. We told him to go and have a look at it. But the war was over, and we muttered and cursed. The Captain told us to shut up and said we could go and find a cup of coffee. Finding a bar, we went in and there were an elderly man and woman. She got on with the stove, and we told them the war was over. They were delighted and the old man ran into the stables to get something and there was a bang and he was killed. The Germans had left a booby-trap as they'd pulled out. This couple, they had gone all through the war and to be killed on Armistice Day like that! Oh, there were hardly any words from the boys, they couldn't speak, they were so upset.

Private Allen Short, 1/8th London Regiment, 1899-2000

On Armistice Day in Blackpool, everyone went stark raving mad, and broke out of hospital. If you could walk, OK, if you could crawl, you did, if you could steal a wheelchair, you would. And we went down and painted the town red. You felt that it was a release from a death penalty, as simple as that.

Private Harold Lawton, 1/4th East Yorkshire Regiment, 1899-
We were getting news in the camp of our military successes. One day in November, the Camp Commandant came round to the parcel hut. He wasn't a bad sort, but he had this domineering way with him, a Berlin swagger. He always wore an impeccable uniform, and every time he managed to rub it in, that we were somehow very lucky to have him there, so I can't say he was popular. He was most congenial on this occasion and asked politely, "Could you let me have some of your English red handkerchiefs?" They were sent out from Britain in our parcels. The sergeant in charge of the hut was most puzzled but agreed, whereupon this officer said, "I should be most grateful if you would let me have nine." The next day the Commandant came in and said, "Look over there," and over the German military section of the camp flew these handkerchiefs, all sewn together into a red flag. Then one day we heard he'd left the camp and had gone into town where he had met some revolutionaries and apparently he must have said something out of place as he was later found in the gutter, badly beaten up, I believe, and his uniform ruined.

Just before we left the camp we had a concert, and the man in charge of the show invited the German officers, and gave them the front row. On top of the stage, when the curtains opened, there was a huge union jack which filled the stage, with a soldier on one side and a sailor on the other and you can imagine what patriotic songs we sang. The Germans knew the war was over, and we did too. It was a wonderful show, and we could see one or two of the officers sitting looking very uncomfortable, but they accepted it.

Private Walter Green, 1/7th Durham Light Infantry, 1897-1998
I'd been ill and was on light fatigues, working at the camp, brushing, tidying up the place, and I was right up against the gate when I heard

some shouting. I looked up and saw two lovely mules in shining harness, pulling a wagon with three German officers in. I stood and admired the mules as they passed me and drew up. The whistles started to blow, which meant that everyone should gather round. Of course there weren't many, as most men were out on work parties. One of these three officers had a lot of papers in his hand, he started to say something but as soon as he opened his mouth there were shouts and yells. You see, a lot of the men had been prisoners for three or four years and understood German very well, so as soon as he said the war was over, they understood without the need for any interpreter. We soon knew what was going on and joined in, caps and hands went in the air and there was pandemonium, absolutely. The German officer tried to speak again but we took no notice of him. He held his hand up and, speaking through an interpreter, told us he would be taking over the camp and that the papers he held in his hand contained all the particulars of our release.

Private Robert Renwick, MM, 16th King's Royal Rifle Corps, 1896-1997

We were in Waterloo Church on the night of 9/10 November. Next morning, we were put on the move again, pushing the wagons, and after doing a few kilometres were halted for a rest when a high ranking officer came galloping up on horseback. There followed what seemed to be a serious discussion and two officers tore off their badges from their uniforms. We sensed that they were admitting defeat at last and that night we were put into a POW camp for the first time. Next morning, we were informed by their interpreter that an Armistice had been agreed and if we pushed their wagons a few more kilometres, we would be set free to make our own way back to the British lines. We objected to this and insisted on our release at once. A few of us made for the gate but the sentry up in his box pointed a rifle towards us, turning us back. However, finding a weak place in the wire at the rear of the camp, we made our escape to freedom at last. It was a white frosty morning and we stood there stunned, you were free but you didn't know exactly where you were or what you were going to do or where to go. It was a strange feeling, standing there in rags and tatters like tramps with no visible means of support. I remember seeing one lad with tears of relief running down his cheeks.

Corporal Joe Armstrong, 1st Loyal North Lancashire Regiment, 1895-1997

In April 1918 I was taken from the farm where I had been for years and transferred to an iron foundry in Hamburg. All the prisoners were in there round the clock, eating there, sleeping there, working there and dying there too. Then in the last week of October I caught dysentery and my weight collapsed. I was carted to hospital in Hamburg, as I was in a bad way. I was dying, no doubt about it.

On Tuesday, about 2am, 12 November, the rumour came round that the Armistice had been signed, well, I didn't know whether to laugh or cry. I can remember shouting, "Stick it, Joe boy, stick it a bit longer. Tha's stuck it fo' over four years, stick it a bit longer." It took six weeks to get home. I arrived on the 18 December and I remember little; I hazily remember being in hospital in Denmark and then we were taken to Leith in Scotland where we were given a bottle of something to drink and a meat pie. I was lying in a bunk and I recall people looking at me as if to say, "he hasn't got long to live". Some time afterwards, I was sent to Ripon in Yorkshire and then allowed to go home. When I got back, my grandmother was there and all she said was, "Good God, his face is less than a baby's." It must have been. I weighed 86 pounds.

Able Seaman Alf Bastin, Hawke Battalion, Royal Naval Volunteer Reserve, 1896-1997

I was out on commando, working on a big estate north of Berlin. For 18 months I had been an assistant gardener, driving a donkey cart and working out on the fields, picking root crops for the house. I used to load the cart up, take it back to the house and store the food where they wanted it.

I was working out on the morning of a miserable, bedraggled day, and suddenly one of the German carters came along. Because it used to be a storage field, they kept the root crops under clumps of earth and straw during the cold spell, and they used to come there for supplies. He came along waving a paper and shouting my nickname, "Nicoli, Nicoli der Krieg ist vorbei," the war is over, and I thought, what the bloody hell is he talking about?

We didn't get any news of the war at all. He came over and produced a special edition of the local newspaper, the *Tagesblatt*, and right across the top "Waffen Stillstand", Armistice. After my initial shock I said, "Good, if so I'm packing up work." We had a conversation and he made a wisecrack to me, I'll never forget. He said, terrible isn't it, for years and years we've been singing "Deutschland, Deutschland über Alles", Germany, Germany above all, and I'll have to change that now to "Deutschland, Deutschland alles über", Germany, Germany, all is over.

It was the 29 December before I got away from there and back to Dyrotz, our last camp, and I was back at Leith on the 2 January 1919. When we got off the ship, we saw trestle tables with telegraph forms on, for us to send a few words home to let them we'd be there in a few days. Then we were taken to a big shed laid out with food all over the place and given a damn good feed.

Private Doug Roberts, 7th Buffs (East Kent Regiment), 1900-2002
When war stopped, I was going to Dieppe with a sergeant to fetch a deserter and it was the first time I'd been in a French train. We stopped at a station and a Frenchman didn't bother to open the door; instead he smashed a window and threw two bottles of wine in and we knew then there'd been an Armistice. We never got the prisoner and I didn't see the sergeant again after that. We stopped in a camp and everyone was getting drunk.

Private Percy Wilson, 21st Manchester Regiment, 1899-2004
The officers called to us to attention and told us there was going to be an Armistice. Two or three near me, one in particular, opened his mouth. "We don't want a bloody Armistice, we want to get over that border and show them what the war's been like."

Private Smiler Marshall, 8th Machine Gun Squadron, Machine Gun Corps (Cavalry), 1897-2005
We thought if we could have a scrap there in Germany, show 'em what war was like, because they never knew what war was like, we wanted to kill a few of them, let them lie about the street, as they did the French. It would have given us some satisfaction, we would have felt cock o' the north, wouldn't we, now we're beating them on their own ground, you see my meaning?

All we were told was that we had to clean ourselves up. We were given three days, all the mud had to be cleaned off, we washed our boots and then we were given a bit of sponge to wipe our breeches down and our puttees, so we were all lovely and clean. You could go to the quartermaster's stores and get a new tunic, bits of cloth, soft soap, and metal polish, shoe polish, three days of nothing but polishing buttons and such like, to impress the Germans.

THE ARMISTICE: IMMEDIATE REACTIONS

Private Archie Richards, 25th Battalion Tank Corps, 1897-1998
The Armistice did not interest me. I had done what I had to do and just wanted to forget about it all. It was a nasty time in my life; I was young and the war had taken away several years. There were lots of celebrations and we made whoopee, but I wanted to get out of it as quick as I could, so I put my name forward for demobilization. I wasn't interested even in medals, I couldn't care less about them. The

sight of medals sickens me and I don't go anywhere near Armistice ceremonies.

Sapper Arthur Halestrap, 46th Division Royal Engineers, 1898-2004
As soon as the Armistice came into force there was a sudden, terrible silence. It was a silence that knocked one silly. It was so sudden. Straightaway we felt that we had nothing to live for. There was nothing in front of us, no objective. Everything you had been working for, for years, had suddenly disappeared. What am I going to do next? What is my future?

A/Captain G B Jameson, MC, C Battery 72nd Brigade, Royal Field Artillery, 1892-1999
You really did just sit down and think, "What the devil am I going to do now? Job's gone." Life had been so full of what you're doing, what you're planning to do, how you'd fill in your recreational time if you had any, then suddenly bang, no need for any of it, you've got to think about something else. That's why first of all there was a real drunken orgy. The Brigade Veterinary Officer arrived back from leave with a case of whiskey. The word got round the Brigade in no time at all, and we descended on the ammunition column and there wasn't much left of his whiskey by the time we'd finished, after which I went to sleep soundly on a stretcher.

You had a very fatalistic view of life. The war had gone on so long that we really couldn't conceive that there would be any other state of affairs at all. We constantly took a bit of the line, then lost it, making good advances, then losing them all, so that we got into a state when we thought no one is going to win, this is going on for God knows how long, there's no end to it. All you thought about was survival, good luck and working your ticket home. When we were on the move and doing well towards the end, we thought, "We've got them on the run, still, he has come back before so he may do it again." You didn't write them off. We had a very healthy respect for the German as a good soldier with a power of recovery even though he was becoming more and more disorganized and dispirited.

Private Joe Yarwood, 34th Division Royal Army Medical Corps, 1896-1995

I felt I'd done a good job, it was over and we were looking forward to going back to Blighty. But I did have that feeling, when we were sitting for a photograph, those of us who came through, that it seemed a pity that having been together for so long and so many of us having remained together, that it was with great regret that we were parting for good.

Private Vic Cole, 1st Queen's Own (Royal West Kent Regiment), 1897-1995

At eleven o'clock on the morning of the eleventh November 1918, I was in the Quarter-Master's stores getting issued with my civilian suit when the bells began to ring and the whistles to blow, the war was over.

It was the Armistice and I was a civilian once again. I had signed on for the duration of the war in Kitchener's Army and had kept the contract to the very hour and the very minute!

On my way to the station, I passed through crowds of cheering boisterous people packed densely in Chatham High Street. I had lots of drinks with men I had never seen before and never saw again, and finally, in my ill-fitting suit, with cloth cap and heavy boots I arrived home to the quiet, orderly and peaceful atmosphere at Gipsy Hill to rest and relax my tired brain and aching back.

Lieutenant Norman Collins, 1/4th Seaforth Highlanders, 1897-1998

On the day of the Armistice, I had a vision. I was standing in a trench. I could not put my head up because I was under fire, but above me, at eye level, walking past, were hundreds and hundreds of boots and puttees. I thought of all those I had known; it was like a panorama of passing people, people from the cadet battalion, through the various training courses and out in France. They went on and on for hours, and I realized it was the dead all walking away and leaving me behind. I felt worried and frightened that they were leaving me by myself. They were marching away into the distance where I would never follow. All the people I knew had gone, except me. That was a vivid dream and I dreamt it on many occasions, although I never told anyone until I was a very old man, because I felt it was a private matter between my old comrades and myself.

COMING HOME

Driver Alfred Henn, 3rd Battery, Warwickshire Royal Horse Artillery, 1897-2000
At Le Havre, some miners were being sent home to the pits in Wales. They were fed up with the war, everyone was. They'd gone down to the sergeants' mess asking for more food. I heard that there was a lot of argument and shouting and this sergeant told them that if they didn't clear off, he'd fight anyone amongst them, so they lynched him. I didn't see this but they said the body was there all right, an officer told us. There was a riot then, they all started. We could hear guns being fired all over the place, they were stealing rifles from everywhere, then a fire engine appeared, coming down from the town, and went inside the camp but the drivers were forced to get out and they ran back home. I was with two mates in a bell tent and we put our kit bags down and lay down behind them to stop the bullets hitting us. Everybody was firing at one another and the canteen, a huge place, got raided. It was full of food. Some Aussies were sent down in a truck with fire extinguishers to put the fires out and they asked us, "What's this all about?" and my mate said, "Oh, it's all about grub, you know, food", and they said, "Oh, we're with you then, cobber." They just chucked

the fire extinguishers out of the truck and loaded up with food and wine and drove off.

The riot lasted a day, and by the next morning the officers were cooking up their own breakfast for the rioters just to keep everyone quiet. There was no punishment at all as far as I know; they just moved the troops that had taken part in it. I don't know if anyone else was killed but I certainly saw some wounded.

Private Fred Lloyd, Army Veterinary Corps, 1898-2005

At Le Havre there was a real mutiny. There was a strike about money the men wanted to spend. They got into the guardroom, set it on fire and picked up rifles and all sorts of things. There was firing all over the place, a terrific night. One or two officers tried to calm the rioters down but it didn't work. It was a hell of a night, machine guns, you could hear them, and bullets were whistling over. It was never in the papers, never reported, but it happened. There were casualties and we heard that some were killed, what did they put that down as, I wonder? Me and another bloke were nosy and went to have a look. There was a shallow trench and my mate said, "Keep your bloody head down." The guardroom lit up what was going on. We were five hundred yards away and watched it from a hill. We could see people running around. We could see one officer standing up and waving his arms about, trying to stop it, but it didn't work.

Private Walter Green, 1/7th Durham Light Infantry, 1897-1998

We came home very slowly, as we were unescorted on our boat and there was the risk of mines in the sea, so I don't think we travelled at more than eight or nine knots all the way. We eventually got to Hull and the quayside was full of people. Everybody was asking, "Do you know Jack or Tom, Jackson, Jones, or Davis? What regiment do you belong to?" They were trying to trace a loved one, a brother who was missing, and they were hoping against hope that he was a prisoner. At the quayside, we were fitted out with clothing. They measured you and gave you an inch on every piece of clothing. We'd say, "Hey, this is too big," and they'd reply, "Yes, but you're going home and they'll fatten you up, and we don't want you back wanting a new set of clothes in eight weeks' time."

On the train, an old lady with a basket came along and gave us each a paper bag with two sandwiches, a piece of cake, a packet of cigarettes and a box of matches.

At the camp, the sergeant major told us that no one was going to be allowed to leave unless they could reach home by 8 pm. We would not be allowed to wander the streets in the early morning, not least because our families didn't know we were coming home.

It was very emotional. I stood across the road from home and I saw that the blackout curtain was still up, but now the war was over my parents hadn't fastened the curtain down the sides, so I was able to see a light on and that somebody was in. I walked to the door, got hold of the rapper and tapped it, then opened the door. I could hear voices and I called out, "Anybody here belonging to me?" Everything went quiet, then I heard my sister shout, "It's our Walt!" and they all left the fireplace and came out. We were all in a heap. You know, everybody wanted to cuddle you, and you wanted to cuddle everybody else. For about five minutes it was just chaotic. They were seeing somebody who was now seven stone and it shocked them because when I left home I was over ten. Poor old mum, she cried. She said she'd see if she could find me something to eat and she went to the pantry and got some cold potatoes and meat and fried it all up, but I couldn't eat it. I only picked at it and then left it and went to bed. The food we had been eating in Germany was rubbish and it had damaged the lining of my stomach.

Dad had missed me more than anything. I was reported missing for three months and they didn't know where I was, dead or alive. I was told that Dad used to go to work at half past seven on a morning and wouldn't speak to anybody. People would call, "Hello, George", and he'd say nothing, wouldn't even say hello, until the day he got a postcard saying I was a POW, when he ran down the middle of the road shouting, "He's a prisoner!" and waving this postcard. He was pleased to tears, if there's such a thing as that.

Private Dick Trafford, 1/2nd Monmouthshire Regiment, 1898-1999
I'll always remember my mother's face. She said, "You lousy devil, all your clothes, dump 'em," she says, "dump 'em, dump 'em! Get one of your old suits. Of course my old suits – I was only young when I joined the army and I'd put weight on, you see, I'd grown. I had nothing to put on so my father had to lend me some clothes while he went to Liverpool to buy me a ready-made suit.

Private Robert Renwick, MM, 16th King's Royal Rifle Corps, 1896-1997
I had a great reception from the village when I came home. I had been reported killed twice and I think the locals wanted to have a look at me. My father met me at Corbridge Station. Mother embraced me and I could feel the tears of joy running down her cheeks. We had a real breakfast of home-cured ham and eggs, and then mother pointed to the kitchen ceiling above which was my bedroom. "Would you like to have a couple of hours in bed now?" I said, "I think I would."

Private Harry Patch, 7th Duke of Cornwall's Light Infantry, 1898-
The day I lost my pals, 22 September 1917 – that is my Remembrance Day, not Armistice Day. The cenotaph service is all right – the rest of it is simply a military show to me. I'm always very, very quiet on that day and I don't want anybody talking to me really. Nearly ninety years after and I always remember it. I shall never forget the three I lost.

Private Ted Francis, 16th Royal Warwickshire Regiment, 1896-1996.
At the end of the war, I remembered my childish dreams of gallant deeds by men on horses and that South African war I'd read all about,

and I thought, "Oh, what a fool I was to taken in by all their propaganda." If there's anyone detested the army in the last months or so, it was me.

Air Mechanic Henry Allingham, No12 Squadron, Royal Naval Air Service, 1896-

You didn't want to think about it any more, you wanted to forget it and I did for eighty-five years and now I talk about it and I get churned up and I didn't see half as much as a lot of men did.

In the RNAS we had it jammy compared to what the other fellows did, and I'm grateful that we did. I don't know that I could have stood what those men stood in the trenches. Poor devils. You don't know what they went through and no one will ever know. And I don't know if they ever got what they deserved.

Private James Hudson, 8th Queen's Own (Royal West Kent Regiment), 1898 2001

I'm not proud to have been trained to kill as a young boy of eighteen. Why should I be? I was quite prepared, obviously, to protect the women and children, which was the stimulating factor in getting one into the army. We hadn't thought about all the horrible things that were going to happen; they were remote, far from one's thinking. I was so young, so naive, and didn't understand much about the world at that age.

Private Dick Barron, 2nd London Mounted Brigade Field Ambulance, Royal Army Medical Corps, 1895-1999

I found I wasn't one of the heroes that warfare is made of. I was not prepared to do anything spectacular, so I wasn't a good soldier. Those who won the war, won the medals, were those who had no imagination, those who were forever cheerful, who could carry on when you had had enough, and would carry your pack and rifle without a second thought.

REMAINING IN KHAKI

Sapper Arthur Halestrap, 46th Division Royal Engineers, 1898-2004
After about a week, waiting for orders to march towards Germany, I began to feel ill. I became so ill that my corporal called for the sergeant, who was so disturbed that he called for the sergeant major, who called for the major. "He's very ill, it's a bad attack of Spanish flu." It was then killing millions in a pandemic. There was no medical unit nearby and even if there had been, it would probably have been too late, so the major said, "Fill him up with rum and let him take his chance. That's all we can do."

I remember a man putting his hand behind my back and sitting me up and holding something to my lips, but that's all I remember until I came to my senses. There was a man sitting at my side and when I came to, he said, "Oh, thank God, we thought you were dead. We couldn't find a pulse and you've been completely out for the count for three days."

I asked for a cup of tea and from that moment felt as well as anything, but since that day I've never been able to bear the smell of rum.

Private Arthur Barraclough, 1/4th Duke of Wellington's Regiment, 1898-2004
I was employed clearing up the battlefield for two or three months. We'd to go scrounging round the old trenches, picking up old rifles, bullets, boxes of ammunition and guns, all sorts of stuff that was lying about. If we found any bodies, we were to report back and we'd leave them for someone else to deal with.

Anyway, a couple of lads from our battalion picked up two artillery shells, and one was carrying them, and as they walked, one of the shells slipped off his arm and burst and killed them both. That was terrible, to go through that war just to be killed then, right at the end.

Private Fred Lloyd, Army Veterinary Corps, 1898-2005

At the depot, we classified the horses to see what was coming home and what wasn't. There were three grades, and peacetime vets were saying which ones were fit to go back to England, these went into quarantine; the next grade was to be sold to the farmers, and the others were for food. A terrific lot of the horses were blind, hundreds of them. They never found out why, perhaps it was exposure to gas. Some of the time, I was leading one awkward horse and three more that were totally blind. If they weren't fit, we'd take them by train or, if they were, we'd take them by road. We used to go right up to Paris with horses, each man leading four to sell to the French for food. In the slaughterhouses, we led them onto scales four at a time and weigh them up. We sold them by weight. It was a bit upsetting.

A/Lance Corporal Cecil Withers, 17th Royal Fusiliers, 1898-2005

As we crossed the border into Germany, it was pouring with rain, pelting down mercilessly. We crossed at the town of Spa and the band struck up 'When we wind up the watch on the Rhine', a popular tune, a German tune turned to our advantage. On our left were some German officers looking on. Nobody said a word, nobody attacked us, and then suddenly we all started to join in this tune in various ways, whistling, singing or humming. We'd won, you see, and they knew it.

Private Frank Sumpter, 1st Rifle Brigade, 1897-1999

The actual army that fought in the war understood the Germans, they knew they'd suffered and they wondered how the hell they ever fought on what they had. They had nothing. When peace was declared and we marched to Germany behind the German army, all we could do was feel sorry for them. They had overcoats made for six foot Prussian Guards, big men, and handed down to small, worn-out soldiers, who had these oversized coats and boots, all wrinkled down at the bottom because they didn't fit them properly. These long coats were all covered in mud round the bottom, a pitiful sight, and we wondered how they had fought that war. They'd do anything for a tin of bully beef. When we got into Germany, it was the posh women who carried on the fight with snide comments, not the men.

Private Smiler Marshall, 8th Machine Gun Squadron, Machine Gun Corps (Cavalry), 1897-2005

The first village we came to in Germany, I'll tell you what we done, we were naughty. We came to a café. The Horse Artillery went there first, they smashed the door down 'cos they couldn't get in, the owner had locked it.

We drank everything, whiskey, schnapps, we just grabbed the bottles, didn't pay for a thing. Then when we'd finished, we lined up all the bottles, and smashed them on the floor, and smashed all the glasses.

When we walked in, the woman and two of her daughters were there, thinking we might want to buy drinks, but as soon as a man of the Queen's Bays, the 2nd Dragoon Guards, jumped over the counter, she scarpered with her daughters and bolted the doors, so we saw nothing of them any more. The rumour was there had been a man there as well but he'd slung his hook as we'd approached the border, and he'd gone off back into Germany somewhere.

It wouldn't have done for a man to have been there, we would have beaten him up, course we would, that's war, isn't it? Why? Are you going to let them off? Ask them if they'd like a bar of chocolate? Is that what you'd do? No, come off it, you'd do the same as your mates are doing, you'd be drinking their ruddy beer, course you would. The officers kept out of the way and I heard, after we'd gone, that they paid for the damage. Officers, that's the difference between us and them.

[Ed. Smiler served with the Occupation until 1919 when he was sent for demobilization. On arrival in England he went home, only to find no one there. As he walked into the kitchen, he saw a coffin on the table and lifting the lid found the body of his father who had only just died.]

Air Mechanic Henry Allingham, No12 Squadron Royal Air Force, 1896-

I was billeted with my officer on a well-to-do jeweller in Rheinberg, not far from Bonn. I'd picked the billet because I wanted something nice and I was fortunate to sleep in a comfy bed, which took some getting used to after all that time.

The father used to speak to his son in German and he would talk to me in French, and he came up on Christmas Eve to ask if I would like to join the family as he presented his staff with Christmas presents. The old gardener came up, cap in hand, and took his present, then he backed out of the room very respectfully, to be followed one by one by all the rest of the staff.

Then the boy was sent to bring his mother up from down stairs. She sat down and listened dutifully to what her husband had to say, and then he gave her a lovely diamond ring. I forget what the boys got for Christmas.

Dorothy, my girlfriend, sent me two jaffa oranges. Where she got those from I wouldn't know, because they were hard to get. She must have made a sacrifice for those. Anyway, these boys, they must have been aged about ten, came up to my room the next morning to wish me Happy Christmas.

I don't know what prompted me to do it, but I was looking round for something to give them and saw these two lovely oranges. I called them over and gave them one each, and do you know what, they couldn't believe it, they really couldn't, honestly, they looked at them and held on to them. They didn't have much to say, but ran down the stairs shouting all the while at the tops of their voices to tell their mother.

They say, you know, "Who gives a child a treat makes church bells ring in heaven's street." I sometimes wonder if those boys are still going – they would be well into their nineties now I suppose – and if they think about the old army man who gave them two jaffa oranges for Christmas.

AFTER THE WAR: BACK TO WORK

Rifleman John Laister, 2nd King's Royal Rifle Corps, 1897-1999
I had three years out of work, so what are you gonna do? What are you gonna do, chum, eh? I wasn't married. I started to play the violin in the streets and in pubs and clubs. I didn't get a lot, just dirty old pennies they used to throw at you. But you couldn't stop and play in the streets, you got to keep on the move then, there was no such thing as playing on the station platform or anything like that. You gotta keep on the move, all the while, because if a copper comes along with 'is cape on his shoulder and you're standing there, he'll 'ave you, see.

Private Joe Yarwood, 31st Division, Royal Army Medical Corps, 1896-1995
The war was a unique experience, a really amazing experience; we were lucky to take part, luckier still to have come through it without any serious injury. And you felt satisfaction that, if only in a very humble degree, you served your country at a very vital time. We all owed a duty to our country without any humbug, and we'd got to jump to it when the situation arose. It was part of the routine, very definitely, part of the routine. I'm being quite sincere about that.

I regretted the waste of time, of three and a half years when I should have been making my way, making some progress in life. I'd nothing to show for it, you see, but it wasn't anybody's fault. I was demobbed in April 1919 and received a bounty of £25. I spent £20 of that having a good suit made because I wanted to be respectably dressed to get a job.

Before the war, I had worked as a travelling representative for a hardware store, and at the end of the war I contacted them about my old job and they wrote to me and said, "Don't be in a hurry back," so I didn't bother writing again. I thought, "Go to hell!" The meanness of it. I heard universities were giving scholarships, and I would have given my right arm to go to university, so I wrote to them asking whether there was any chance of me applying for one of these scholarships and they didn't reply, so I wrote a rude letter saying I was good enough to serve the country for three and a half years and they hadn't the decency to respond. That caused a bit of a stink.

I tried hard but I couldn't get a job. It was very frustrating, a very rough period, and then in September, I met this man, a Frenchman, and he was in the automatic machine business. He'd got a map of the Western Front, if you please, and he'd designed little bulbs which would light up and you could pick out a town, say Verdun, and information would be given about the town and the year of fighting there.

It was quite a good idea, and I was taken on to try and sell it, but who wanted to hear about the war after four years of fighting? I worked all week, evenings and weekends without a penny overtime, but in the end it was a wash-out.

Private Vic Cole, 1st Queen's Own (Royal West Kent Regiment), 1897-1995
In May 1919, I went ashore, down Macquary Street in Montreal, which runs parallel to the river, and a band was coming and people were lining the street. I asked someone, "What's up, who's coming?" and I was told, "The boys are coming home from France, the war's over, you know. and the boys are coming home." So I lined up and along came the Canadian troops, marching, band playing, people cheering, and a bloke prodded me and said, "Hey, take your hat off when they pass. Those boys have been over in France fighting for you."

I didn't say anything to him but I wished I'd been wearing my medals. I'd been over there serving for a full two years before most of those buggers ever arrived. Anyway, I took my hat off to these gallant Canadians who had been over in France fighting for me, and went back to my ship.

Private Edward White, 10th King's Royal Rifle Corps, 1897–1999

After I was badly wounded on the Somme I never soldiered again, my arm was too badly damaged. But after the war I had to get a job, so I had to try and give myself at least an arm and a half. I got some boxing gloves and swung my arm about and got some movement, and I was happy. But it's when I found myself out in the labour market and couldn't find a job, couldn't find anything, then I started to wonder. Your pension will be so and so, and I found myself with fifteen shillings a week. What can I do with fifteen shillings?

The landlord came up to me one day and said, " I want you out." I was very annoyed. I said, "Where am I going to go?" He said, "That's not my trouble." I had to find a place, with one arm, when I was out in the street.

This was the glorious country, and I was sleeping in shop doorways, going down to public lavatories to have a wash. I walked, walked, walked, first to Leicester, then from one town to another, cleaned stables. I did mushroom picking in Cheshire. I went to Liverpool docks and ended up back in London. Then I went to the pension offices to draw my pension because I'd no money left, but they'd stopped it. They asked:

"Why haven't you drawn your pension?"

"I've been looking for work."

"Looking for work? Where?"

"All over England."

"You got proof? That you've been looking for work?"

I told them I'd just gone round asking for casual work. How could I prove that?

"You been in prison?"

I said, "What? I've been looking for work!"

It took a long time to convince them that I hadn't been in prison.

In the end they said, "We'll give you a few shillings now and the rest of the money will be at the Post Office on Wednesday."

In the end, I got four shillings and sixpence a day looking after a billiard hall, brushing the tables. I used to go in the mornings and sweep the floor. They were quite pleased with me, all the hours I was putting in.

Private Vic Cole, 1st Queen's Own (Royal West Kent Regiment), 1897-1995

When I went to sea, working as a wireless operator for Marconi, the men told me about the dangers they'd been through, how they'd once seen a periscope one day, the dreadful moment when they'd seen the periscope come up, and they'd turned the ship around and gone away, and somebody got torpedoed. I looked at them in amazement, with their nice bunks to sleep in and their three meals a day. In 1919 they were still on war bonus, getting an extra amount every month because there were a few floating mines. When I started telling them about Ypres and walking over the dead bodies and bones, they used to look at me in disbelief, they thought I was telling bloody lies, and they used to walk away, so I gave up speaking about it. I didn't care in those days; after the experience of that war, you learnt that. Whatever happened to me in life after that First War, it couldn't be any worse than what I'd already been through, so I didn't care.

Flight Sergeant Bill Hall, No16 Squadron, Royal Air Force, 1898-1999

I was glad the war was over in one sense, but peace really cut down a lot on my activities, my excitement. I had to come down and I merely became a clerk in an office, vastly different from a month or two before, when I was flying and bombing. Peace was an anti-climax, I'd been so active, doing what I wanted to do. There was no war, so the RAF didn't want me and I was demobilised. I was finished and I simply went back to work.

Private Ted Francis 16th Royal Warwickshire Regiment, 1896-1996

It was difficult to get back into civilian life again. The Prime Minister had got on his feet and said, "Welcome home, lads, you've come to a land fit for heroes", and he was the best liar I've ever heard. When I got back, I naturally approached my old firm, the little factory, to get my job back.

They looked at me like I was a complete stranger. There was hardly anyone I recognized and they almost pushed me out of the door, saying, "We've got no job for you." Yes, I was bitter. What would anyone's feelings be, when the fellow who is walking up the gutter trying to sell matches has no arm or leg? It was two or three years before I landed a job.

Private Dick Trafford, 1/2nd Monmouthshire Regiment, 1898-1999
There was one chap, he lived next door to us, and he wore a silver plate in his head where he'd been hit by a lump of shrapnel. He'd lost all use of one arm and most of the feeling in one leg which he dragged along when he walked. But he lived for a few years like that. You'd come outside and see him going down the street and you'd think, "Thank God I'm not like that."

There was another man I knew, he owned a public house on Church Street in Ormskirk, Peter Burke, he was shot through the buttocks and he could never sit down properly, and then you'd see a man, he was an officer, Lieutenant Watson, he was a grammar school teacher in Ormskirk, he couldn't walk properly because he'd been wounded in the leg.

You saw something everyday that reminded you of the war, it brought bad memories back, you couldn't avoid it. But they were alive and those on the Somme and Passchendaele weren't.

Private Arthur Burge, 2/5th East Surrey Regiment, 1895-1999
After the war, I could not bring myself to do anything. I had always wanted to be a chemist but the thought of it in 1918 was beyond me. I couldn't pass the exams because I couldn't concentrate.

My father got me a job amongst a lot of women, just working on my own, checking ledgers. It was a simple job that any fool could do, no brainwork to it, just accuracy. I did that for two years while I got over my experiences. My nerves were bad. I took up dancing which helped me an awful lot.

Even so, I still have nightmares, even today, those sights still haven't left me completely. What disgusting sights I saw, oh, the curse of it all.